mobile MAGAZINE Guide to BlackBerry®

Bill Foust

800 East 96th Street,
Indianapolis, Indiana 46240

MOBILE GUIDE TO BLACKBERRY®

Copyright © 2005 by Que Publishing

All rights reserved. No part of this book shall be reproduced, stored in a retrieval system, or transmitted by any means, electronic, mechanical, photocopying, recording, or otherwise, without written permission from the publisher. No patent liability is assumed with respect to the use of the information contained herein. Although every precaution has been taken in the preparation of this book, the publisher and author assume no responsibility for errors or omissions. Nor is any liability assumed for damages resulting from the use of the information contained herein.

International Standard Book Number: 0-7897-3343-9

Library of Congress Catalog Card Number: 2004116491

Printed in the United States of America

First Printing: May 2005

08 07 06 05   4 3 2 1

Trademarks

All terms mentioned in this book that are known to be trademarks or service marks have been appropriately capitalized. Que Publishing cannot attest to the accuracy of this information. Use of a term in this book should not be regarded as affecting the validity of any trademark or service mark.

BlackBerry is a registered trademark of Research In Motion Limited.

Warning and Disclaimer

Every effort has been made to make this book as complete and as accurate as possible, but no warranty or fitness is implied. The information provided is on an "as is" basis. The author and the publisher shall have neither liability nor responsibility to any person or entity with respect to any loss or damages arising from the information contained in this book.

Bulk Sales

Que Publishing offers excellent discounts on this book when ordered in quantity for bulk purchases or special sales. For more information, please contact

    U.S. Corporate and Government Sales
    1-800-382-3419
    corpsales@pearsontechgroup.com

Associate Publisher
Greg Wiegand

Acquisitions Editor
Todd Green

Development Editor
Laura Norman

Managing Editor
Charlotte Clapp

Project Editor
Tonya Simpson

Production Editor
Benjamin Berg

Indexer
Chris Barrick

Proofreader
Andy Beaster

Technical Editor
Richard Evers

Publishing Coordinator
Sharry Lee Gregory

Interior Designer
Anne Jones

Cover Designer
Anne Jones

Page Layout
Kelly Maish

Introduction, 1

Part I **Getting Familiar with BlackBerry**
1 Touring the BlackBerry Handheld, 5
2 Interacting with Your BlackBerry Handheld, 15

Part II **What To Do After You Open the Box**
3 Installing and Configuring the Desktop Manager, 29
4 Personalizing Your Device, 55

Part III **The "Killer" Applications**
5 Composing and Sending Messages, 73
6 Managing Your Messages, 87
7 Message Attachments, 103
8 Browsing the Internet Wirelessly, 111
9 Making Phone Calls, 127

Part IV **BlackBerry PIM Applications**
10 Using the Address Book, 147
11 Using the Calendar, 161
12 Managing Tasks, 173

Part V **Advanced Topics**
13 Other Applications on Your BlackBerry, 179
14 Finding and Installing Third-Party Applications, 191

Part VI **Appendixes**
A Considering an Upgrade?, 207
B BlackBerry Behind the Scenes, 211

Index, 215

Introduction 1
  About This Book 1
  Which Versions Are Supported 2
  Who This Book Is For 2

I GETTING FAMILIAR WITH BLACKBERRY 3

1 Touring the BlackBerry Handheld 5
  Anatomy of a BlackBerry Handheld 5
  Welcome to the World of Thumb Typing 9
  Navigating the BlackBerry Keyboard 12

2 Interacting with Your BlackBerry Handheld 15
  The BlackBerry Home Screen 15
  Interacting with a BlackBerry Application 18

II WHAT TO DO AFTER YOU OPEN THE BOX 27

3 Installing and Configuring the Desktop Manager 29
  What Is the Desktop Manager? 29
  Redirecting Messages to the BlackBerry 29
  Installing the Desktop Manager 31
  Configuring the Desktop Manager 33
  Using the Desktop Redirector 35
  Upgrading Your Handheld Software 36
  Working with the Desktop Manager Applets 37

4 Personalizing Your Device 55
  Setting the Time and Date 55
  Add Identifying Information 56
  Securing Your Data 57
  Saving the Battery 59
  Selecting a Profile 60
  Changing the Display 63

Organizing the Home Screen 65
Choosing a Theme in Version 4.0 66
Setting Your Home Screen and Standby Image in Version 4.0 68
Using Help in Version 4.0 69

III THE "KILLER" APPLICATIONS 71

5 Composing and Sending Messages 73
Why Messages and Not Emails? 73
Composing a Message 74
AutoText: Fixing Your Typos 82
Sending More Email: Replies and Forwarding 83

6 Managing Your Messages 87
Working with the Message List 87
Opening Messages 88
Accessing Other Messages from Within a Message 94
Deleting Messages 94
Organizing Email Messages with Folders 95
Saving Messages 96
Using the Search Function to Find Messages 97
Message List Options 99

7 Message Attachments 103
Working with Email Attachments 103
Viewing Attachments 107

8 Browsing the Internet Wirelessly 111
Web Browsers for the BlackBerry 111
Surfing the Web with Your BlackBerry 112
Using Bookmarks 117
Installing a New Ringtone 120
Saving Pictures on Your Handheld 121
Changing Browser Options 122
Clearing the Browser Cache 125

9 Making Phone Calls ... 127
- The Recent Call List ... 127
- The Call Screen ... 131
- Phone Options ... 137
- Phone Status ... 143

IV BLACKBERRY PIM APPLICATIONS ... 145

10 Using the Address Book ... 147
- Using the Address List ... 147
- Creating a New Address Entry ... 148
- Managing Addresses ... 149
- Grouping Multiple Addresses ... 150
- Understanding Categories ... 152
- Finding an Address ... 154
- Using Lookups on BES ... 155
- Contacting an Address ... 156
- Address Book Options ... 157
- Accessing the SIM Phone Book ... 158

11 Using the Calendar ... 161
- Working with Calendar Views ... 161
- Creating a New Appointment ... 164
- Creating Recurring Appointments ... 167
- Managing Appointments ... 170
- Setting Calendar Options ... 171

12 Managing Tasks ... 173
- Using the Tasks List ... 173
- Creating a New Task ... 174
- Editing a Task ... 175
- Deleting a Task ... 175
- Finding a Task ... 176
- Task Options ... 176

V ADVANCED TOPICS 177

13 Other Applications on Your BlackBerry 179
Why Use MemoPad? 179
Setting an Alarm 182
Using the Calculator 183
Keeping Passwords Safe with Password Keeper 185
Playing BrickBreaker 188

14 Finding and Installing Third-Party Applications 191
What Kind of Applications Run on a BlackBerry? 191
Finding Third-Party Applications 192
Helpful Third-Party Applications 195
Creating Your Own Applications 200
Installing a Third-Party Application 200

VI APPENDIXES 205

A Considering an Upgrade? 207
Comparing the Devices as Phones 207
Comparing the Devices as PDAs 208
Let's Talk About Form Factor 208
Just How Hard Is It to Use That Keypad? 209
Bluetooth Support 210

B BlackBerry Behind the Scenes 211
From Server to Handheld 211
From Handheld to Server 213

Index 215

ABOUT THE AUTHOR

Bill Foust has been a recognized activist and consultant specializing in the RIM BlackBerry for more than five years. He's an active participant in BlackBerry developer forums and the BlackBerry-users Yahoo! group. He has written many BlackBerry applications including ExpenseMinder and EzToDo, which were two of the best-selling applications at Handango.com. He also had one of the first websites devoted to helping developers at www.rimdev.com.

DEDICATION

This book is dedicated to my wonderful family, for without their support and patience, it never would have been completed.

MOBILE magazine is the world's leading authority on mobile technology. Every month, MOBILE delivers incisive reviews and in-depth how-to stories on the latest portable gadgets and gear, from cell phones and PDAs to notebooks and digital cameras. Find out more by visiting www.mobilemagazine.com!

ACKNOWLEDGMENTS

So many people deserve credit for helping to make this book a reality. First and foremost, credit goes to God Almighty and his son Jesus who orchestrate all our steps.

I'd like to thank my wife Angela and daughter Alexandra for letting me take the time I needed to write this book. I'd like to thank my extended family as well for their support and encouragement, especially my mother-in-law Evelyn Meyers for helping me test some things.

Special thanks go to Richard Evers for his technical support and answering my many, many emails.

Of course, Todd Green deserves special note for being patient with me when I needed it and not being patient with me when I needed that as well. Also thanks to Laura Norman for her many great suggestions during the editing process.

I'd like to thank everyone else at Pearson Education and the folks at *Mobile* magazine for all their efforts, and my agent at Studio B for making this all come together.

Finally, I'd like to give some special thanks to Vern Weitzman at Itrezzo, Inc. for hosting my website and BlackBerry on their servers. I wouldn't have been able to do this without it.

Thanks!

WE WANT TO HEAR FROM YOU!

As the reader of this book, *you* are our most important critic and commentator. We value your opinion and want to know what we're doing right, what we could do better, what areas you'd like to see us publish in, and any other words of wisdom you're willing to pass our way.

As an associate publisher for Que, I welcome your comments. You can email or write me directly to let me know what you did or didn't like about this book—as well as what we can do to make our books better.

Please note that I cannot help you with technical problems related to the topic of this book. We do have a User Services group, however, where I will forward specific technical questions related to the book.

When you write, please be sure to include this book's title and author as well as your name, email address, and phone number. I will carefully review your comments and share them with the author and editors who worked on the book.

Email: feedback@quepublishing.com

Mail: Greg Wiegand
         Associate Publisher
         Que Publishing
         800 East 96th Street
         Indianapolis, IN 46240 USA

For more information about this book or another Que Publishing title, visit our Web site at www.quepublishing.com. Type the ISBN (excluding hyphens) or the title of a book in the Search field to find the page you're looking for.

INTRODUCTION

The first time you heard someone talking about their "BlackBerry," you were probably pretty confused. You could tell, however, that they were excited about it and before long you were sitting there next to them getting a first-hand demonstration. Then, even though you didn't fully understand it, you were trying to explain to your boss how this "BlackBerry" thing worked and trying to get one for yourself. Am I right?

The BlackBerry handhelds just seem to have that effect on people. They are stylish, sophisticated, and best of all, somehow get your email onto them in a way that makes you not miss your desktop email client.

I know. That was me once, too.

So now you have one or maybe you are trying to learn more so you can get your own handheld. Whatever the case may be, let me say "Thanks!" for taking the time to look at this book. I truly hope that it helps you to make the most of your handheld.

ABOUT THIS BOOK

This book is organized into chapters that each cover roughly one application or topic area of the BlackBerry software. While there are some interrelated portions, feel free to skip ahead to a chapter that you are particularly interested in, or maybe a specific topic you just have a question about.

If you have never used a BlackBerry handheld before, please make sure that you read Chapter 2, "Interacting with Your BlackBerry Handheld," before any of the chapters on the handheld software. The rest of the book will use phrases such as "Select the field Name" or "Click the New menu item," and Chapter 2 lays the foundation on how to perform these common operations.

WHICH VERSIONS ARE SUPPORTED

When I started writing this book, the 7100 series handhelds were not yet released. As a result, the 7200 series handhelds were chosen as the newest yet most representative of the handheld models available. For this reason, the majority of the figures show a 7200 handheld.

This book then is based on the 3.7 version of the handheld software. 3.7 is the version most color handhelds use and is not significantly different than the previous version, 3.6, which most of the monochrome handhelds used.

During the writing of this book, the 7100 series handhelds came out with version 4.0 of the handheld software. Version 4.0 introduces some new features as well as adds support for the new 7100 series handhelds. These new features are covered in sections that specifically indicate that they are part of the new version 4.0 handheld software. In addition, the 7100 series handhelds behave a little differently than the other handheld models available in some areas. These differences are often noted in special notes. When something works in a different way on a model 7100 handheld, I say so.

WHO THIS BOOK IS FOR

Like any book introducing a topic, I've tried not to assume anything when talking about the handheld. The handhelds must be connected to a PC at some point, however, so I assume that you have at least some basic PC experience. Specifically, you need to be able to install software on a PC, launch an application, and understand how to interact with that application. Also, since the handheld must be physically connected to the PC with a cable, I assume that you know how to make these connections without destroying the PC.

Overall, however, this book is focused on new users. Maybe you just got your first BlackBerry and need to learn how to use it quickly. Or maybe you have had a BlackBerry for some time, but know that you aren't using all of the features to their fullest. Whatever the case may be, this book is written and organized to help you get from the very first step of having a brand new handheld to learning in depth how the applications work.

If you are already familiar with your handheld and just want to learn about a particular aspect in more detail, you can jump ahead to a chapter to quickly learn about it.

There are also two appendices that you may be interested in. Appendix A is my honest review of the 7100v and how it compared to my 7280. Appendix B is a little "behind the scenes" look at how an email message actually gets from your server to your handheld. Of course, these aren't required to understand how to use your handheld; however, you might find this information helpful.

Part I
GETTING FAMILIAR WITH BLACKBERRY

1   Touring the BlackBerry Handheld

2   Interacting with Your BlackBerry Handheld

Chapter 1

TOURING THE BLACKBERRY HANDHELD

BLACKBERRY BASICS:

- From the holster to the SIM card, you need to know what's what on the BlackBerry and how to find it.

- Learn the ins and outs of typing on a BlackBerry keyboard—it's okay if you're all thumbs.

Congratulations, and welcome to the wirelessly connected world. As promoted by RIM, the "Always on, Always connected" lifestyle is now within your reach. Of course, in order to achieve this virtual Nirvana of connectivity, you will need to hone your thumb-typing skills and master the labyrinth of features inside that innocent-looking device.

Interesting analogies aside, the first step to understanding is analysis. So let's start by examining the physical features of a BlackBerry handheld. As you may know, there are many versions of BlackBerry handhelds available. The biggest difference between handhelds lies on the inside in terms of the wireless modem used to communicate with various wireless carriers. There are differences on the outside as well. There may be a difference in screen size, whether the screen is color, and whether the device uses a cradle or just a plug to communicate to the desktop PC. Of course, there are some standard features that make a handheld a BlackBerry handheld, so we'll delve into those features now.

ANATOMY OF A BLACKBERRY HANDHELD

Most of the rest of this book will focus on the functions and the applications found on your BlackBerry. Before we get to that, though, you really need to be familiar with the physical features of the handheld. Things such as connection ports and the power button vary slightly between models, so the following sections will give you a quick introduction to where everything is and a brief overview of how the BlackBerry works.

TURNING THE DARN THING ON

The On button is cleverly hidden on most models. For all but the newest 7100 model, you'll find it in the lower-right corner of the keyboard. It is either silver colored or has an image of a sun or light bulb on it (see Figure 1.1). This button is also used to enable and disable the backlight feature.

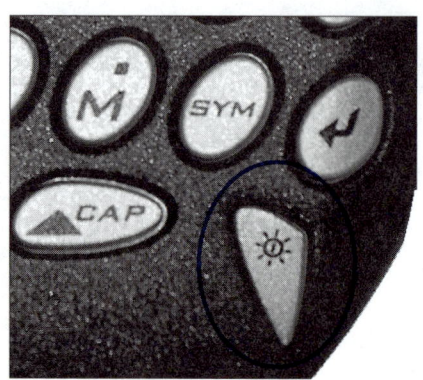

FIGURE 1.1
The Power button.

7100 If you have one of the 7100 series handhelds, the power button is in a different location. It is the small recessed button on the top face of the handheld. It is a plain black color and has no other markings on it. On 7100 series handhelds, the backlight comes on automatically any time you interact with the handheld, so there is no button to turn on the backlighting feature.

To turn the handheld on, simply press and hold the power button for a short period of time. You should see a splash screen to let you know that the handheld is now on and in the process of booting up. It can take a few moments for it to completely turn on and launch all of the software needed to use the handheld.

The Power button can also be used to turn off the device by pressing and holding it down for about 5 seconds. If you're working in an application and get ready to shut down, it's just as easy to use the icon on the Home screen to do this or to configure the software to automatically turn itself off at certain times.

THE DISPLAY SCREEN

There isn't much to say about screens on BlackBerry devices, except that every model has one and that they don't have touch-screen capability. There are varying screen sizes among the available models and they may be color or black and white. The screens on BlackBerry handhelds have always been sharper than handhelds with a touch-screen, and the screens on all BlackBerry handhelds can be backlit for reading in low light. See Figure 1.2 for examples of some of the screens used on various BlackBerry models.

THE QWERTY KEYBOARD

For a long time, BlackBerry handhelds were the only handhelds with a complete miniature QWERTY keyboard. It's a testament to the value of having a keyboard that many other devices are now including them. That value is seen most clearly when it comes to creating messages. Plain and simple, devices without a keyboard just aren't as easy to use when it comes to creating messages. The keyboard is always located on the front face of the handheld at the bottom. We'll look at the keyboard and the special keys on it in more detail later in the "Welcome to the World of Thumb Typing" section.

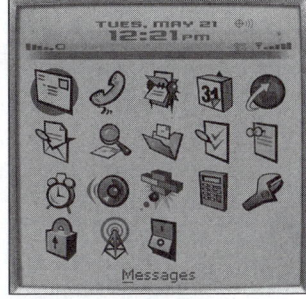

FIGURE 1.2
Three sample screens as seen on various BlackBerry handhelds.

The exception to this, however, is the new BlackBerry 7100 models, which have a modified 20-key keyboard. On these devices, each key represents up to two characters and the handheld uses a dictionary to make intelligent guesses about what you are really trying to type. The letters are still arranged in the same manner as a traditional keyboard, however, which makes it easy to adapt to.

THE TRACKWHEEL AND ESCAPE BUTTON

A keyboard is important, but there must still be a way to navigate the many features and screens that are necessary in any complex system. That is the job of the trackwheel and Escape button. They are always located on the right face of the handheld (see Figure 1.3)—a real sticking point for all you lefties out there, but that's just the way it is.

The trackwheel can be used in two ways. Not only does it roll up and down, but you can also click it by pressing on the wheel. Rolling the trackwheel is used to navigate around the screens, and clicks are used to select or activate things such as menus. As the name implies, the Escape button is used to cancel actions. We will go over both of these functions in more detail in Chapter 2, "Interacting with Your BlackBerry Handheld."

FIGURE 1.3
The trackwheel and Escape button are easy to locate but not as intuitive as you might expect.

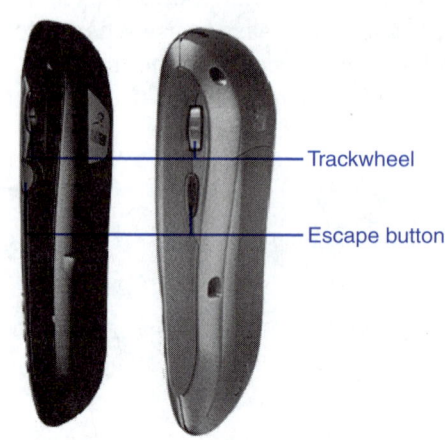

— Trackwheel

— Escape button

> **note** Just in case you were wondering why some models come with a cradle and others don't, they did away with the cradle-integrated connector because people didn't like traveling with a cradle. A small cord is easier to deal with on the road.
>
> Another little item related to using your BlackBerry as a phone is found on the top face of the handheld. Some models include a button in the center of the top face that lets you jump straight to the phone feature without having to use the trackwheel to select the phone application or the Escape button to exit a current application.

CONNECTION PORTS

Even though the main purpose of a BlackBerry is to be away from your desktop, it must still be hooked up to your PC for initialization and probably for synchronization (with the right server configuration, you can synchronize wirelessly as well). For this reason, all BlackBerry handhelds have a connection port. The connection port is also used to recharge the handheld's battery.

The connection port is one of two kinds. It is either a special serial port on the bottom face of the handheld that is designed to be dropped into a cradle, or it is a small USB connection on the left face of the handheld.

MICROPHONE, SPEAKER, AND/OR EARBUD CONNECTOR

Almost every BlackBerry handheld has an integrated cellular phone that has a speaker and microphone, earbud connector, or both. If the handheld has a speaker and microphone, the speaker on the front face above the screen and the microphone is below the keyboard so you can hold the handheld to your head like a normal phone. If the handheld has an earbud connector it is usually located on the left face (though some older models had it on the top face).

REMOVABLE BATTERY/SIM CARD ACCESS PANEL

The back face of the handheld is usually reserved for an access panel to access the SIM card and/or removable battery. Not all models have these features, but if they do, the back face is where you will find them.

Also on the back face or under the access panel, you will find a small hole labeled Reset. Ideally, you will never need to reset your handheld, but if you ever find your handheld locked up and other methods of turning off the device do not work, you can insert the end of a paperclip into the hole to force a reboot of your handheld. This should only be used as a last resort, however!

WHAT'S IN A SIM?

The SIM card contains information about your account with your wireless carrier and some limited storage capabilities. It allows you to change devices easily by simply transferring the SIM card to the new device. That new device then will instantly have access to your phone number, minutes, and all the features of your account.

All GSM devices from all carriers use a SIM card, so you would think that it would be easy to get a device from, say, Cingular, and use it with Verizon by simply transferring your SIM card into the device. Unfortunately, the carriers use a system of device locking that causes a device to use SIM cards from only that carrier to prevent this very thing. Even the exact same model of device can be made to work with only a particular network through device locking.

Device locks exist for all GSM devices and not just BlackBerry handhelds. For many of the devices there are unlock codes available on websites to disable the device locks, but BlackBerry handhelds are not listed and no information could be found at the time of this writing.

MORE THAN JUST A HOLSTER

One last seemingly innocent piece of hardware is the holster used to carry your handheld around. It may seem silly to point it out, but the holster actually plays a very important role. The holster actually contains a small magnet that the handheld uses to sense when it is in the holster.

Among other things, the sensor tells the software to automatically jump to the newest email when you pull your handheld out of the holder. It also allows the software to notify you one way if the device is holstered and another if it is not. Lastly, it helps improve the battery life by deactivating non-essential functions while it is in the holster, such as the display and keyboard.

WELCOME TO THE WORLD OF THUMB TYPING

You may be wondering how you can actually type on such on a small keyboard using a traditional touch typing position for your fingers—you can't. Instead, you have to use a technique called thumb typing. Thumb typing is essentially using only one or two thumbs to do all of the typing. Your other fingers are just used to hold the handheld.

7100 With the more compact keyboard the 7100 models sport, even thumb typing is difficult. You'll likely resort to the typical cell phone typing method—hunt and peck with one finger while cradling the device in the other hand.

There are three ways to position your hands to thumb type, and you may have done them all naturally without thinking about it. In fact, you will probably switch between the three styles often depending on what you are doing.

The first way is the two-thumb typing position. This position is the most effective for composing a message quickly because it uses both thumbs for typing which gives quick access to any keys you need. However, if you use this typing position, you cannot use the trackwheel to navigate. Figure 1.4 shows an example of this position.

FIGURE 1.4
The two-thumbed typing position.

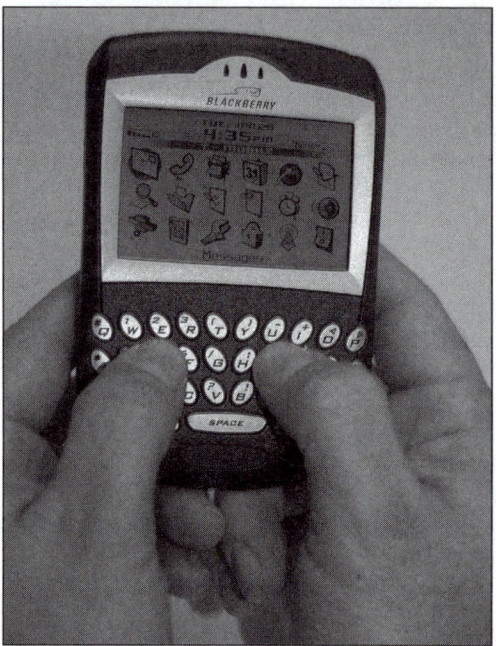

The second way is the two-handed navigating position. This way puts your right thumb on the trackwheel for quick navigation. The other thumb is available for typing, but it is not the most efficient position. Still, it is a good compromise between the need to navigate and the need to type. Figure 1.5 shows an example of this position.

The third way is the one-handed position. This way uses only your right hand to hold the device and your right thumb for both navigating and typing, shown in Figure 1.6. This position can be pretty awkward at times, but it is the only real way to use your handheld when you need your other hand for another task—such as driving. Now, I don't recommend this approach at all, but I know you will be tempted to experiment and it's best to show you the right way to do something you shouldn't be doing.

You may see pictures of people trying to use their index finger to type while holding the device in the other hand. While this may look good in a picture, it just doesn't work practically. Go ahead and try it and you will see I'm right.

WELCOME TO THE WORLD OF THUMB TYPING

FIGURE 1.5
The one-thumbed navigating position.

FIGURE 1.6
The one-handed position.

NAVIGATING THE BLACKBERRY KEYBOARD

It may seem pretty obvious how to use the keyboard since it is a standard QWERTY keyboard, but it is important to point out that the keyboard is not a *full* keyboard. It has no numeric keys and very few symbol keys. Of course, you can get to these other characters, but it takes some special key combinations to do so. Figure 1.7 shows the keyboard and labels all of the special keys. The 7100 series handhelds have a slightly different keyboard and some new buttons. Figure 1.8 shows a 7100v and labels the special keys on it.

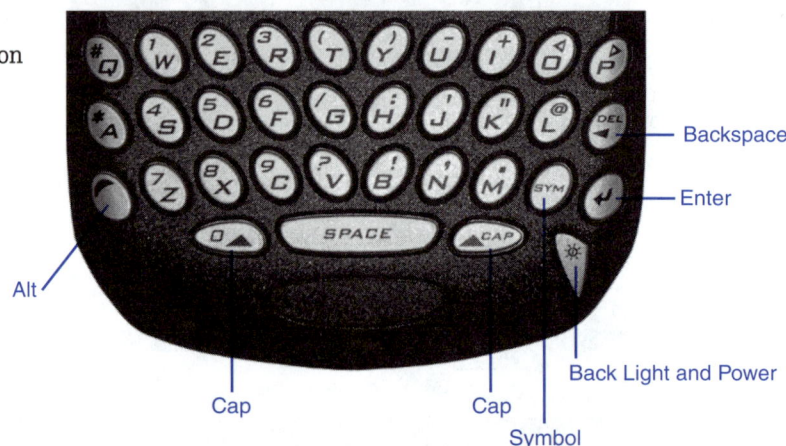

FIGURE 1.7
The special keys on the keyboard.

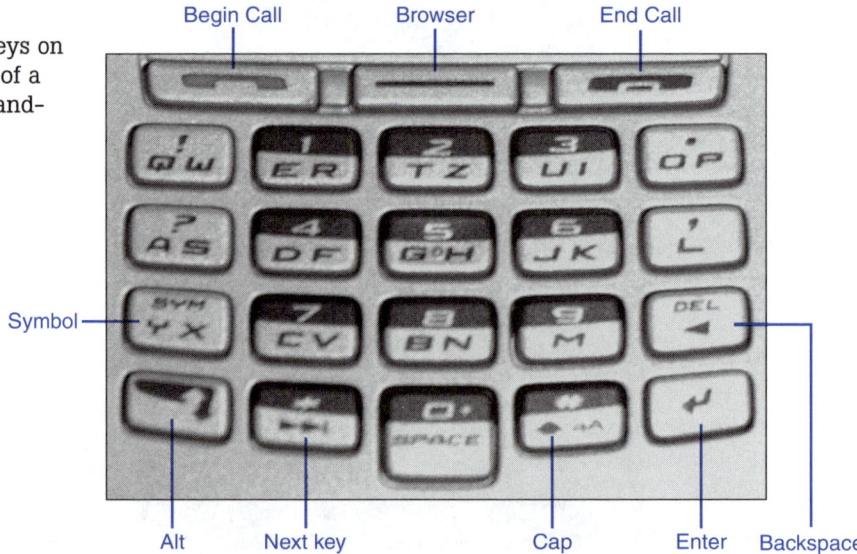

FIGURE 1.8
The special keys on the keyboard of a 7100 series handheld.

THE CAP KEYS

The Cap keys function just like the Shift keys on a traditional keyboard. Press either one of the Cap keys and notice that an icon appears in the upper-right corner that resembles the Cap key, as shown in Figure 1.9. Pressing a letter key produces the uppercase version of that letter and the icon disappears. This way, you can use only one finger to make uppercase characters. You can also press and hold the Cap key if you want to type multiple uppercase characters in a row.

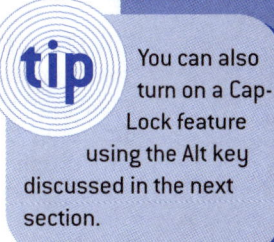

tip You can also turn on a Cap-Lock feature using the Alt key discussed in the next section.

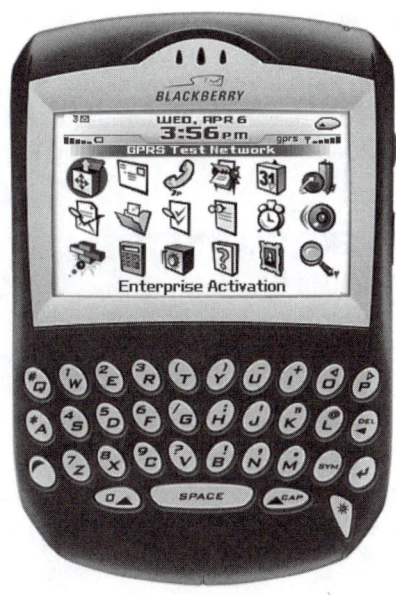

FIGURE 1.9
The Caps indicator is seen in the upper-right corner of the screen.

THE ALT KEY

The Alt key is the primary tool used to access alternative characters and functionality in the BlackBerry keyboard. Notice that each key on the keyboard has another character printed on the top of the key, as shown in Figure 1.10. These are the characters that are generated when that key is used in conjunction with the Alt key. The Alt key behaves in the same way as the Cap keys in that pressing it shows an icon in the upper-right portion of the screen.

Pressing Alt and Cap keys together typically turns the Cap-Lock on. Just like a full QWERTY keyboard, this will cause key presses to generate the capital version of the pressed key. Cap-Lock is turned off my pressing the Cap key again. Some models also support a Num-Lock as well, so be sure to check out the users guide for specifics.

14 CHAPTER 1 TOURING THE BLACKBERRY HANDHELD

FIGURE 1.10
The alternate characters are positioned differently on the keys of some models.

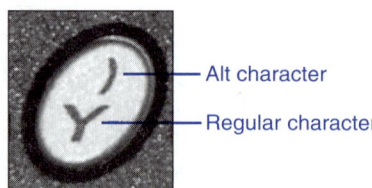
— Alt character
— Regular character

> **note** On handhelds that have the 4.0 version of the software, you can also display the symbol dialog by clicking the Show Symbols menu item, which we will talk more about in Chapter 2.

THE SYMBOL KEY

The Symbol key is used to get to even more characters that are used infrequently. On some models, the Symbol key is a combination of the Alt and Space keys or Alt and ZX key, but on most handhelds there is a dedicated key labeled SYM. Pressing the Symbol key shows a dialog that lists several symbols above a letter from the standard keyboard. You can choose the symbol by pressing the corresponding key under the symbol you want.

BEGIN CALL AND END CALL KEYS

The Begin Call and End Call keys exist only on 7100 series handhelds and are there to give the user an easy way to work with the phone feature. Pressing the Begin Call button will launch the New Call application if it is not already displayed. Once a phone number is entered, pressing the Begin Call button will attempt to place that call.

Once a call is underway, pressing the End Call button will disconnect the call and return you to the Home Screen. In fact, pressing the End Call button any other time (even when the Call application is not in use) will take you to the Home Screen as well.

BROWSER KEY

The Browser key is another key that only exists on 7100 series handhelds. It is located between the Begin Call and End Call keys and often is marked with a single line or a trademark symbol of the carrier network. Pressing the key is the same as launching the browser using the icon on the Home screen. Again, this is covered in detail in Chapter 2.

NEXT KEY

There is one more key that is only available on the 7100 series handhelds. The Next key has two arrows pointing to the right followed by a line. Clicking this key is the same as scrolling the trackwheel down. There is no key that is equivalent to scrolling the trackwheel up, however.

Chapter 2

INTERACTING WITH YOUR BLACKBERRY HANDHELD

BLACKBERRY BASICS:

- The Home Screen is the screen with icons you can click on to open an application.

- Most screens display a menu when you click the trackwheel. These menu items perform actions in the application.

- List, Choice, Button, and Edit fields are common screen elements used in most applications.

- You can cut, copy, and paste on many fields through menu items.

This chapter focuses on the very basics of how to interact with your BlackBerry handheld, such as how to open a menu, select an item, and navigate around the screen. For those of you who are already familiar with the basic functionality of your BlackBerry, you should still skim the chapter to pick up tips and tricks for using your BlackBerry effectively that you might not already know.

THE BLACKBERRY HOME SCREEN

When you turn your BlackBerry on for the first time, you will find yourself at the home screen (see Figure 2.1).

FIGURE 2.1
The BlackBerry handheld home screen shown on a model 7280.

The home screen displays a lot of information. The largest part of the screen is given to displaying icons representing tasks or actions you can do. The header at the top displays notification icons, the current date and time, as well as signal and battery strength.

> **note** On devices without color, the currently selected icon is the negative of the original icon.

> **7100** On 7100 series handhelds, some of the applications may be organized into folders. These folders can be opened by scrolling the trackwheel to select one, and then clicking it. When a folder is opened, the contents of the folder are displayed in the same way as the Home screen. Pressing the Escape key closes the folder and returns you to the Home screen.

> **note** It is possible to remove the shortcuts from the main screen through a configuration setting. Please see "General Options" in Chapter 9 for more information on this.

The icon list, sometimes called the application list, generally represents the different applications that are available on your handheld. These include Messages, Address Book, and others. There are also icons for commonly accessed features such as Compose and Profiles, which are actually portions of other applications.

INTERACTING WITH THE APPLICATION ICONS

Start by scrolling the trackwheel up or down. Notice that the icon changes slightly as you scroll the trackwheel. Exactly how the icon changes depends on the device, but in general there will be some kind of highlight. The highlight acts as a "selection indicator," letting you know which application is selected and will be activated if you click the trackwheel.

In case you hadn't noticed, the trackwheel can be pressed in so that it has a "click" feel to it. This is what "clicking the trackwheel" means. Now, let's launch an application. Move the selection indicator to the Messages application and click the trackwheel.

At this point, you should see the Messages application on the screen. (Don't worry if you accidentally scrolled the trackwheel at the same time that you clicked and ended up with a different application open. It happens to the best of us from time to time.) Okay, so right now you aren't interested in checking new messages or composing a new message—no problem. There is an Escape button on the side of the handheld below the trackwheel that is used to cancel an action or "back up" a screen. Press the Escape button and you should once again see the home screen.

ICON SHORTCUTS

As you scroll the trackwheel back and forth through the icon list, notice that the name of the icon is shown below the icon list. This is another identifying feature to let you know what the icon does because initially some icons may not be obvious just by looking at them.

Scroll the trackwheel to the Messages icon again. Notice that the text indicator for the Messages icon is "Messages." The underlined letter means that the icon has a shortcut character associated with it (similar to what you find in Microsoft Windows applications). For instance, a shortcut character means that if you press that key while on the home screen, the icon will be selected and launched. So in this example, pressing the M key while the home screen is displayed will cause the Messages icon to be selected and then launched, just like we had done previously by scrolling to the icon and clicking the trackwheel.

Not all icons have a shortcut character. Table 2.1 is a list of the standard icons for the BlackBerry Handheld Software, their shortcuts, and descriptions.

THE BLACKBERRY HOME SCREEN

Table 2.1—Standard Icon Shortcuts

Icon	Name	Shortcut	Description
	Messages	M	Read and manage messages
	Phone	P	Call history
	Address Book	A	View and manage address information
	Calendar	L	View and manage calendar information
	Browser	B	The BlackBerry web browser
	Compose	C	Jump to the Compose Messages screen
	Search Messages	S	Jump to the Search Messages screen
	Saved Messages	V	Access your Saved Messages folder
	Tasks	T	View and manage your To Do list
	MemoPad	D	A simple notepad
	Alarm	R	A simple alarm clock
	Profiles	F	Manage your profiles
	Calculator	U	A simple calculator
	Options	O	Many configuration settings
	Keyboard Lock	K	Enables the Keyboard Lock
	Turn Wireless Off	<none>	Turns off just the wireless
	Turn Power Off	<none>	Powers down the device

If you have a 7100 with version 4.0, the software has themes that can be provided by your carrier. Themes can change everything on your Home screen, including the icons for applications. As a result, the icons on your handheld may not look exactly like the icons in Table 2.1. (We will talk more about themes in Chapter 4, "Personalizing Your Device.")

The 4.0 version of the handheld software adds three new icons to your screen, as shown in Table 2.2.

7100 The 7100 series handhelds do not use the keyboard shortcuts because of the smaller keyboard on those handhelds. Instead, pressing a key will display the Call Log application and begin the process of placing a call. We will talk more about placing a call in Chapter 9, "Making Phone Calls."

CHAPTER 2 INTERACTING WITH YOUR BLACKBERRY HANDHELD

Table 2.2—Additional Icons in Version 4.0			
Icon	Name	Shortcut	Description
	Password Keeper	<none>	Store and manage your passwords
	Pictures	<none>	View and manage pictures
	Help	<none>	Online help

INTERACTING WITH A BLACKBERRY APPLICATION

Now that you can launch an application, lets take a few moments and discuss the standard components, or fields, that make up most applications. These components are the building blocks for many of the applications in the BlackBerry handheld software and understanding how to work with them is an important step.

There are five main components that can appear in a BlackBerry application. They are

- **Menu**—Bringing up a menu for more actions
- **List**—Displays a list of items
- **Button**—A clickable button
- **Choice**—A short selectable list of values
- **Edit**—Field for entering text

One or more of these fields can appear together on a screen in any order. Because user input can only go to one field at a time, there is a field selector that is part of the screen as well. Only one field can be selected at a time. You can change the selected field by scrolling the trackwheel up or down. The input portion of the selected field is drawn in reverse, or if it is an edit field, a cursor appears in it. (The cursor is a little different than in your standard software application. Rather than a blinking line, it is a solid rectangle that moves as you input text.) Figure 2.2 shows a screen where the selected field is the Snooze field.

The next few sections take a closer look at each of the five main component types you'll find when working with BlackBerry applications.

MENUS

All BlackBerry applications display something and do something. The "do something" part is usually done by displaying a menu then reacting to the menu item you select. To display a menu in an open application, simply click the trackwheel. Not all applications use a menu, but if it does, this should display it. Figure 2.3 shows the Phone application menu as an example.

INTERACTING WITH A BLACKBERRY APPLICATION

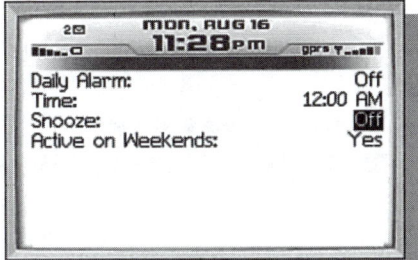

FIGURE 2.2
Toggle the Snooze field to On by clicking the trackwheel.

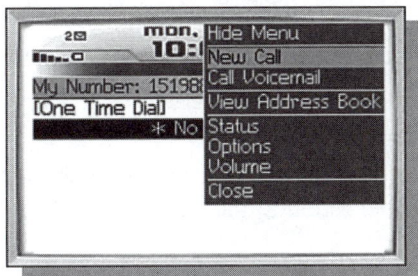

FIGURE 2.3
A menu being displayed.

While the menu is displayed, scrolling the trackwheel up and down moves the selection indicator up and down in the menu. The menu item that has been highlighted (or reversed to white, on black-and-white models) is the selected item.

The Hide Menu menu item is common to all application menus. Clicking this item causes the menu to close. You can also click the Escape key (located below the trackwheel) to close the menu display.

Menu items can be any action that the application can do and are not configurable by a user. Different menu items may be displayed, depending on conditions in the screen or what field is selected. For instance, in the Address Book application, if there are no contacts, the menu will show only a New Address menu item, and will not show Edit Address or Delete Address menu items because there are no items in the list to edit or delete. Selecting a menu item can also cause another menu to be displayed, but this is not a normal operation.

> **tip** Some applications that have a specialized screen, such as the Home Screen, may use an Alt-click to display the menu.

LISTS

Lists are some of the most common components used in applications that display a lot of information. For instance, the Messages application displays a list of messages. The list tends to be the only element on the screen because it usually can be added to and may grow to be bigger than the screen. When this happens it becomes

> **note** Some menus have different menu items depending on which item in the list is selected.

scrollable. Figure 2.4 shows an example of a list. To change the selected item in the list, just scroll the trackwheel up or down.

FIGURE 2.4
Example of a list on the Messages screen.

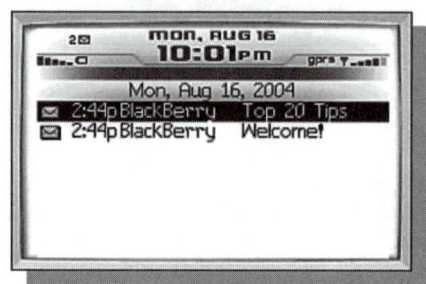

If the list has more elements than can fit on a single screen, small arrows appear on the right side of the screen indicating that there are items above and/or below the screen.

Some lists allow you to select more than a single item. Do this by holding the CAP key while scrolling the trackwheel.

> **tip** For lists that are very long, scrolling through the list one item at a time can be very painful. Fortunately, you can scroll the list one screen at a time by scrolling with the Alt key pressed in.
>
> Another way to activate a button is to press the Enter key when the button is selected.

BUTTONS

Buttons are not used as often as other components, but they have special behavior that should be addressed. As you would expect, a button can be clicked, which is done by clicking the trackwheel or pressing the Enter key. If the screen has a menu, clicking the trackwheel would normally display it. However, if a button is selected, clicking the trackwheel will "click" the button instead. Whatever action the button does is executed right away. This is basically the same as displaying the menu and selecting a menu item, so a button is used when a menu isn't the best way to trigger an action—which isn't often. Figure 2.5 shows a screen with a button labeled Preview.

FIGURE 2.5
An active (highlighted) button's action occurs as soon as you click the trackwheel.

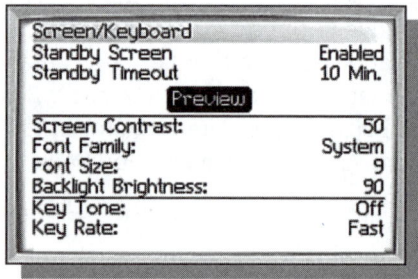

CHOICE FIELDS

Choice fields are used in many applications where there is a small list of acceptable values. For instance, selecting a time display format would have only two acceptable values, "24 hour" and "12 hour." Not surprisingly, these are very common in configuration screens. Figure 2.6 is shows an example of a screen with a Choice field.

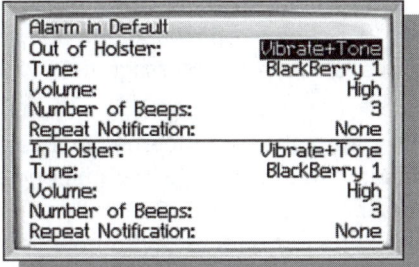

FIGURE 2.6
Example of a Choice field.

When working with a Choice field, there are two ways to switch the values. The first is through a menu labeled Change Option that is displayed automatically in the menu if the selected field is a Choice field.

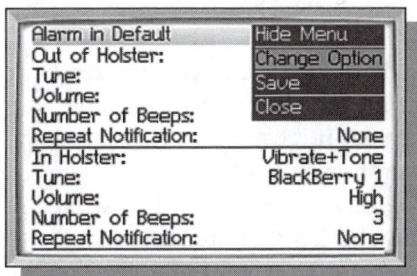

FIGURE 2.7
Example of the Change Option menu item.

The second method is to hold down the Alt key while scrolling the trackwheel in a Choice field. Either method should display a small dialog with the short list of values allowing you to scroll through the list and click to select a value.

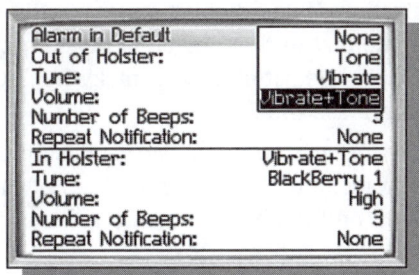

FIGURE 2.8
Choice fields have two or more options that you can select from.

If the Change Option menu was used, the selection can be made by either clicking the trackwheel or pressing the Enter key. Pressing the Escape key cancels the operation.

> **tip** Another way to change the value is to press the Space key with the Choice field selected. This will cause the selection to change to the next value.

If the Alt+Scroll method was used, releasing the Alt key sets the selected value.

EDIT FIELDS

Edit fields are used whenever there is a need to enter data that cannot be narrowed down to a choice. An example of an edit field is the address field of the Address Book or the Message field when composing a new message.

The Edit field has a number of properties that can be used to limit the type of information entered, such as the numeric only property which allows only numbers to be entered. Generally you will not notice these properties because they do not interfere with how you type in the information.

However, they can help you out in many ways to make entering text easier. In the example of the numeric only property, you do not have to use the Alt+char key combination: Simply pressing the key will cause the proper number to appear. Often people use this without even thinking about it. Fields that are used to collect web addresses or email addresses have special properties as well that will make the Space key automatically insert an "@" or "." character as appropriate.

If the Edit field already has text in it, you can scroll through the existing text by scrolling the trackwheel up and down. Notice that as you go up, the cursor stays in the same column if it can, but when scrolling down, the cursor jumps to the end of the text on each line. Moving the cursor to some text in the middle of the line can be tricky, but it's not impossible. Some newer devices have keys for moving right and left that are reached through the Alt key. If not, pressing and holding the Alt button while scrolling the trackwheel will move the cursor right and left also.

COPY AND PASTING

Edit fields also have the ability to cut/copy and paste. Only one bit of text can be copied at a time, but this can be a very useful feature. There are two ways to start the copy selection. If you display a menu while an Edit field is selected and that field has some text in it, a Select menu is shown. You can also press and hold the Shift key while scrolling the trackwheel. Once the copy selection has started, you can release the Shift key.

The same rules apply for moving the cursor as described previously, even the Alt+scroll rule. As you move the cursor around, all of the text between the starting cursor location and the current cursor location is highlighted as shown in Figure 2.9.

Once some text is selected, bringing up a menu shows new menu items—Copy, Cut, and Cancel Selection. The Cut menu item is only shown if the Edit field you have selected text from is not read only. In this example, the message is read only, so no Cut menu item is shown in Figure 2.10.

INTERACTING WITH A BLACKBERRY APPLICATION

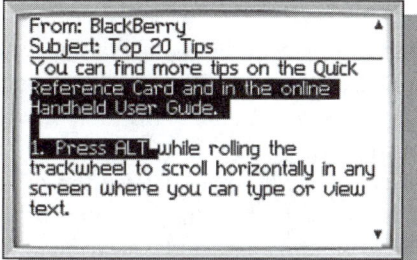

FIGURE 2.9
Some text selected in a message.

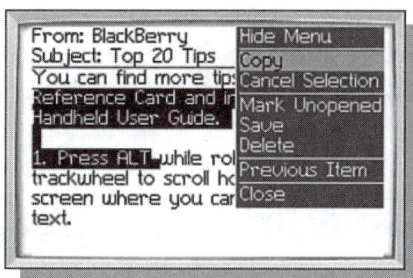

FIGURE 2.10
The Copy menu once text has been selected.

Selecting the Cancel Selection menu item or pressing the Escape key will cancel the selection. Selecting the Copy menu item cancels the selection too, but the copied text is also placed in the clipboard. Selecting the Cut menu item removes the selected text and adds it to the clipboard. The text then stays in the clipboard until another copy selection is made.

Once some text is copied, a new Paste menu item shows up when the menu is displayed and an Edit field is selected. When the menu item is selected, the text in the clipboard is pasted into the Edit field at the current cursor location.

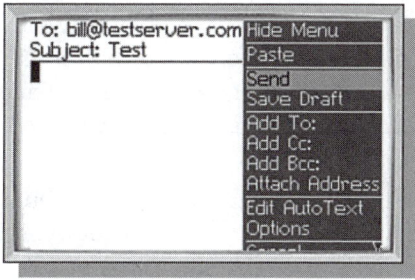

FIGURE 2.11
The Paste menu item is available once text has been copied.

SURETYPE AND MULTITAP

Because the 7100 series handhelds have more than one letter per key, there must be some way to make specific words from the series of keypresses that happens when a person types. There are actually two ways that you can do this. These are called SureType and MultiTap.

SureType is a method that uses a dictionary to make accurate guesses as to what word you are really wanting when you type. Using SureType, you only have to press each key you want once, and the software does the rest. For instance, if you press the keys, TY, GH, UI, and AS, the software would produce a guess of "THIS." It is able to do this because the other possible combinations of letters do not make words that are as common as "THIS." The words "THUS" and "THIA" would be offered as alternatives because they are either valid but less common words, or are the closest possible combination that could be part of another word. Figure 2.12 shows the word being entered and the possible alternatives under it.

FIGURE 2.12
The software provides a guess of "THIS" and lists other possible alternatives.

Notice that the word "THIS" is underlined. When the word is underlined, it means that the word is a guess given by the software. Scrolling the trackwheel up or down moves the selection indicator in the list of possible guesses below and changes the word on the edit field. Clicking the trackwheel or pressing the Space key accepts the selected word and resets the software to begin making guesses on the next word.

Sometimes you may not want to use SureType. If the word you want to enter is not in the dictionary, it may be difficult to get the software to make a proper guess. You may also not want to use SureType out of personal preference. In this case, you can turn off SureType (through configuration options or using a menu item) and switch to MultiTap mode.

When an edit field is in MultiTap mode, an "ABC" indicator is shown in the upper-right corner of the screen, as seen in Figure 2.13. Some fields, such as password fields, only work in MultiTap mode because showing the whole word without the password masking would be insecure.

INTERACTING WITH A BLACKBERRY APPLICATION

FIGURE 2.13
When an Edit field is in MultiTap mode, a special indicator is shown in the upper-right corner of the screen.

To enter a word using MultiTap mode, you sometimes need to press a key more than once. Pressing a key with two characters on it will cause the left character to be shown. Pressing the same key again will cause the character to change to the other character on the key.

For instance, pressing the ER key will first produce the E character. Pressing the ER key again quickly will change the E character to the R character. When a character is being entered, it is shown with an underline in the same way as when using SureType. This means the character can be changed by pressing the same key again. The character will only remain underlined for about a second, however, so you need to be quick about pressing the key again to change the character.

So, if we go back to our previous example, to type the word "THIS" in MultiType mode, you would have to press the keys TY, GH, GH, UI, UI, AS, AS. This means you have to do more keystrokes to enter the word, but it also means that you can be confident about the resulting word.

> **7100** Some fields are designed to only allow numbers to be entered, such as a phone number field. On these fields, a numeric indicator with the number "123" on it is shown in the upper-right corner. When this is shown, pressing any key will default to the number on the key instead of the letter.

Part II

WHAT TO DO AFTER YOU OPEN THE BOX

3 Installing and Configuring the Desktop Manager

4 Personalizing Your Device

Chapter 3

INSTALLING AND CONFIGURING THE DESKTOP MANAGER

BLACKBERRY BASICS:

- The Desktop Manager is an important tool for managing and configuring your handheld.

- There are three different ways that you can redirect email messages to your handheld—BlackBerry Enterprise Server, BlackBerry Desktop Redirector, and BlackBerry Web Client.

- You can set filters in the Redirector Settings Applet to help combat spam email.

- When you set up your handheld for the first time, you must generate a security key.

WHAT IS THE DESKTOP MANAGER?

Like most handheld devices that synchronize data with your PC, there is a component that needs to be installed on your PC to help manage your handheld. This piece is called the BlackBerry Desktop Manager and is included on the CD that shipped with your handheld. The Desktop Manager's first job is to set up your handheld and configure it so you can start to receive messages.

Afterward, the Desktop Manager handles the maintenance tasks such as backup/restore, synchronization with your email server, and loading new applications.

REDIRECTING MESSAGES TO THE BLACKBERRY

The first thing to look at when setting up your device is to decide how emails will get to your device. As you may expect, some piece of software must be there to cause your messages to be sent from wherever they are to your handheld. This process is referred to as "redirecting your messages."

There are three ways to accomplish the redirection of messages:

- BlackBerry Enterprise Server (BES)
- BlackBerry Web Client
- BlackBerry Desktop Redirector

Generally there is only one right way for you, but choosing the right method can be difficult if you are not familiar with why there are three ways and what the differences are.

BLACKBERRY ENTERPRISE SERVER

The BlackBerry Enterprise Server is a server component that is purchased separately from your handheld. It provides tight integration between BlackBerry handhelds and your corporate email server. It is installed on a server at your corporate offices and allows the Information Technologies staff additional management control features over your handheld, and can provide additional services because of the tight integration. Redirection of your email is done by the server.

Companies that want to give BlackBerry handhelds to many employees often have a BlackBerry Enterprise Server installed. It only works with Microsoft Exchange and Lotus Notes Email servers, and users have to use either Microsoft Outlook or the Lotus Notes Client to access their email.

If you use a company-provided BlackBerry then this is the option you should use, but you will likely also receive additional instructions from your IT staff. If you are unsure whether your company has a BlackBerry Enterprise Server installed, ask your IT staff.

BLACKBERRY WEB CLIENT

Another common choice is the BlackBerry Web Client. The Web Client is basically a BlackBerry Enterprise Server that is run by an ISP or your wireless provider. You will typically be given an email address from that provider to be used with your BlackBerry, and that address will most likely be different than the email address that you use on your desktop PC currently.

DESKTOP REDIRECTOR

If you use Microsoft Outlook as your email client and do not have a BlackBerry Enterprise Server or Microsoft Exchange server, then the BlackBerry Desktop Redirector is your redirection method. Unlike the BlackBerry Enterprise Server, which does redirection at an email server, the Desktop Redirector does it at your desktop PC. The Desktop Redirector is a separate program that runs on your desktop PC and integrates with Microsoft Outlook to redirect email messages that the email client retrieves.

Because the Desktop Redirector runs on your desktop PC, the desktop PC must be on and connected to the Internet for you to receive emails on your handheld. If your desktop PC is a laptop that you take with you, then this method will not work and you need to look at setting up a dedicated system to run the Desktop Redirector or consider installing a BlackBerry Enterprise Server. Setting up a dedicated system usually means setting up an old PC or purchasing an inexpensive PC to run the Desktop Redirector on.

The nice thing about using Desktop Redirector is that you can configure Outlook to retrieve messages from multiple providers using the POP3 protocol and have all of them delivered to your handheld. When you reply, however, only one reply address will be used. If you want to get email from your account at AOL or Yahoo!, you must use the Desktop Redirector, even if you have access to a BlackBerry Enterprise Server.

note Your handheld can be used with both a BlackBerry Web Client and the BlackBerry Enterprise Server. If you want to do this, configure the Desktop Manager to use the BlackBerry Enterprise Server first, then use the BlackBerry Web Client to configure your handheld to use that also.

INSTALLING THE DESKTOP MANAGER

To Install the Desktop Manager on your PC, you should simply have to insert the CD. The installer should start up right away. If it does not, you will need to launch it manually by clicking the Start button and then selecting the Run button. A small dialog will open that looks like the one shown in Figure 3.1.

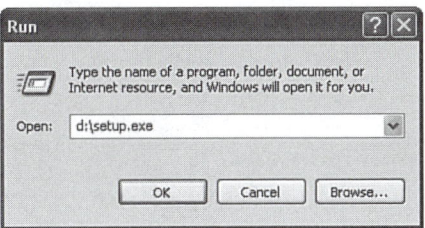

FIGURE 3.1
Open the Windows Run dialog to start the CD if it does not start automatically.

Enter D:\Setup.exe and click the OK Button. The installer should start up with a splash screen and then display the welcome screen to the Install Wizard (see Figure 3.2).

The next few steps are pretty standard for installing Windows applications. Step through the screens, answering the questions as appropriate, and clicking Next until you get to the step shown in Figure 3.3, which asks you what kind of installation you will be doing.

note — There are really no differences between installing version 3.6 or 3.7 of the Desktop Manager software, so this information should apply to you regardless of which one you are installing.

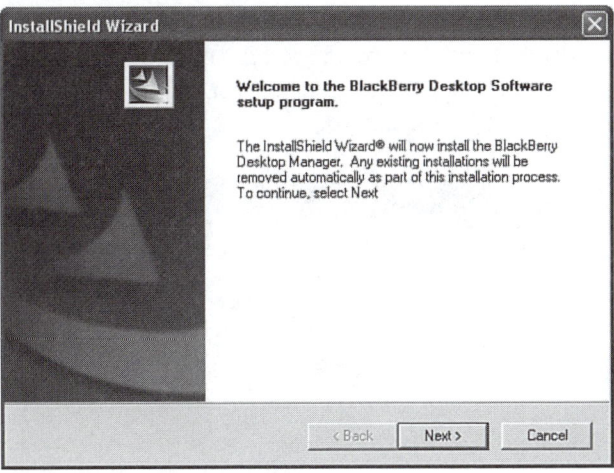

FIGURE 3.2
The installation process begins with the welcome screen.

This is the first of three screens with questions to answer how your Desktop Manager will be configured. This screen is asking whether you want to the Desktop Manager to integrate with an email client or server. If you were given a BlackBerry Web Client address and want to use only that address, select the

Integrate with a New or Existing ISP Email Account option and click the Next button to continue with the installation wizard.

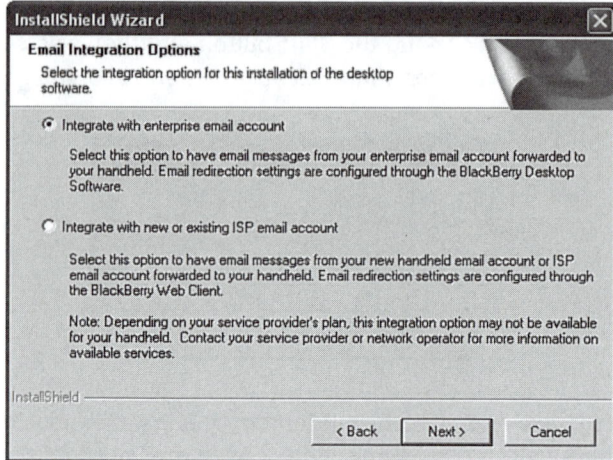

FIGURE 3.3
Selecting the email integration for your Desktop Manager.

If you want the Desktop Manager to integrate with an Email client or server, then select the Integrate with Enterprise Email Account option and click the Next button.

The next step in the wizard, shown in Figure 3.4, asks which email system you are going to work with. The only two options are Microsoft Exchange and Lotus Notes. As we mentioned before, these are the only two supported systems and you should know which one you are going to use. Select the appropriate email system and click the Next button. If you plan to use the Desktop Redirector, select the Microsoft Exchange option at this screen, even if you do not have access to a Microsoft Exchange server. If you selected Lotus Notes, continue with the installation wizard.

FIGURE 3.4
Selecting the email system.

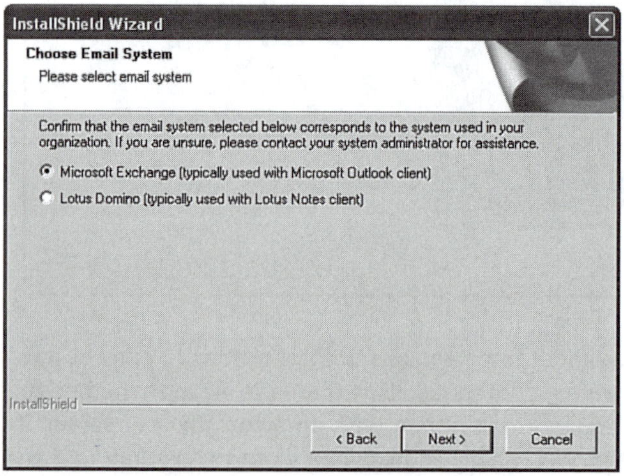

CONFIGURING THE DESKTOP MANAGER

The last screen, shown in Figure 3.5, asks what redirection method you want to use. If you want redirection to happen at the server and know that your company has installed a BlackBerry Enterprise Server, choose the Redirect Email Using the BlackBerry Enterprise Server option and click the Next button. If you want to use the Desktop Redirector, select the Redirect Email Using the BlackBerry Desktop Redirector option and click the Next button.

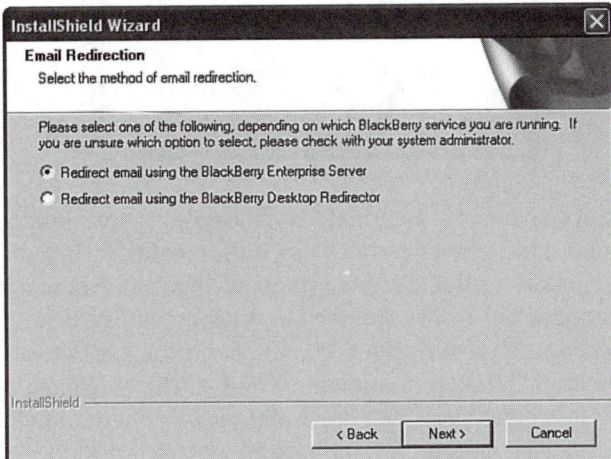

FIGURE 3.5
Select an email redirection method.

The rest of the installation wizard contains many screens that are common to Windows installers. Continue the installation wizard, answering questions as appropriate.

CONFIGURING THE DESKTOP MANAGER

After the installation is done and you launch the Desktop Manager for the first time, you might have to provide additional information or want to change some of the settings. The following sections cover some of the most common scenarios.

SETTING THE COMMUNICATIONS PORT

Your handheld must be connected to your computer via a USB or serial cable for the Desktop Manager to do anything with it. When you install the Desktop Manager, the default port may be incorrect. If you get a dialog similar to the one shown in Figure 3.6, you need to change the connection settings.

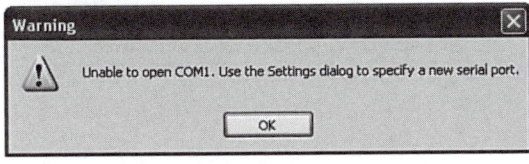

FIGURE 3.6
The Unable to Connect message means the port that is selected is not the one that communicates with your BlackBerry.

CHAPTER 3 INSTALLING AND CONFIGURING THE DESKTOP MANAGER

You can change this by selecting the Option menu, and then the Connection Settings menu item. That will display a dialog similar to the one seen in Figure 3.7.

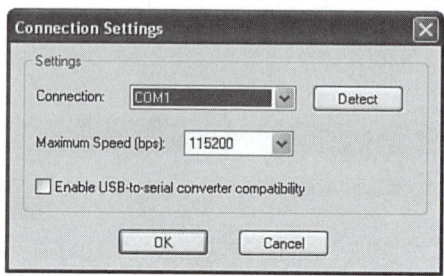

FIGURE 3.7
The Connection Settings dialog enables you to correct the port setting.

You should know how your handheld is connected to the desktop PC, but generally speaking, most newer devices use USB to connect. If your handheld uses a serial cable, make sure you know which COM port it is connected to. You can change the connection in the Connection drop-down list. If your device is already plugged in to your desktop PC, you can click the Detect button and allow the Desktop Manager to attempt to find it. The Maximum speed setting is used with serial connections, but generally you should not need to change it. Lastly, if your device uses a USB connection, but your desktop PC does not have a USB port, you can buy a USB-to-serial converter. If you have this, you should check the Enable USB-to-serial Converter Compatibility check box.

CONNECTING TO THE EMAIL SYSTEM

If you are integrating with an email system, the Desktop Manager will attempt to connect to that email system when it is launched. You will see a dialog telling you that the connection is being established.

When connecting to a Microsoft Exchange server using Outlook, you will have to choose the profile that will be used for the connection. In this case, a dialog like Figure 3.8 will be shown. Generally, there will be only one profile in the list and you can simply use that. However, if there is more than one listed and you do not know which one to use, you should ask your IT department.

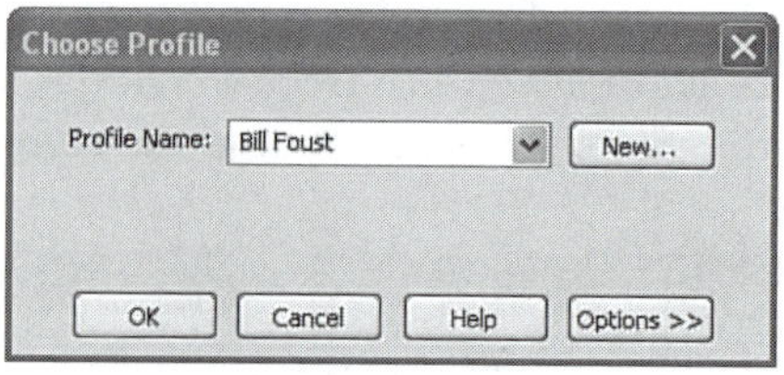

FIGURE 3.8
The Connection Settings dialog.

OTHER CONFIGURATION OPTIONS

There are only two other things that you can configure in the Desktop Manager without using one of the applets. The first is the view style of the icons. Like Windows Explorer, you can view the icons of the applets as Large or Small. You can change this setting through the View menu by selecting either the Large Icons or Small Icons menu items.

The other option you can configure is the location of the files that the Desktop Manager creates during the Intellisync process and for configuration files.

Click the Options menu and select the Data Folder Settings menu item. The dialog, shown in Figure 3.9, shows the current folder being used. To specify another directory, click the Use This Specified Folder radio button and click the Browse button to select a different folder.

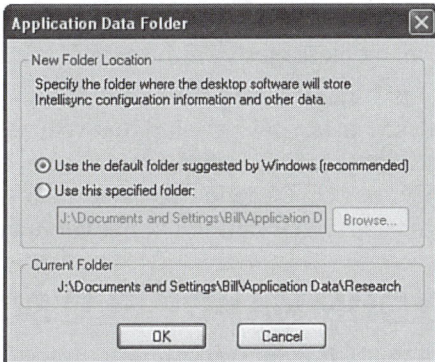

FIGURE 3.9
Changing the location of the Application Data folder.

USING THE DESKTOP REDIRECTOR

The Desktop Redirector is a relatively simple piece of software that works with Microsoft Outlook. It is responsible for gathering new messages from Outlook and sending them to your handheld. In order to do this effectively, it must be running all the time.

There aren't many things that you can do with the Desktop Redirector. Its screen simply shows a lot of statistics that you can't change, and there are only a few menu items available. The Desktop Redirector is shown in Figure 3.10.

> **note** Even though you can run the Desktop Redirector if you are configured to a BlackBerry Enterprise Server, there really isn't any benefit in doing this.

There are just a few menu items available under the Options menu, which we will discuss next. The first of these is Hide When Minimized. You may have noticed that the Desktop Redirector displays an icon in the system tray when it is launched. Clicking the menu item causes the check box next to the menu item to toggle on and off. When the check box is shown, minimizing the Desktop Redirector causes the application to not be shown on the task bar.

This leaves only the icon on the system tray showing, and helps to keep your desktop clean. Double-clicking on the icon in the system tray will display the Desktop Redirector screen again.

FIGURE 3.10
The Desktop Redirector shows many statistics about messages that have been redirected.

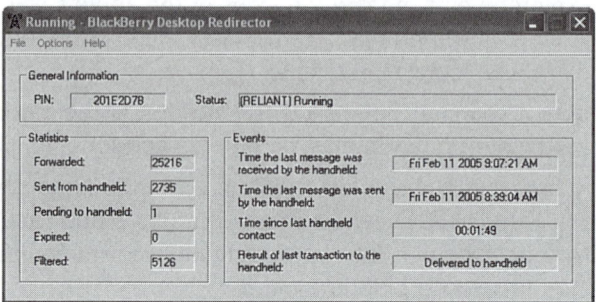

The second menu item is Clear Statistics. Clicking this menu item will reset all the counts of how many messages have been sent, filtered, and so on, to 0.

The last menu item is Purge Pending Messages. For a number of reasons, it is possible to have several messages pending that will never be delivered. One of the most common is because the destination device is lost or broken and you will be getting a new device. Clicking this menu item will purge all of the messages that were sent to that device but not yet delivered to it.

UPGRADING YOUR HANDHELD SOFTWARE

You might not have realized it, but you can also use the Desktop Manager to install new software onto your handheld. There are new versions of the BlackBerry handheld software released periodically, and there may be some real benefits in upgrading to the latest version. Getting the software, however, can sometimes be rather difficult.

You can only get the latest software from your carrier, and not all carriers are open or enthusiastic about supporting new versions. Your best bet is to search the support website of your carrier or call the customer support group.

When you get the new software, it will most likely be in a setup package that you must install. The installer doesn't install the software on your handheld directly, however. Instead, it installs the software onto your hard drive as part of the Desktop Manager. Then later when you run the Desktop Manager, it will install the software on your handheld.

After you have installed the new handheld software, launch the Desktop Manager and connect your handheld to the desktop PC. The Desktop Manager will notice that there is a new version of software available and display a prompt asking if you would like to install the new software. This prompt is shown in Figure 3.11.

WORKING WITH THE DESKTOP MANAGER APPLETS

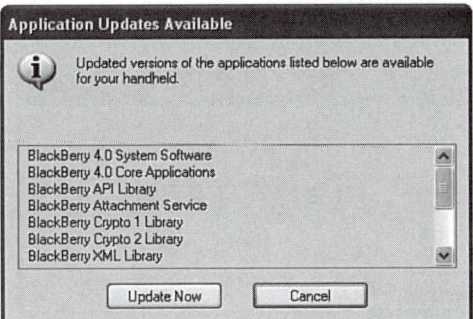

FIGURE 3.11
The Desktop Manager automatically prompts asking if you would like to install new versions of the handheld software.

Installing new handheld software is a complicated process that involves several steps in order to get your handheld back to the same state where it was when you started. During the process, your handheld will be wiped completely clean, so a complete backup and restore are essential parts of the process. Once the process starts, the dialog seen in Figure 3.12 is shown to display the status of each step as it progresses through the upgrade.

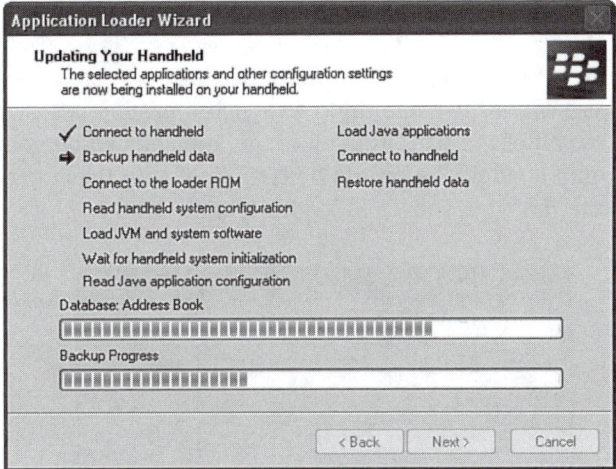

FIGURE 3.12
This dialog shows the progress of each step that is required when installing a new version of handheld software.

Once it's all done, make sure to take some time to explore what is new in the handheld software.

WORKING WITH THE DESKTOP MANAGER APPLETS

The BlackBerry Desktop Manager is basically a collection of applets that each offer more specific functionality. There are four standard applets that you should see: Application Loader, Backup/Restore, Intellisync, and Redirector

Settings. These are shown in Figure 3.13. We'll spend some time going over each of these applets in more detail below.

FIGURE 3.13
The Desktop Manager contains four standard applets.

APPLICATION LOADER

Chapter 14, "Finding and Installing Third-Party Applications," is devoted to third-party applications and how to load them using the Application Loader, so we won't go into detail on that here. Just suffice it to say that the Application Loader is used to add, update, or remove other applications from your handheld.

BACKUP/RESTORE

The Backup/Restore applet handles doing backups or restores to your device. Backup/Restore is not the same thing as synchronization with your email system. This takes all of the data from all of the applications on your handheld and saves it into a single file on the hard drive of your desktop computer. The Backup/Restore dialog is shown in Figure 3.14.

FIGURE 3.14
Backup/Restore enables you to manage the data that you keep on your BlackBerry.

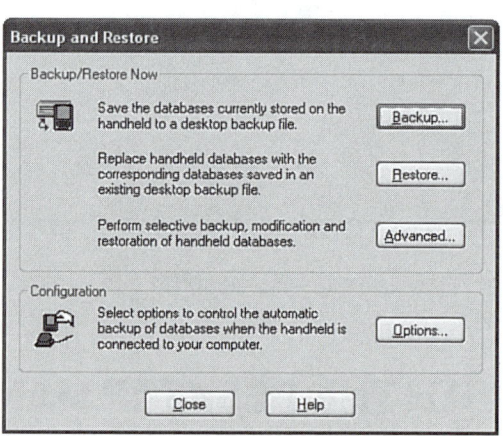

Making a backup is always a good idea. Backing up your handheld can make the process of moving to a new device with all of your data intact very easy if you ever break or lose your handheld...not to mention those accidental deletions that happen.

WORKING WITH THE DESKTOP MANAGER APPLETS

Data on BlackBerry handhelds is stored in databases and each one is given a name. Applications are not required to create a database, but if the application needs to save any data, it will have at least one. There is no limit to the number of databases that an application can create, however. Typically the database name will be related to the application name, such as "Memos" and "Memopad Options," which are the two databases that the Memopad application uses.

During a backup or restore, the contents of these databases are transferred between the handheld and a file on your computer. The details of backing up the data and restoring it to your handheld are covered in the following sections.

PERFORMING A BACKUP OF YOUR BLACKBERRY DATA

To perform a backup, simply click the Backup button on the Backup/Restore screen. If the Backup button is not enabled, it means that your handheld is not connected to the desktop PC, or that the connection is not recognized.

A standard Save File dialog is displayed, asking what to name your backup file. It defaults to the My Documents folder, which is fine for most people. The suggested filename includes the PIN of the device and the date. Click the Save button to begin the Backup.

Another dialog is displayed detailing the progress of the backup for each database that exists on the handheld. If you have a lot of messages or contacts, the backup process can take a long time.

RESTORING DATA TO THE BLACKBERRY

Restoring is just as easy as backing up. Click the Restore button on the Backup/Restore screen. A standard Open File dialog is shown, which lists the .IPD files in the My Documents folder (or whatever folder you saved the backup to). Select the one you want to restore from and click the Open button to begin the restore.

If the PIN of the device that is currently connected to the desktop PC is different than the PIN of the device that the backup was made from, you will get a message box asking if you want to proceed. This can help prevent errors if you use multiple devices, and is allowed as a way to let you restore the data into a new device should the other one need to be replaced.

ADVANCED BACKUP/RESTORE OPTIONS

Occasionally you will want to back up or restore just specific databases on your handheld. The Advanced feature is for just this situation. Clicking the Advanced button on the Backup/Restore screen displays the Advanced Backup and Restore screen, shown in Figure 3.15. The pane on the right side of the screen lists all of the databases on your handheld at that moment. The pane on the left side lists all of the databases in the backup file.

CHAPTER 3 INSTALLING AND CONFIGURING THE DESKTOP MANAGER

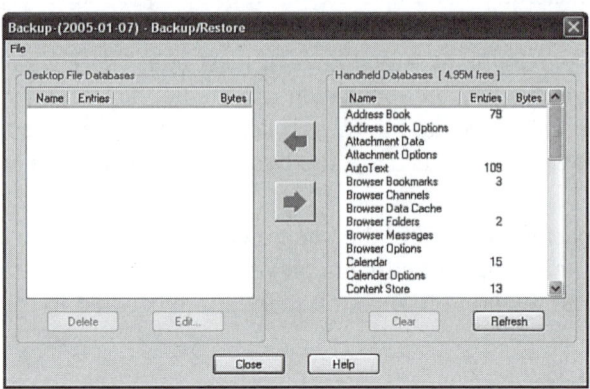

FIGURE 3.15
The Advanced Backup/Restore feature gives you some additional flexibility to help you manage your BlackBerry data.

> **caution** Be careful when using the Advanced Restore option, because restoring a database will cause the existing database on the handheld to be deleted first. If you overwrite the data on the device, you cannot get it back (unless you happen to have another backup that predates the one you restored from).

To back up a specific database, click the database name from the list in the right pane and click the left arrow button in the center of the dialog. This puts an entry for that database in the list in the left pane, if one is not already there.

To restore a specific database, you will need to load a backup file first by choosing File, Open. Select the desired file and click the Open button.

Once a backup file has been loaded, the databases included in that backup file are added to the list in the left pane. Select the database that is to be restored, and click the right arrow in the center of the dialog. If the database to be restored already exists on the handheld, a dialog will be displayed asking you to confirm the restore.

Finally, if you are ever in a position where you want to delete a database from the handheld, you can do that in the Advanced Backup/Restore screen as well. Simply select the database from the list in the right pane, and click the Clear button at the bottom of the list.

CONFIGURING BACKUP/RESTORE OPTIONS

It's easy to forget to do backups of things, and your handheld is no exception. Fortunately, you can set up the Backup/Restore applet to automatically create backups for you at regular intervals. This is done through the Options screen.

Click the Options button on the Backup/Restore screen to display the Backup and Restore Options dialog, shown in Figure 3.16.

To enable a regular automatic backup of your handheld, check the Automatically Backup my Handheld check box at the top of the dialog. Then specify the number of days between backups in the Every field at the end of the check box.

Most likely, you will want to back up all of the data. However, you can choose not to do a backup of your messages and PIM data because they are already backed up in your email system.

WORKING WITH THE DESKTOP MANAGER APPLETS

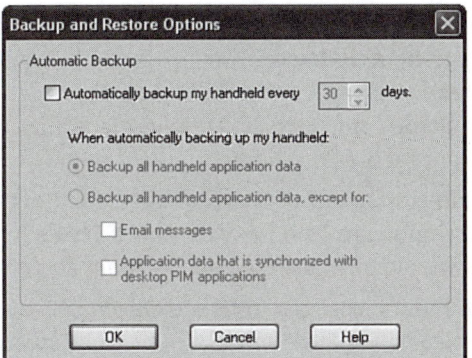

FIGURE 3.16
The Backup/Restore Options dialog allows you to set your BlackBerry for a regular backup schedule.

If you want to back up all of your data, select the radio button Backup All Handheld Application Data. If you want to not back up either the message or PIM data, or both, select the Backup All Handheld Application Data, Except For radio button. The two check boxes at the bottom of the dialog will become enabled. To not back up your messages, check the Email Messages check box. To not back up your PIM data (Contacts, Appointments, and so forth) check the Application Data That Is Synchronized with Desktop PIM Applications check box.

INTELLISYNC

The Intellisync applet, shown in Figure 3.17, sets up and handles synchronization of your handheld to your email system. Synchronization basically means it will make your handheld and your email system contain the same data. For instance, if you added a contact to the Address Book on your handheld, it will make a copy of that contact in your email system as well.

FIGURE 3.17
The Intellisync applet handles the synchronization of your data between the PC and the BlackBerry.

SYNCHRONIZING YOUR DATA

The installer sets up a standard configuration, so you should not need to change anything to be able to synchronize your handheld. There are, however, a lot of areas where you can customize the synchronization process if you want to. The dialog is divided into two sections—Synchronize Now at the top of the screen and Configuration at the bottom.

There are four things that can be synchronized each time a synchronization is done. These four things are listed as four check boxes in the Synchronize Now section. You can enable and disable each of them as you need.

If you want your email messages to be synchronized, click the Reconcile Email check box. This basically makes sure that the email messages on your handheld are the same as the email messages on your email system. Depending on how it is configured, this will mean that email messages that are deleted or moved to another folder on one end will be deleted or moved on the other. For example, if you delete messages from your inbox on your PC, then those messages will also be deleted from the Message list on the BlackBerry and vice versa.

If you want your contacts and appointments to be synchronized, click the Synchronize PIM check box. Unlike synchronizing email messages, synchronizing PIM data will also update any existing contacts and appointments if they have been changed on the other system.

The last thing that can be synchronized is your handheld's date and time. You can easily configure your desktop PC to update its time periodically to ensure that time is always correct. If you want to update your handheld's date and time whenever a synchronization is done, check the Update the Handheld's Date and Time check box.

There are only two ways to do a synchronization, and one of them is by clicking the Synchronize Now button. When you click the Synchronize Now button, the software analyzes the data on your handheld and the data in your email system and makes changes to both of them at the same. It takes some time to do all of this, though, and a progress dialog is shown while it works.

Once the analysis is complete, another dialog is sometimes displayed, showing a summary of the actions that will be taken (see Figure 3.18). The summary lists the number of records that will be added to both the handheld and the desktop systems. If you want to see exactly what data is being synchronized, you can click the Details button. The dialog shown is different for each kind of data being synchronized and lists the individual records being synchronized. There is no way to modify the list and choose individual records at this point. The only thing you can do is cancel the synchronization.

> **tip** It is possible for other companies to write small programs, or add-ins, that can also participate in the synchronization process. There aren't any used with the Desktop Manager out of the box, but if you install a software package that uses an add-in, you may need to check the Execute Add-in Actions check box in order for these add-ins to be run.

WORKING WITH THE DESKTOP MANAGER APPLETS

FIGURE 3.18
Summary of synchronization changes.

CONFIGURING SYNCHRONIZATION

The rest of the Intellisync dialog is devoted to several buttons that you can click to configure the various aspects of the synchronization process. The buttons roughly correspond to the four synchronization actions discussed in the previous section. As a general rule, you should not need to make any changes to these configurations. The synchronization process is complex and you should only make changes here if you know what you are doing.

If you checked the Reconcile Email check box in the synchronize options then you can configure just how that email is reconciled by clicking the Configure Email button (see Figure 3.19).

FIGURE 3.19
Choose your email synchronization options.

The top set of radio buttons allows you to specify how email messages in a folder will be synchronized. Check the topmost radio button, labeled Import Moves and Deletes to Handheld Only, if you want your handheld to always be the same as your desktop email system. Using this synchronization method, if you move an email message to a folder on your handheld, that move will be ignored when your handheld is synchronized and the message on your handheld will be moved to the folder in which the message exists on your computer's email system.

If you want changes made on your handheld to also be made on your computer's email system, check the Synchronize Moves and Deletes radio button. Two other radio buttons are now enabled. In the event that the same message was moved to two different folders on the handheld and the desktop email systems, Intellisync will use these settings to determine which is the correct folder to use. This is also sometimes called a *synchronization conflict*.

In this situation, you have two choices: Either the email system is correct and the handheld needs to be changed, or the handheld is correct and the email system needs to be changed. If the email system is correct, check the Mailbox Wins radio button. If the handheld is correct, check Handheld Wins.

The middle section is simply a notification as to whether wireless synchronization is enabled or not. Wireless synchronization is only available for users who are using the BlackBerry Enterprise Server for email redirection.

You can also synchronize Personal Folders as well as your inbox. If you would like to include a Personal Folder in the synchronization process, select it from the list.

Much like the Email Synchronization, the Personal Information Management (PIM) Synchronization has many options for how to synchronize the PIM data. To configure these, click the Configure PIM button in the Intellisync dialog (see Figure 3.20).

FIGURE 3.20
Configuring PIM Synchronization advanced settings.

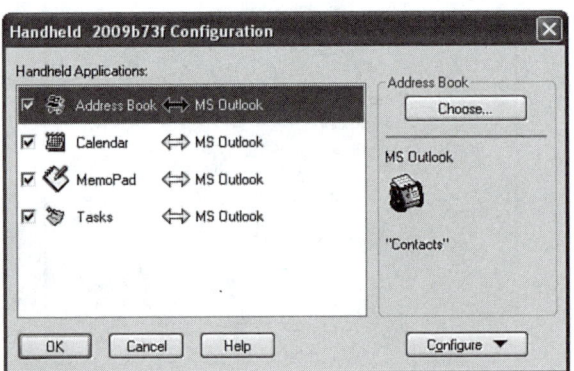

This screen lists the four kinds of PIM data that can be synchronized from your handheld: Address Book, Calendar, Memopad, and Tasks. To the left of each kind of data is a check box. If you do not want to synchronize the data from this application, simply uncheck the check box next to it. To the right of each kind of data are some arrows to indicate how the data is to be synchronized and what the source of the data is. To change how an application is synchronized or the source of that data, click the Choose button in the upper-right part of the dialog.

The next dialog shown lists all of the of the possible sources of data that can be used (see Figure 3.21). This list, called a list of translators, may contain different items depending on which type of data you chose. For instance, Address Book has more translators available than the MemoPad.

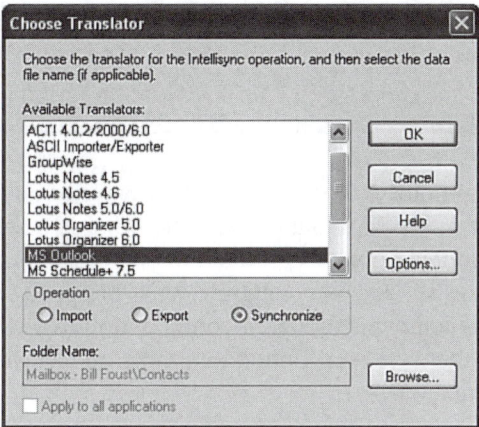

FIGURE 3.21
Choosing a translator for synchronization.

A translator is simply a small program that knows how to convert, or translate, data from one format to another. Most of the time you won't need to change these. If you installed the Desktop Manager to use Outlook, the Microsoft Outlook translators will be configured. If you chose Lotus Notes, then the Notes translators will be configured. There are many other translators, however, to common systems such as Act! and Groupwise. You can select one of these other translators if you want to synchronize your data with the other program.

Each translator can operate on the data in one of three ways: Import, Export, and Synchronize. Under the translator list are three radio buttons that correspond to these operations. If you want to simply import the data from the email system to the handheld, check the Import radio button. This is shown in the list of PIM applications as an arrow pointing left next to the translator. If you want to simply export the data from the handheld to the email system, check the Export radio button. This is shown as an arrow pointing to the right in the PIM list. If you want to synchronize both the handheld and the email system, check the Synchronize radio button. This is shown as a two-headed arrow pointing both right and left in the PIM list.

If you are using some software that uses add-ins, you can configure them by clicking the Configure Add-Ins button. This displays a screen like the one shown in Figure 3.22, which will list each of the add-ins installed on your desktop PC. To configure the add-in, select it from the list and click the Configure button. The add-in will display its configuration screen.

FIGURE 3.22
Configuring the synchronization of add-ins.

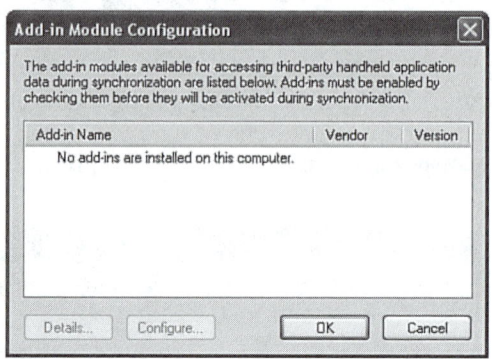

As mentioned previously, there are only two ways to do a synchronization. The first is the Synchronize Now button, and the other is a synchronization that can be started by connecting your handheld to your desktop computer, if you have configured it to do so. You can configure what happens when the handheld is connected to the computer though a configuration called Auto start. To set up Auto start, click the Auto start button and a dialog like the one shown in Figure 3.23 will be displayed.

FIGURE 3.23
Setting up Auto start.

Just like the Synchronize Now section of the dialog, there are four actions that can be taken each time the handheld is connected to the computer: Reconcile Email, Synchronize PIM, Execute Add-in Action, and Update Handheld's Date and Time. To enable one of these four actions, check the check box next to it. Then, the next time your handheld is connected to your computer, a synchronization will occur. Depending on how often you connect your handheld, you may want a full synchronization or you may want nothing to happen. Some people like the idea that all they have to do is connect their device with their computer and a synchronization will start. Others who connect and disconnect their handheld often probably want nothing to happen when they reconnect.

REDIRECTOR SETTINGS

The Redirector Settings applet is used to configure how email messages are redirected from your email system to your handheld, as well as some appearance settings and filtering. When you first set up your handheld, you must use the Redirector Settings applet to generate a security key.

The Redirector Settings dialog has four tabs, each of which configures a different aspect of the redirection process. Generally, you will not need to reset these settings.

> **note** If you are using the BlackBerry Web Client and are not integrating with an email system, all of the redirecting is configured by the ISP and therefore you will not see this applet.

REDIRECTOR GENERAL SETTINGS

When you launch the Redirector Settings applet, the General tab, shown in Figure 3.24, is displayed by default. The top of the dialog shows the PIN of the handheld that is currently attached to the computer. Even though it appears that you can change the PIN, you can't, so don't try.

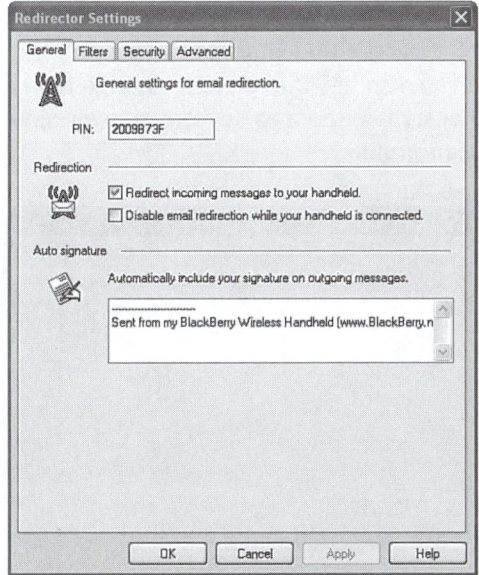

FIGURE 3.24
Redirector General settings are fairly straightforward.

The middle section has two check boxes for when to redirect email messages to your handheld. The first check box, called Redirect Incoming Messages to Your Handheld, is checked by default. If for some strange reason you don't want email messages to be redirected to your handheld, uncheck this check box.

The second check box is only enabled when the first is checked. If you spend most of your time at your desktop PC, it can get annoying having to take care of messages appearing on your handheld when you are right there and able to

> **tip** It might be useful to let people know that you are responding using a mobile device. This can discourage them from creating unnecessarily long messages or even to not bother you any more and solve the problem themselves!

take care of them on your computer. If this is the case, you can make sure that your handheld is connected to the desktop PC and check the Disable Email Redirection While Your Handheld Is Connected check box. Then when you do need the redirection activated, simply disconnect the handheld from your desktop PC and take it with you. While you are away, messages will be redirected to you until you can get back and reconnect the handheld.

The last and most commonly changed setting is Auto Signature. The auto signature is a small message that is attached to all of the outgoing email messages that are sent from your handheld. This signature is different and separate from a signature that might be applied by your email system. The default auto signature lets people know that you are working on a BlackBerry and supplies the web address so they can get one too. This is great PR for BlackBerry, but probably not as useful to you.

REDIRECTOR FILTERS

With the huge and rampant abundance of spam, the last thing you need is to get it on your handheld. Of course there are many methods out there to combat spam, but you can consider the Filters tab to be your last line of defense (see Figure 3.25). You can also use the filters to change how some email messages are handled and designate them as Level 1 messages, which can be given a different notification profile.

FIGURE 3.25
Redirector Filters settings.

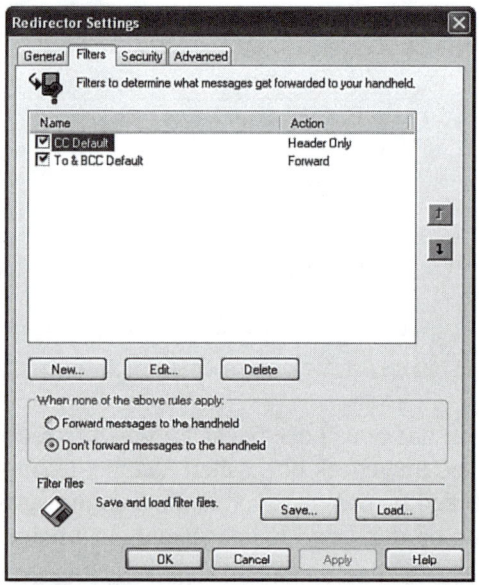

Two filters are created by default, called CC Default and To & BCC Default. These filters give you the most commonly expected behavior for how messages should be sent to your handheld. Each filter can be enabled or disabled. To disable a filter, uncheck the check box next to the filter name in the filter list.

The order of the filters is important as well. When there is a new message, the filters are checked in order from top to bottom. If the criteria of the filter matches the message, the action of the filter is taken and processing is stopped. The rest of the filters are never given an opportunity to process the message even if there are other filters that would match. You can adjust the order of the filters by clicking the up or down arrows on the right side of the dialog. The selected filter will be moved up or down in the filter list accordingly.

Aside from the filters, you can also specify what happens if none of the filters apply to a message. The radio buttons in the group box below the filter list allow you to specify whether a message should be forwarded or not if none of the filters match.

The default filters along with the default setting of these radio buttons basically impose a filter that only forwards email messages that are addressed to you directly either in the To, CC, or BCC fields. If your company uses distribution lists extensively, you may need to change these rules to allow the distribution lists.

To create a new filter, click the New button under the filter list (see Figure 3.26).

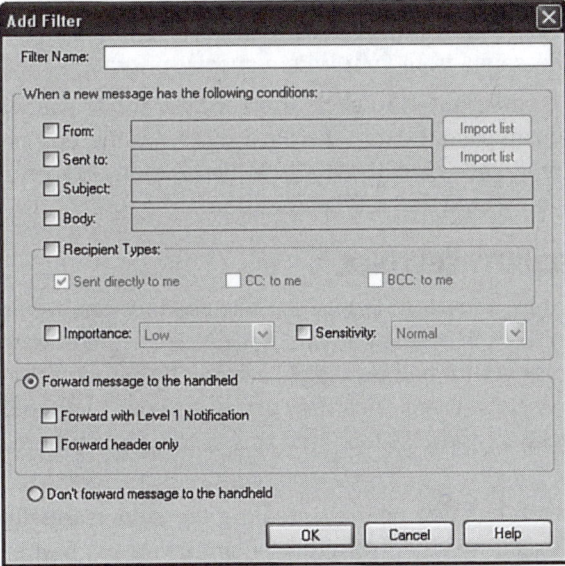

FIGURE 3.26
Adding a new filter gives you additional control over your messages.

Each filter has three general sections. The first is the name of the filter. The filter name is not important for any of the processing, but is there to provide a readable description of what the filter does.

The second is a matching section where you can specify criteria of what the email message must have in order to be considered a match for this filter. You can specify as many matching elements as you want to make the matching as specific as necessary. Each possible matching element has a check box next to it. Checking the check box activates that matching element and allows you to provide the matching string.

For instance, let's say you wanted to make a filter that doesn't forward any messages sent from your cousin. You know the one who is constantly sending you junk email? First check the check box next to the From field. That field is now enabled, allowing you to enter your cousin's email address. If you have it in your address book, you can click the Import List button to view the address book of your email system and select it from there. If you happen to have a second annoying cousin you want to ignore in the same way, you can add his email address to the line as well; just put a semicolon between the email addresses.

> **note** Level 1 notifications are basically special flags on your email messages that are specific to BlackBerry. In Chapter 4, "Personalizing Your Device," we talk more about notification profiles on your handheld. Basically, however, you can configure your handheld to give you a different notification if a message arrives that has a Level 1 notification specifier.

The last section is what should be done with messages—basically, deciding whether the message should be forwarded or not and how it should be forwarded. In the case of our example, you would click the Don't Forward This Message to the Handheld radio button.

On the other hand, let's say you wanted to make a filter that forwarded any email messages from your wife as high-priority messages. In this case you would click the Forward This Message to the Handheld radio button. When this is checked, the two check boxes below it become enabled. You would also check the Forward with Level 1 Notification check box to give those messages from your wife a special priority.

Lastly, if you wanted to back up your filter list or share it with other people, you can save it using the Save button at the bottom of the dialog. Similarly, if you were given a filter list or want to restore a backup of your filters, you would use the Load button.

REDIRECTOR SECURITY SETTINGS

The Security tab, shown in Figure 3.27, is used for one thing—creating a new security key. The security key is another name for the encryption key that is used to encrypt your email messages as they fly through the wireless networks, then decrypt them once they arrive on your handheld. You were always told that BlackBerry was secure, and this is the place where that security is created.

The Security tab has two options, creating the keys manually or automatically. Generating a security key automatically simply means that every 31 days, the Desktop Manager will prompt you to create a new security key. To activate this option, click the Generate Keys Automatically radio button.

WORKING WITH THE DESKTOP MANAGER APPLETS

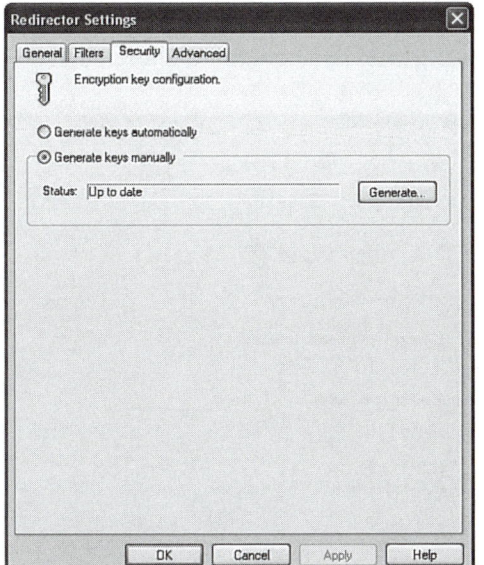

FIGURE 3.27
Redirector security settings create the security key to encrypt and decrypt your messages.

If you do not want to be bothered by the Desktop Manager, you can click the Generate Keys Manually radio button and generate new keys yourself whenever you feel it is necessary. You can generate a new key by clicking the Generate button. When you do that, a screen like the one shown in Figure 3.28 is shown, instructing you to randomly move the mouse around the screen. The Desktop Manager uses this random movement to generate the new security key, which is then shared with your handheld.

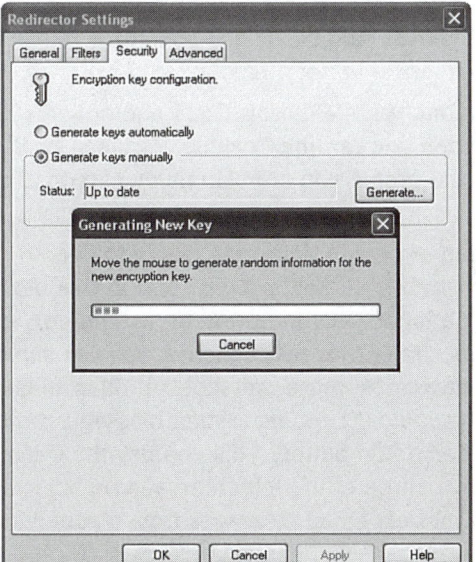

FIGURE 3.28
Generating a new security key.

REDIRECTOR ADVANCED SETTINGS

The last tab is the Advanced tab, shown in Figure 3.29. This tab contains five settings that a user generally shouldn't need to change.

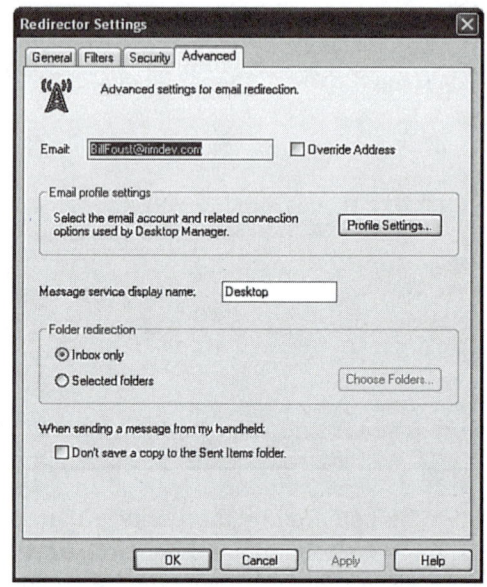

FIGURE 3.29
Redirector Advanced settings should most likely be left at the defaults unless you are directed by an IT manager or ISP to make changes.

The first setting is the email address that will be used as the ReplyTo address of email messages sent from your handheld. This setting is only available to users who use Microsoft Exchange and a BlackBerry Enterprise Server to redirect their email messages. This defaults to the email address for the email system you are connected to, but if it is not what you want you can change it. First check the Override Address check box. Once this is done, you can modify the email address inside the edit box.

If you are integrating with Microsoft Exchange or Lotus Notes, you selected a profile or user when you ran the Desktop Manager for the first time. If you need to change the profile you are using, you can do it by clicking the Profile Settings button.

If you are the kind of person who uses lots of folders to sort your Inbox then you may need to utilize the folder redirection in this next section. The default selection is for the Inbox Only radio button, which only examines new messages in your Inbox folder for redirection. If you use server-side rules to sort incoming email messages, those messages in other folders would not be redirected to your handheld. To redirect email messages from other folders, click the Selected Folders radio button. This enables the Choose Folders button. Clicking it displays a tree of the folders in your email system with check boxes next to each. To redirect email messages from a subfolder, check the check box next to it.

If you send a lot of email messages from your handheld, you may not want to save copies of them in the Sent Items folder of your email system. This is particularly true if it is difficult to empty the Sent Items folder regularly. If this is the case, check the Don't Save a Copy to the Sent Items Folder check box.

When you are all done making changes to these configuration settings, don't forget to click the OK button to save them. Now get out there and enjoy your new handheld!

Chapter 4

PERSONALIZING YOUR DEVICE

BLACKBERRY BASICS:

- There are some things you need to do to set up your handheld when you first get it—such as setting the time, entering the owner information, and more.

- You can set up security settings and passwords to keep the information on your handheld secure.

- Profiles are used to control how the handheld alerts you when you need to be notified of something.

- The Auto Off feature should be used to automatically turn your device off when you do not need it to save battery life.

Now that the Desktop Manager is set up and you have email delivery working, it is time to set it up in the way that best suits you and the way you will be using the BlackBerry handheld.

The BlackBerry handheld software has many ways to personalize your BlackBerry, ranging from utility features such as password protection to cosmetic features such as the order in which the main screen icons appear.

SETTING THE TIME AND DATE

Most likely your BlackBerry will automatically get the time and date information from your wireless carrier, but you may still need to set the time zone. At the very least, you will want to make sure that the date/time information is set correctly.

Start by opening the Options application. If you recall from Chapter 2, you can do this by scrolling the trackwheel up or down until the Options application is selected on the Home screen. The icon for the Options application looks like a wrench or pocketknife, depending on your model. Next, scroll the trackwheel down to select the Date/Time item from the list and click the trackwheel to show the screen seen in Figure 4.1.

Each of the fields on this screen are Choice fields. Again, if you recall from Chapter 2, a Choice field is a field that lets you select one of many possible values from a small list. The Date and Time fields are actually several Choice fields put together. The hour, minute, month, day, and year are all separate fields. The easiest way to change a Choice field is to click the trackwheel to display the menu and select the Change Option menu item. This will display a small window showing the complete list of values for the selected field. You can then scroll through the list to find the desired value and click the trackwheel again to select it. Or, rather then use the menu item to display the list, you can simply press the space key to select the next value in the list.

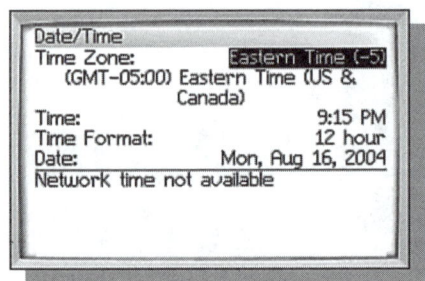

FIGURE 4.1
Setting the date and time manually.

> **tip** Pressing any letter will advance the selection to the next value that begins with that letter as well.

In the case of time zone, the list displayed shows the name of the time zone and its time difference compared to GMT (Greenwich Mean Time). For instance, Eastern time zone is shown as Eastern (–5), meaning if you take GMT and subtract five hours, you will have the current time in the Eastern time zone.

Some entries are not real time zones, but special cases that do not fit into another category, usually because different regions have their own rules about daylight saving time. For instance, Indiana is really in the Eastern time zone, but has its own entry in this time zone list because Indiana does not observe daylight saving time like the rest of the Eastern time zone.

Notice that as you change the time zone, the current time will also be changed. This is because nearly all of the times used by the BlackBerry are stored in GMT and adjusted based on your time zone setting.

The Time and Date fields behave a little differently than a standard Choice field. This is because the list of values being displayed in the window could be quite large, especially for the Minute field. Instead, a small window is shown and scrolling the trackwheel up or down causes the selected value to change in place as you scroll.

> **tip** It is likely that someone who finds your BlackBerry may not know where to find the owner information. In that case, you should put a small sticker physically on the handheld somewhere. If your handheld is one with a removable battery, then under the battery cover is an ideal place. Otherwise, the back of the handheld is probably the best location.

If your handheld has gotten the date and time from your wireless carrier, these values are shown in the bottom portion of the screen. You cannot change the values: They are there for informational purposes only. If your current time is not the same as the network time and you want to set it to be the same, you can simply click the Copy Network Time menu item.

ADD IDENTIFYING INFORMATION

No one wants to think about what might happen if you were to lose your handheld, but it is a possibility. The simplest thing you can do is put your name and telephone number on the device somewhere so that if a good Samaritan were to find it, they can reach you.

The BlackBerry has a spot where you can save this information in the Options application under the Owner item.

SECURING YOUR DATA

FIGURE 4.2
Setting the owner information.

Enter your name and whatever information might be relevant. At the very least, put your phone number and/or email address where someone can reach you, and remember to update it!

SECURING YOUR DATA

Of course we all believe that the information we carry on our handhelds is critically important, but realistically it probably is not. I have no doubt, however, that someone out there does have information of national importance on their handheld. For those people, and the paranoid person inside all of us, the BlackBerry can be set up to automatically password-protect the handheld after a period of inactivity.

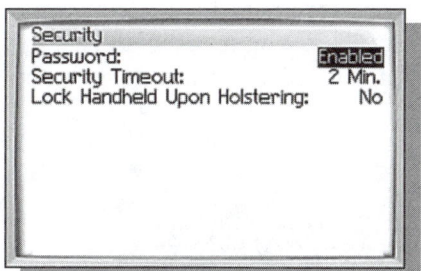

FIGURE 4.3
A look at the Security options.

In the Options application under the Security item, you have the option of enabling the password protection, setting an idle timeout, and choosing to automatically secure the handheld when it is put back into the holster.

When you save the configuration enabling the password protection, you will be prompted for the password and asked to verify it.

From this point on when the handheld has been secured and you go to access it, you will see a screen like the one in Figure 4.5.

note On some handhelds, this may not be configurable. This is one of the items your information technology department can configure for you if your company is running a BlackBerry Enterprise Server.

FIGURE 4.4
Setting the password.

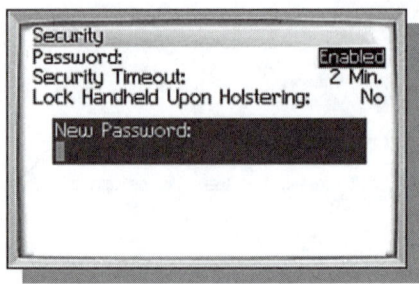

FIGURE 4.5
The screen of a locked handheld.

It is important to note that while the handheld is still secured, you can see the owner information on the screen. If you start typing, the password entry box is displayed and you can enter your password and click the trackwheel or press the Enter key when you are done. If the trackwheel is moved, a dialog is displayed giving the user the option to make an emergency call as shown in Figure 4.6. Doing this will call 112, which is the international GSM standard emergency number.

FIGURE 4.6
The emergency call prompt is displayed after clicking the trackwheel while the device is locked.

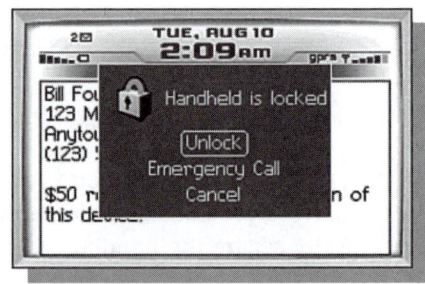

caution If you (or another person) enters the password incorrectly 10 times, all of the memory on that handheld will be erased!

If you decide that you want to disable the security on the handheld, you can do so the same way you set it, by going to the Security item under Options and just changing Enabled field to Disabled. When the new changes are saved, the password verification dialog will be shown again as in Figure 4.7.

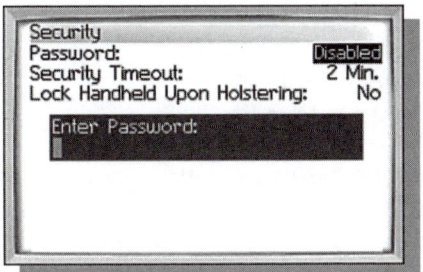

FIGURE 4.7
Disabling the password prompts for the current password one last time.

SAVING THE BATTERY

One of the strong points of the BlackBerry has always been outstanding battery performance. Even with such great performance, there are things that you can and should do to further maximize the battery life.

The simplest of these is to configure it to automatically turn off at times when you are not likely to use it, or do not want to be disturbed—such as when you are sleeping.

Let's not forget how this can save your marriage, too. So what does this have to do with your marriage? Well, just leave your pager on at night and let your spouse be awoken at 3 a.m. by the handheld buzzing away on the nightstand to let you know that you just received a piece of spam email. See where I'm headed here?

So take care of that right now by opening the Options application and selecting the Auto On/Off item. As you can see in Figure 4.8, there are two parts of the screen. The top part sets up the On/Off behavior on the weekday and the bottom part is for the weekend.

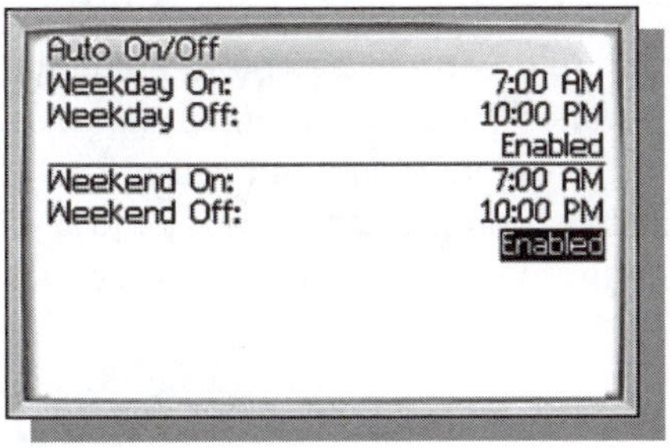

FIGURE 4.8
Configuring the Auto On/Off screen.

The On and Off times should be something sane that reflects your work habits. For most people an On time of 7 a.m. and an Off time of 10 p.m. should work out fine. Lastly, change the Disabled Field to read Enabled. Make similar changes for the On and Off times during the weekend.

> **note** The Auto On/Off times are always the local time on the handheld. Changing the time zone does not cause these times to change.

One last thing to remember: If you get a lot of messages, you should be prepared for a number of alerts to hit in succession when the handheld is automatically turned on.

SELECTING A PROFILE

One of the areas that people can express themselves the most is the way in which their handheld alerts them. On cellular phones, this is most often through the wide variety of ring tones available. Unfortunately, the BlackBerry does not offer the same level of variety. There are some ringtones, but they are pretty bland.

The good news is that there are many ways to customize the various alerts that your handheld can generate. To start, select the Profiles application (the one that looks like a speaker), or the choose the Options application and select the Profiles item. Either path results in a screen like the one shown in Figure 4.9.

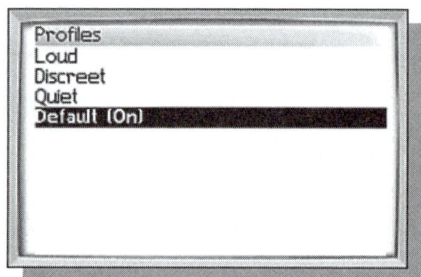

FIGURE 4.9
The list of BlackBerry profiles.

WHAT IS A PROFILE?

A profile determines how you are alerted by the BlackBerry when various events happen, such a message arriving or being notified that it is time for your next meeting. By choosing a different profile, you can easily change the behavior of your handheld without having to reconfigure every application that can alert you. For instance, when going to an important meeting, you can change the profile to Quiet, which will cause the handheld to vibrate no matter what alert is firing. Later, when going out in the warehouse, you can change the profile to Loud so the alerts can be heard above the noise in the warehouse.

> **note** To quickly change the enabled profile, select a profile and press the Space key. This will enable the selected profile and return to the previous screen as well.

EXPLORING THE BLACKBERRY PROFILES

The current profile is the one with (On) status next to the name in the list. In the case of Figure 4.9, the current profile is the Default profile. To change the profile, move the selection to another profile, for instance Quiet, and click the Enable menu item as in Figure 4.10.

SELECTING A PROFILE

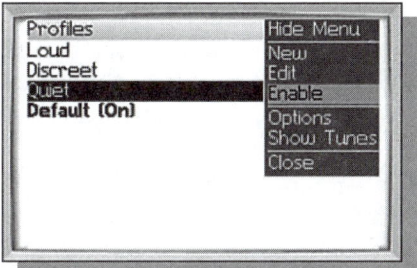

FIGURE 4.10
Changing the default profile.

Generally speaking, you will probably edit the Default profile to fit the way you want the BlackBerry configured the majority of the time, but if you need to (or if you just have to buck the system), you can create custom profiles.

To get a better feel for how this works, let's look in more detail at the Default profile. Click the Edit menu item to see the screen shown in Figure 4.11.

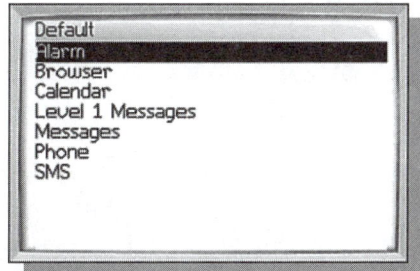

FIGURE 4.11
Showing the list of notification types.

This list shows all of the circumstances that may cause an alert to happen. Most of the items are self-explanatory.

Each of these circumstances, or notification types, can be edited to potentially provide a unique way of alerting you. Select the Messages notification type and click the Edit menu item to see the screen shown in Figure 4.12.

For each notification type, there are two basic rules that can be defined—a rule determines what happens when the handheld is in the holster, and what happens when it is not. The upper part of the screen defines the Out of Holster rule and the lower defines the In Holster rule.

The rules are as follows:

- **None**—When this rule is selected there is no alert given for that notification type. So, if you have Messages set to None, then you will not be alerted when a new message is received.

- **Tone**—Selecting this rule causes the BlackBerry to alert you with a tone when the notification occurs. You can also change the

note There is an item that you might not figure out on your own—Level 1 Notifications. Level 1 messages are messages with a special flag meaning they are more important. You can set up special filters in the Desktop Manager to redirect messages as Level 1 messages. Also, PIN messages (a special kind of handheld to handheld message we will talk about more in Chapter 5, "Composing and Sending Messages") are considered Level 1 messages.

type of tone that is used for this rule, how loud it will be, and how many times it will play.

- **Vibrate**—Pretty obvious. The one thing you probably don't know is that the BlackBerry will vibrate two times and only two times. This unfortunately is not configurable. On the upside, though, Vibrate alerts use less power than Tone alerts.
- **Vibrate+Tone**—Select this rule if you are afraid you'll be in a noisy situation and won't catch just one type of alert. The BlackBerry will vibrate first, and then play the tone (according to the settings you've chosen for Tone)—the vibrate and tone alerts will not happen at the same time.

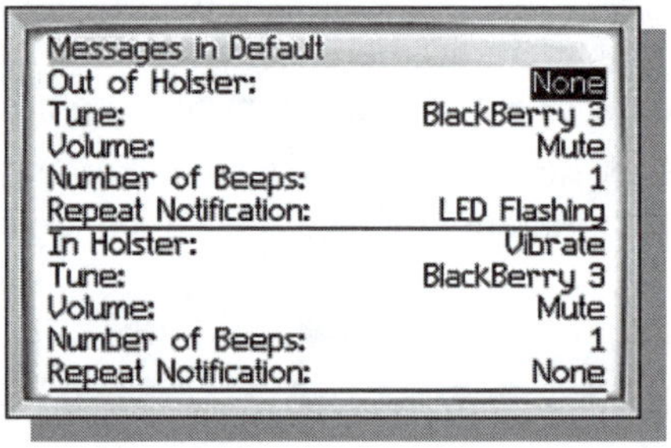

FIGURE 4.12
Changing the notification.

Repeat Notification is another setting that can be configured for each notification type. If you are changing this rule to LED Flashing, you will only get the alert once. After that, until you interact with the handheld in some way, the LED flashes instead of giving the initial alert again (such as playing the tune). This setting is nice in those situations where your handheld is already out and on the table or in your hand but you aren't in a position to respond to the alert immediately.

In addition, the Phone notification type has one setting the others do not, called Do Not Disturb, as shown in Figure 4.13.

FIGURE 4.13
Notice the Do Not Disturb choice.

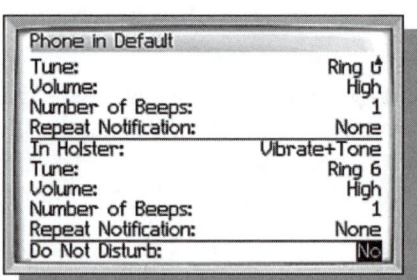

If the Do Not Disturb setting is set to Yes, the call will immediately roll over to voice mail or your carrier's unavailable message. This is different from having the rule set to None. If the rule is set None, the handheld will still give you chance to answer the call by displaying the incoming call dialog box and the caller will hear rings while the handheld waits a response. With Do Not Disturb activated, you don't even get a notification that someone is calling.

To create a new profile, click the New menu item from the list of profiles. This will copy the default profile (including any changes you may have made to it) into a new unnamed profile and begin editing it. The top of the screen has a Name field where you can type in the new name. Editing each of the notification types works the same as before.

One profile you may want to consider is a No Vibration profile. This is the same as the default profile except incoming messages do not alert you by vibrate mode. This is one way to be able to leave your handheld on at night (maybe because you still need to receive phone calls) and not be bothered by it vibrating while you are asleep.

CHANGING THE DISPLAY

In addition to changing the way you are alerted by your BlackBerry, you may want to change the way the words are displayed on the screen. The BlackBerry models have an impressive collection of fonts and sizes available. Whether you want the font to be larger and easier to read or tiny so more text can fit on the screen, you can do it. You can also change the screen saver settings and do keyboard tuning in the same place. Open the Options application and select the Screen/Keyboard options group (see Figure 4.14).

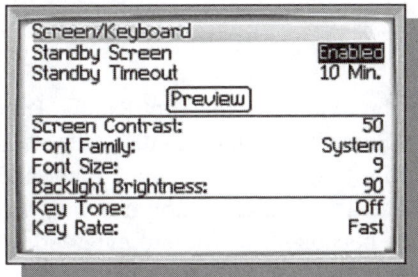

FIGURE 4.14
A look at the Screen/Keyboard options.

This screen is divided into three sections. The top section has the screen saver settings, the middle contains font settings, and the bottom has keyboard settings.

SCREEN SAVER SETTINGS

The screen saver is a small graphic that is displayed after a period of inactivity when your BlackBerry handheld is out of its holster. A default graphic is set by your wireless provider and is unchangeable on older versions of the handheld software. On handhelds with version 4.0 of the handheld software however, you can specify a different image to use. The section "Setting Your Home Screen and Standby Image" later in this chapter discusses this in more detail.

7100 The 7100 series handhelds do not have a screen saver, so these options will not be shown.

You can configure the inactivity time required to display it or disable it completely. If you have never seen it before, you can select the Preview button and click the trackwheel to activate the screen saver. The biggest value I see in having the screen saver is to keep wandering eyes from viewing the screen if you set your handheld down for a while.

FIGURE 4.15
The screen saver is activated.

FONT SETTINGS

This section allows you to change the Font Family, Font Size, and possibly the Font Style. The BlackBerry has several fonts available with several font sizes for each. To change the font, select the Font Family and click the Change Option menu item. The list of fonts is shown in a typical chooser. This one, however, is very nice because the font is previewed onscreen as you scroll up and down in the font list so you can see what the font looks like.

The Font Size choice behaves similarly. The font sizes available depend on the font family you chose.

Some Font Families also allow you to choose a Font Style—typically these are the Font Families with names beginning with BB. There are three styles to choose from—Plain, Bold, and Italic. Again, the Font Style you've selected is previewed onscreen so you can make sure it's a choice you want to stick with. Some models of BlackBerry handhelds do not have fonts with a Font Style.

KEYBOARD SETTINGS

Finally, you can change the way the keyboard behaves, but only slightly. The first option turns on or off the keyboard tone. The keyboard tone is a small "click" sound that simulates the sound made by older tactile PC keyboards.

The second option, Key Rate, is how fast keystrokes happen if you simply hold down a particular key. This primarily affects the Backspace key and how fast characters are erased when you press and hold it down. If you often find yourself accidentally erasing text you didn't want to when holding down the Backspace key, I would change this option to Slow; otherwise, don't worry about it.

ORGANIZING THE HOME SCREEN

The Home screen with the icons for each application is the central hub of your BlackBerry experience, so it makes sense that you can organize it so you can work more efficiently. Although you can use the Home screen shortcuts to quickly navigate from one application to another, there are times when rearranging the order of the icons is beneficial. For instance, if you happen to use the Calculator application more than the ToDo application, you may want to consider moving Calculator to be closer to the other applications that you use most frequently.

To accomplish this, select the icon you wish to move. Then, with the Alt key pressed, click the trackwheel to display a menu. Release the Alt key, and select the Move Icon menu item. The icon will be now have a box around it. Scroll the trackwheel up or down. As you do, the icon will move around the screen. Clicking the Escape key stops the move and saves the new icon order (see Figure 4.16).

FIGURE 4.16
Moving the Calculator application.

Another way to customize the Home screen is to remove the applications that you do not use. For instance, you may want to remove the Profiles icon once you have it customized, because it is also available in the Options application. To do this, select the icon to hide. Then bring up the Home screen menu by clicking the trackwheel while pressing the Alt key. Select the Hide Icon menu item (see Figure 4.17).

Of course, once you have hidden an icon, you need to be able to bring it back. After an icon has been hidden, a new Show All menu item is available on the main screen menu. Clicking this menu item will cause any previously hidden icons to be shown again, but now the hidden icons have a white "X" through them (see Figure 4.18).

FIGURE 4.17
The Profiles icon is now hidden.

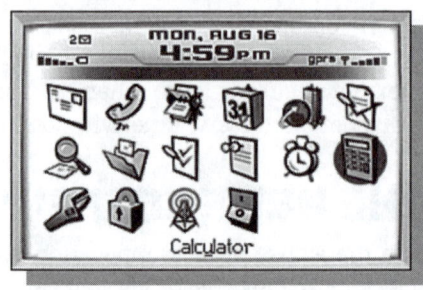

FIGURE 4.18
The Profiles icon has an "X" through it to show it is hidden.

To unhide the icon, select it and then display the main screen menu. The Hide Icon and Show All menu items both have checks next to them, indicating that those features are currently activated. To unhide an icon or turn off the Show All option, click the appropriate menu item.

After all of these changes have been made, it is probably comforting to know that next time the device is reset the new order will be preserved.

CHOOSING A THEME IN VERSION 4.0

One of the new features with version 4.0 of the handheld software is *themes*. In much the same way that Microsoft Windows has themes, the BlackBerry themes are a way to change the look of your handheld. This includes everything from the color scheme to the application icons and more. Even the way that the battery and signal strength indicators are displayed can be changed by a theme.

The bad news to all this is that you probably only have a choice between two themes, if you have a choice at all. This is because themes are provided by your wireless carrier, so if you have one, it will be designed to how they want it to look. The only other alternative is the Default theme, which is essentially the same as having no theme. Themes are only generally available on 7100 model handhelds, but they are supported on all handhelds with version 4.0 of the software installed.

You can view the themes on your handheld by opening the Options application and selecting the Themes option group. This displays a screen that lists the names of each of the themes, as shown in Figure 4.19. The theme that is currently active will have (Active) next to the theme name.

FIGURE 4.19
Viewing the list of themes installed on your handheld.

To start using a different theme, scroll the selection indicator to the new theme and click the Activate menu item. It can take some time for all of the changes to take effect once the menu item is clicked. Figure 4.20 shows an example of the Default and the Vodafone theme on a 7100v.

FIGURE 4.20
The Vodafone and Default themes shown on a BlackBerry 7100v.

SETTING YOUR HOME SCREEN AND STANDBY IMAGE IN VERSION 4.0

Another neat feature that version 4.0 adds is the ability to store and view pictures on your handheld. You can also choose one of them to be the background image of your Home screen.

Your handheld may not have any pictures on it when you get it, but don't worry: You can add some by saving them from web pages. (We talk more about how to do this in Chapter 8.)

You can view the pictures that are saved on your handheld by opening the Pictures application from the Home screen. The next screen, shown in Figure 4.21, shows a list of the pictures that have been saved on your handheld. Each line shows a thumbnail of the picture, the name of the picture, and the amount of memory used by the picture.

FIGURE 4.21
The Pictures application shows the pictures that have been saved on your handheld.

Sometimes a thumbnail image just isn't enough or you simply want to view the full image. To do this, scroll the trackwheel so that the picture is selected and click the Open menu item. Another screen will appear that shows the image in full size.

You can specify an image to be the background image on the Home screen or the standby image that is shown when the screen saver is activated. To set an image as the background image, click the Set As Home Screen Image menu item from the image list screen or while viewing an image. The standby image is set in the same way, by clicking the Set As Standby Screen menu item. If you decide that you do not want a background image or standby image, you can reset the settings by clicking the Reset Home Screen Image or Reset Standby Screen image menu items, as appropriate.

USING HELP IN VERSION 4.0

Version 4.0 of the handheld software also comes with a Help application. It provides help on a wide variety of topics that are organized into a browsable index, shown in Figure 4.22. To view a topic, scroll the trackwheel to it and click the trackwheel. If the topic has subtopics, you will see another list of topics that you can scroll and click in the same way.

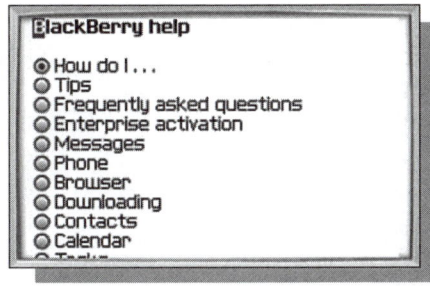

FIGURE 4.22
Version 4.0 of the handheld software provides a Help application.

If you click the trackwheel while the selection is not on a topic, a menu will be shown. You can also display the menu by pressing and holding the Alt key while clicking the trackwheel.

You can search the current screen for some text by clicking the Find menu item. A dialog will be shown asking for the search text; clicking the trackwheel will start the search.

There are two menu items that help you with navigating in the Help application as well. The Index menu item is always available and clicking it will return you to the main index of help topics. If you currently have a help topic open, a menu item will be shown that is the title of the previous list of subtopics. The menu item name will be the name of the topic list. For example, if you are viewing a topic chosen from the Tips subtopic, the menu item shown will be called Tips.

> **note** The Find menu item does not search all of the help topics. Instead it simply searches the text currently displayed on the screen for specified text.

Part III

THE "KILLER" APPLICATIONS

- **5** Composing and Sending Messages
- **6** Managing Messages
- **7** Message Attachments
- **8** Browsing the Internet Wirelessly
- **9** Making Phone Calls

Chapter 5

COMPOSING AND SENDING MESSAGES

BLACKBERRY BASICS:

- A BlackBerry handles more than just email messages. It also handles PIN messages, SMS messages, and phone calls. These are generically called messages.

- PIN messages are like email messages, but do not travel through an email server. Instead they are sent directly to the other device within the wireless network.

- You can use the Compose icon on the home screen or the Compose menu item to start composing a new message.

- Received messages can be replied to and forwarded to other people.

This is it. This is the heart of the BlackBerry system and the reason you got a BlackBerry in the first place. Of all the applications and features of the handheld, this is the one you will use the most. It should be no surprise then that the Messages application is the most complex and has the most features of any of the applications on the handheld. That isn't to say that it is hard to use; in fact it is quite easy to use and I believe you will be surprised at how much thought and effort has gone into designing this software.

One thing that you will see many times in this chapter is that there is almost never just one way to do something. Instead, common features can be accessed in several ways and on multiple screens. This may seem confusing at first, but once you get the hang of it, it is very intuitive to use.

WHY MESSAGES AND NOT EMAILS?

So why is it called Messages and not Emails? Quite simply, a message is more than just an email. A message can be an SMS message, a PIN message, or a phone call, as well as an email message, and all of these show up in the Message List—subject to configurations of course. Let's take a look at each kind of message in more detail:

- **S**hort **M**essage **S**ervice Message—SMS is an acronym for Short Message Service. Every cellular carrier supports sending and receiving SMS messages on your cellular phone. Since nearly all BlackBerry handhelds have a cellular phone built into them, support for SMS messages is necessary. SMS messages are addressed to phone numbers and are very short, typically less than 150 characters.

- Phone Call—A Phone call message is really a call log entry. It contains information about a placed or received call such as start and stop time. It also has a section for adding notes about the call.

CHAPTER 5 COMPOSING AND SENDING MESSAGES

> **note** Because PIN messages do not rely on an email server at all, they are sometimes used as a way to notify users of email server issues. They also can be used as part of a disaster recovery plan. There have been several articles about how people were still able to communicate with their BlackBerry handhelds even when the wireless systems were overloaded and voice calls were not possible.

- Email—An Email message is the standard email we know and love (except for spam email). These messages may be sent or received emails.

- PIN Message—PIN messages are messages that can only be sent between BlackBerry handhelds. Every BlackBerry device has a PIN assigned to it that is unique. PIN messages are addressed to the PIN of a device. They are very similar to Email messages, except that they are treated with a higher priority by the BlackBerry delivery system. PIN messages also share information about the state of the message such as if the message has been successfully delivered to the destination handheld.

Now that you've seen the various types of messages, let's jump right in and look at sending messages. When you start the Messages application, you are shown a screen I call the Message list. There are a lot of things you can do from this screen, but for now we will be focusing on the menu items for sending messages.

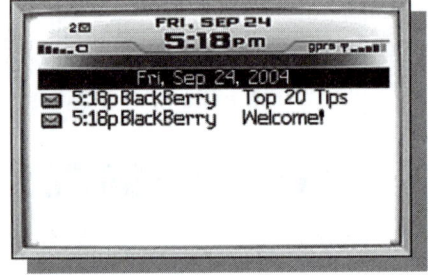

FIGURE 5.1
A look at the Message list of a new device.

> **note** It may seem strange to "compose" a call, but that is the best way to describe it since the BlackBerry software considers a call to be a message and the process is nearly the same as composing an email.

COMPOSING A MESSAGE

Composing a message is one of those actions that can be done in many different ways. You have the option of composing a message while viewing the Message list, or you can also compose a message by opening the Compose application.

STARTING AT THE MESSAGE SCREEN

From the Message screen's menu, you can compose messages using one of the four available message types—Email, Call, SMS, and PIN (see Figure 5.2). Selecting the Compose Email, Compose PIN, Place Call, or Compose SMS menu item begins the process to create the selected type of message.

Selecting any of the menu's compose options will display the Address Book. We haven't discussed the Address Book yet, but once you have some items in the Address Book, they will be displayed here so you can choose the recipient of the message. For now, we will focus only on the special [Use Once] recipient. The rest of the options will be covered in detail in Chapter 10, "Using the Address Book."

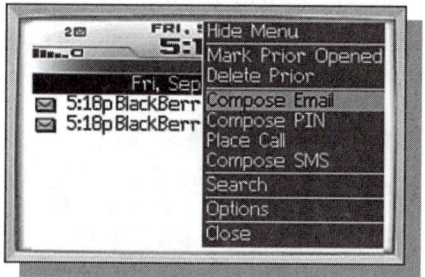

FIGURE 5.2
The Compose menu items available on the Message screen menu.

At the top of the Address Book screen is a special entry called [Use Once], as shown in Figure 5.3. This special item is only shown when you select one of the Compose menu items and is used to enter an address that you don't want to keep in your address book—something you only intend to use once.

Select the [Use Once] item and click the trackwheel to show a menu related to the message type you previously selected. For instance, if you chose Compose Email, the menu item shown with [Use Once] will be "Email…". If you chose Compose PIN, the menu will be "PIN…".

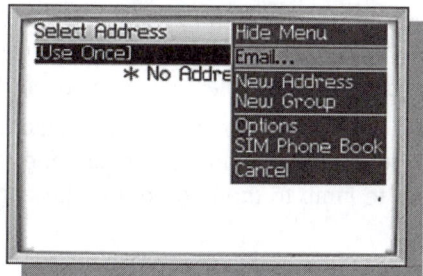

FIGURE 5.3
The [Use Once] enables you to send a message to someone who is not in your Address Book.

While this feature is designed for use when you intend to use the recipient's contact information only once, the screen does save the contact information you used the last time you sent a message using [Use Once]. You can clear the field either by pressing the Backspace key repeatedly or selecting the Clear Field menu item. Once you have entered a recipient's address or phone number, select the Continue menu item to continue composing the message.

> **tip**
> If you are using your handheld in a corporate environment with a BES server, you can look up the names of other people in your company using the Lookup menu. This is covered in more detail in Chapter 10.

STARTING FROM THE COMPOSE APPLICATION

You may also remember that there is an icon on the Home screen that is labeled Compose. You can select this icon to begin composing a message. Notice however that you didn't have to specify a message type. Opening the menu while [Use Once] is selected in the Address Book screen shows a menu item for each message type available, as shown in Figure 5.4.

From this point on, the compose screens are somewhat different based on the message type selected. We will cover each of them in more detail.

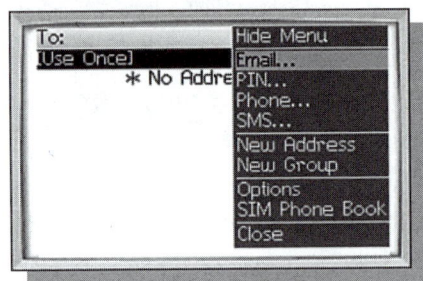

FIGURE 5.4
The [Use Once] recipient when selected from the Compose application.

> **note** If the address exists in the Address Book, it will display the "friendly name" of the recipient, such as "John Doe" instead of the true address of "JohnDoe@nowhere.com."

COMPOSING AN EMAIL OR PIN MESSAGE

Composing email messages and PIN messages use the same screen, have the same features, and will therefore be covered together. For this section, the terms email and PIN will be interchangeable.

Once you have entered the recipient address and selected the message type, the Compose Email screen is displayed. This screen should look similar to any standard email client. It has fields for the subject and body of the email and shows the selected recipient in the To: field.

When you start composing a message, the cursor is already placed in the Subject: field. Pressing the Enter key or scrolling the trackwheel down will cause the cursor to jump to the body of the message. Figure 5.5 shows a basic message.

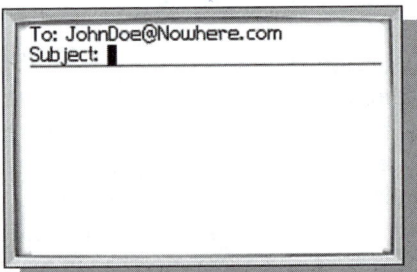

FIGURE 5.5
Composing a simple email message.

COMPOSING A MESSAGE

ADDING ADDITIONAL RECIPIENTS

Sometimes you want to send a message to more than one person at a time. You can always copy the text of the message and create another message with a different recipient, but there are better ways. Clicking the trackwheel on any part of the screen shows three menu items to handle this. Add To:, Add Cc:, and Add Bcc: can be used to add other addresses to the message (see Figure 5.6). These terms are standard email terms, but if you are unfamiliar with them, the sidebar discusses their usage and definition.

> **7100** You can change the keypad mode between SureType and MultiTap from the Compose Email screen. If you are in SureType mode, clicking the Enable MultiTap menu item will change the mode to MultiTap and display the ABC indicator in the upper right corner. To change it back, click the Enable SureType menu item.
>
> Changing the keypad mode is not just for composing the current email message. The keypad mode you select will remain active until you set it again.

EMAIL 101

The terms To:, Cc:, and Bcc: are used to describe who should receive the message and what their role is on the topic. To: is of course the main recipient of the message. There can be more than one address on the To: line, as in instances where a message is sent to an entire team.

Cc: means *carbon copy*, a term that goes back to the days when copies were made with carbon paper. Cc: recipients are people who have an interest in the message, but who are not directly responsible for the content of it. In the previous example, the team manager may be a Cc: recipient of the message to the team.

Bcc: means *blind carbon copy*. The word blind here means that the To: and Cc: recipients will not see any recipients on the Bcc: list in the message header. Essentially, Bcc: recipients receive a copy of the message secretly. In the previous example, the company president may be a Bcc: recipient if the issue is important enough, but the sender doesn't want the other recipients to know that the president is receiving the same message.

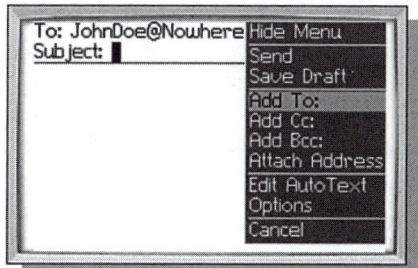

FIGURE 5.6
Menus for adding additional recipients to an email message.

Selecting one of the Add menu items will repeat the process of selecting the recipient. First the Address Book is shown, you choose the recipient, or, if the [Use Once] item is selected, you enter the address information. When this is done, a new line is added to the header of the message showing the new recipient.

You can change or remove recipients by scrolling the trackwheel to select the recipient to change or remove, and then clicking the trackwheel to show the menu with several new menu items.

CHAPTER 5 COMPOSING AND SENDING MESSAGES

> **note** Messages cannot be created with recipients of different types. For instance even though PIN and email are composed using the same screen, you cannot create a message with both a PIN recipient and an email recipient. Once the message composition has begun, the message type is set and only recipients of that type can be added.

The Change Address menu item goes back through the process of selecting a recipient that was outlined above by displaying the Address Book and so on. In this case, the original recipient is simply changed to the new address.

The Delete Field menu item can be used to remove any of the recipients from the message. It is important to note, however, that you cannot remove the last To: recipient. The Delete Field menu will not be shown if there is only one To: recipient.

CHANGING THE PRIORITY LEVEL OF THE EMAIL

Most email clients support message importance. This is simply an indicator set by the sender to let the recipients know at a glance if the message needs immediate attention. In practice, it is rarely used, but all good email clients support it, including the BlackBerry software.

To set the message importance, click the trackwheel anywhere on the screen and select the Options menu item. This will display the Current Message Options screen, as shown in Figure 5.7, which contains a single field—Importance. The default is Normal, but you can change the value to either Low or High by selecting the Change Option menu or pressing the Space key to advance the selected value. Selecting the Save menu item will save the changes and return you to the Compose Message screen. This setting is made only for the current message. The next time you compose an email message, the Importance will be set to Normal again.

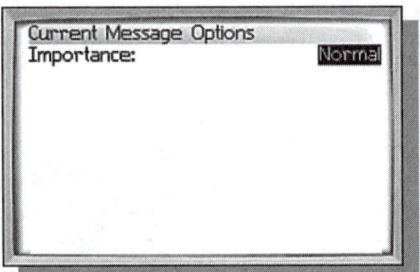

FIGURE 5.7
Choosing the importance level for a message using the Current Message Options screen.

ATTACHING AN ADDRESS

There are occasions when you need to share an address and other contact information with someone else. The BlackBerry software makes this easy with built-in support for V-Cards, both while composing and viewing email messages.

The Attach Address menu item is used to create a V-Card formatted attachment on the email message you are composing. This menu displays the Address Book, so you can select which address to include. You must click Continue after selecting the address to be attached. (The [Use Once] menu is not available for this operation.) When an address is selected, the attachment is shown at the bottom of the body of the message as shown in Figure 5.8.

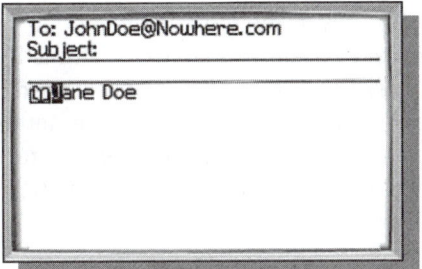

FIGURE 5.8
Composing a message with an address attachment.

The nice thing about V-Cards is that they are a standard that most email clients implement. You can send them to BlackBerry as well as non-BlackBerry users with some degree of confidence that the user will be able to import the data in without difficulty.

Deleting the address attachment is simple as well. Scroll the trackwheel to the line with the address attachment, click the trackwheel, and then select the Delete Field menu item.

SAVING A MESSAGE IN PROGRESS

We've all had it happen. You are in the middle of composing an email and something pops up the requires your immediate attention. Fortunately, there is a way to save your work and exit the Compose Email screen through the Save Draft menu.

When a message is saved, it shows up in the Message list with a different icon indicating that it is a draft, as shown in Figure 5.9. To resume the composition, select the message in the Message list, click the trackwheel, and then select the Open menu item. This will return you to Compose Email Message screen where you can finish the email.

tip Hold ALT down, and then press ESC to trackwheel-scroll between tasks. This allows you to leave any app you're in (and running) to go to whatever you want.

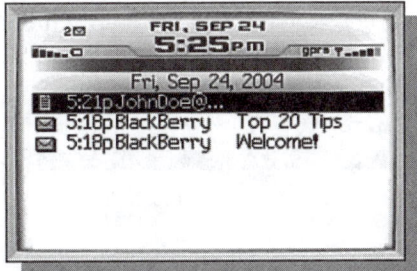

FIGURE 5.9
A draft message is saved in the Message list.

DISCARDING A MESSAGE WHILE COMPOSING

Another thing that is sure to happen sometime is wanting to throw away the email you are currently composing. Do this by selecting the Cancel menu item or by pressing the ESC key. If the message has been changed, you will get a dialog asking if you really want to save the draft instead of canceling the composition or if you really want to go ahead and discard the changes. Figure 5.10 shows an example of this. Select the appropriate button by scrolling the trackwheel up or down and clicking the trackwheel or pressing the Enter key. If you got to this dialog accidentally, select the Cancel button to return to the Compose Email screen.

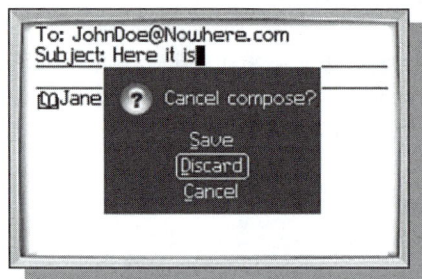

FIGURE 5.10
Cancel Compose dialog box.

SENDING THE MESSAGE

When the email is finally done and ready to be sent, select the Send menu item to send it.

That doesn't mean that the message is immediately sent, however; it simply means that the message is saved into the Message list and is marked as waiting to be sent. This is done because you may not have the wireless modem activated or you may be out of coverage area and unable to send. While the message is waiting to be sent, it has an icon that looks like a small clock. You do not have to do anything to send the message once the wireless modem is activated or back in coverage. The software will automatically try to send the message periodically. When it does try to send the message, the icon will show a series of curves getting bigger. Finally, when the message is sent, the icon changes to a check mark. Figures 5.11 and 5.12 show these icons.

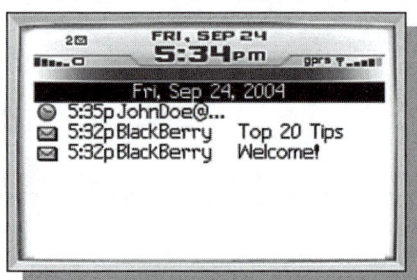

FIGURE 5.11
A message not yet sent shows a "clock" icon in the Message list.

COMPOSING A MESSAGE

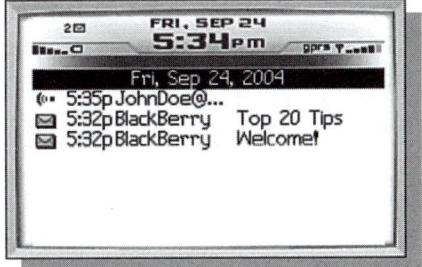

FIGURE 5.12
A message attempting to be sent as seen in the Message list.

COMPOSING AN SMS MESSAGE

Composing an SMS message is very similar to composing an email or PIN message. An SMS message has only a body, however, and the number of characters is limited. The Compose SMS screen shows the number of available characters that can be sent in the upper-right portion of the screen (see Figure 5.13). This number is entirely dependent on the wireless carrier's limitations.

Saving a draft and sending the SMS message behave the same as saving and sending an email or PIN message, but these are the only common features between these types of messages.

FIGURE 5.13
Composing an SMS message.

CHANGING THE RECIPIENT OF AN SMS MESSAGE

Unlike email or PIN messages, SMS messages cannot have multiple recipients. The only thing you can do is change the recipient to another one. You can do this by scrolling the trackwheel up to the recipient's name or number, clicking the trackwheel, and then selecting the Change Number menu. This will once again show the Address Book, where you can select a new recipient or enter the number through the [Use Once] item.

PLACING A CALL

Placing a call begins just like composing any other message: The Address Book is displayed and you select an entry or fill in the recipient in the [Use Once] screen, in this case by entering a phone number. At this point, though, the composing is done and the call is placed. We'll cover calls and placing calls in more depth in Chapter 9, "Making Phone Calls."

AUTOTEXT: FIXING YOUR TYPOS

The complete QWERTY keyboard is a great feature of BlackBerry Handhelds, but let's face it: It is easy to make mistakes on the small keyboard—not to mention that most people are not spelling bee champions. Fortunately, the AutoText feature is there to help you out by correcting commonly misspelled words, and providing shortcuts for words that require the Alt or SYM keys.

AutoText really applies to almost any area of the BlackBerry software where you can enter text, but you will use it the most when composing messages because this is where you will be doing the most typing.

Even with a new device, there is an impressive set of AutoText rules to fix many common mistakes such as changing "hte" to "the" and "acn" to "can". Oftentimes, you may not even notice that you ever made a typo!

There are also rules to make typing a bit easier, such as automatically adding an apostrophe to words so you don't have to press the Alt key combination to insert one manually. Changes like "dont" to "don't" and "cant" to "can't" help you to not look like an fool and still type quickly. Beware, though, some of the AutoText rules are not as obvious. Typing "ill" will not yield "I'll" because "ill" is a valid word. Instead you can type "il" to have AutoText change it into "I'll". It's a good idea to spend some time looking at the AutoText rules to get the most out of this feature and make your typing as easy as possible.

There are two ways to open the AutoText rules list. When composing an email or PIN message, you can select the Edit AutoText menu item or you can open the Options application and select AutoText item from the list. Figure 5.14 shows the AutoText screen.

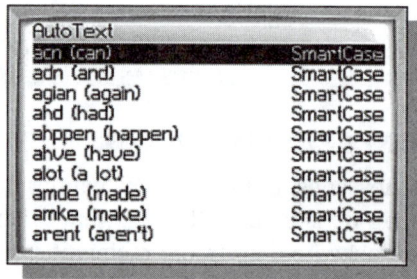

FIGURE 5.14
The AutoText rules list.

CREATING A NEW RULE

One of the rules I think should be included automatically is a rule that converts "bb" to "BlackBerry". To create this rule click the New menu item to show the New Rule screen. Figure 5.15 shows the screen with the new rule filled in.

The Replace: field contains the text that causes the rule to activate. When the rule activates, it deletes the Replace text and inserts the With text.

FORWARDING A CALL MESSAGE

So that we avoid any confusion here, forwarding a Call message is *not the same* as call forwarding. Remember that a Call message is really more of a log of the call, and not the call itself. Forwarding the Call message is simply creating an email that contains the information about the call in the body of the email. This includes any notes that may have been added as well.

To do this, select the Call message in the Message list, click the trackwheel, and then select the Forward menu item, or open the Call message and then select the Forward menu item. This will show the Address Book (with the [Use Once] address), allowing you to select a recipient or enter an email address. You must choose an email address as the recipient.

The Compose Email screen will be shown with the subject and body of the email already filled in with the information from the Call message. If you don't like the pre-populated text, you can edit it before sending the email. Figure 5.16 shows an example of a forwarded Call message.

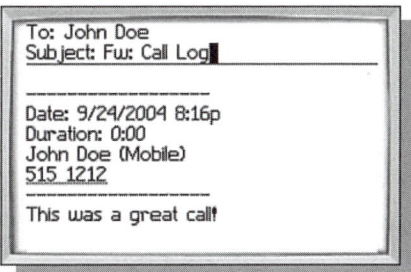

FIGURE 5.16
Default email generated when forwarding a Call message.

Chapter 6

MANAGING YOUR MESSAGES

BLACKBERRY BASICS:

- The Message list is the screen you see when you open the Messages application. It is where all of your messages are shown in a list.

- Each message type has an icon next to it to help you quickly identify what kind of message it is.

- You can delete all of the messages older than a specific date by using the Delete Prior menu.

- You can use folders to sort your messages.

- There is a powerful Search screen to help you find messages in the Message list.

WORKING WITH THE MESSAGE LIST

Now that we've covered how to create and send email, it is time to look at all the other features that are available in the Messages application. Figure 6.1 shows the Message list as you get it with a new handheld. The top portion of the Message screen is the same as the top of the main screen with all the icons. You may not have noticed, but the Phone application is the only other application to do this.

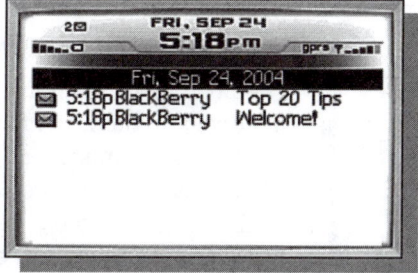

FIGURE 6.1
A look at the Message list of a new handheld.

The Message list shows you all of the messages that have been sent or received each day. At the top of the list is a line that contains only a date. This is called the date header. Below the date header are the individual messages that were sent or received on that date, sorted by time. Each message has an icon and a subject. Depending on the options configured, there may also be the name of the sender and/or the time. This is followed by another date header for the previous day and the messages for that date, and so on.

tip Remember back to Chapter 2 when we talked about lists? The Message list is of course a List field, and all of the tips and tricks mentioned there work here. Of course there are a ton of keyboard shortcuts that we'll go over later as well.

You can also open the selected message by pressing the Enter key while in the Message list.

OPENING MESSAGES

One of things you do most often from the Message screen is view an existing message that you have received. All messages are viewed the same way, but the kind of information displayed is different depending on what the message type is.

In the Message list, scroll the trackwheel up or down to select the desired message, click, and then select the Open menu item to open the message for viewing.

OPENING AN EMAIL OR PIN MESSAGE

Email and PIN messages look and behave the same when opened. The View Email screen also looks similar to the Compose Email screen. The actions and menu items that are available, however, are completely different.

When you first open the View Email screen, you can see the sender, subject, and first portion of the email message. Scrolling the trackwheel up or down scrolls the screen displaying more information. Obviously, you can read the body of the message here, but there are many more things you can do as well. The following sections talk about some of the things you can do once an email or PIN message has been opened.

VIEWING MORE TEXT IN A LONG EMAIL

The body of an email message is not always delivered completely to the handheld. In order to improve the efficiency of the system, only the first 2,000 or so characters of an email message actually reside on the handheld. When this happens, the bottom of the message displays the text "More Available: XXXX bytes" and two new menu items are added, More and More All. Figure 6.2 shows an example of this in a message.

Selecting one of these menu items causes a request to be sent from your handheld to the server asking for more text of the email message. The More menu item simply asks for one piece (about 2,000 characters). The More All menu item tells the server to send as many pieces as necessary to completely deliver the email message.

note The BlackBerry Message Viewer will not display HTML message content. If a message is a MIME multi-part message with HTML content, the HTML is removed and the plain text portion of the email is delivered to the handheld.

FIGURE 6.2
This newsletter is broken into multiple pieces. The More Available line is shown at the bottom of this screen.

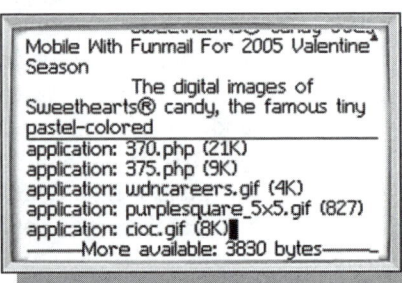

Why is this necessary in the first place? Well, some email messages can be very large and most wireless plans limit the amount of data that you can transfer in a month. Also, transferring a lot of data can take a long time. To save on both time and data transferred, only one part of large messages is sent to the device automatically. If you want the rest of the message, you can get it, but if you don't, then you've saved both time and money.

SEARCHING TEXT OF AN EMAIL OR PIN MESSAGE

Eventually there will come a time when you need to find something in an email or PIN message. The Find menu item is there for just such an occasion. When you select the Find menu item, a small dialog appears asking for the text to find, as shown in Figure 6.3. Enter the text and click the trackwheel (or press the Enter key) to do the search.

> **note** By default, scrolling to the More Available line automatically requests the next piece of the email message, but this option can be disabled, in which case you can only access the rest of the message using the More and More All items in the menu.

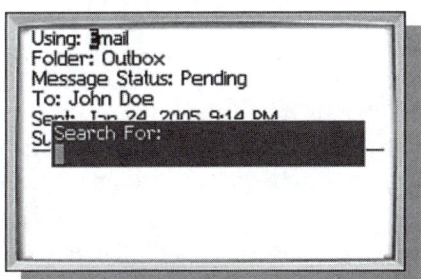

FIGURE 6.3
Entering the text to find.

The cursor will be placed at the beginning of the first occurrence of the text found. Selecting the Find Next menu item will continue the search as you would expect. When the last occurrence has been found, a small information dialog saying simply "Not Found" is shown.

Once the Not Found dialog is shown, the Find criterion is reset. That means that the Find Next menu item is not there and selecting the Find menu item will once again show the dialog asking for the text to find.

VIEWING MESSAGE HEADER INFORMATION

As I mentioned earlier, when entering the View Email screen, the cursor is positioned so you can see some of the header information (specifically the sender and subject), and the rest of the screen is devoted to the body of the email.

There is other information in the message header, though, and you can bring that into view by scrolling the trackwheel up (see Figure 6.4). This information includes other recipients, date and time, the read status, and the folder the message is stored in.

> **note** The search is always case-insensitive and does not need to match the whole word. There are no options available to change these parameters. Also, it is also not possible to search up; you can only search down. For this reason, you should have the cursor at the top of the message when using the Find feature.

FIGURE 6.4
Viewing all of the headers in an email message.

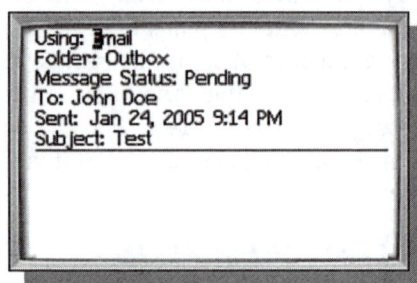

Each of these fields in the header is selectable, and some have special menu items that are only available when that field is selected.

One handy menu item is the Copy menu item. This menu is available on the To:, Cc:, Bcc:, Reply-To:, From:, and Sent: fields. Since these fields are not selectable, it's not possible to highlight them to copy the values. The Copy menu item does that for you.

Another menu item that is very handy is shown when an address is selected. The text of the menu item is dynamic and says Email *WhateverNameIsSelected*. This is useful when you want to send an email to only one person in a long list of recipients or when the Reply-To: is set to an address other than the sender's address.

If the address of the selected address field matches an entry in your Address Book, there will also be menu called View Contact that enables you to display that Address Book entry. If the Address Book also contains information necessary to create other kinds of messages, those appropriate menus will be shown, such as PIN, Call, or SMS. For instance, if you have John Doe in your address book and have only his email and phone number, then selecting John Doe from one of the header fields will show the menu items Email John Doe, Call John Doe, or SMS John Doe.

If the address in the selected address field is not found in your Address Book, there will be an Add to Address Book menu item available to create a new entry with that information.

FRIENDLY NAME AND REAL ADDRESS

Most of the addresses that are displayed are really two pieces of information—the email address and the friendly name. The friendly name is intended to be a name that someone will recognize so they do not have to memorize the email addresses of their friends. For instance "John Doe" is much easier to read and understand than "John_D1234-40@cc.eng.myttech.edu".

The View Email message screen shows the friendly name whenever possible, but there may be times when you want to see the real address instead. For any address field (To:, From:, CC:, or BCC:) that is selected, the menu item Show Address is available. This option will change that address field to only display the real address, as shown in Figure 6.5. The next time you bring up the menu item, Show Name is available to change it back.

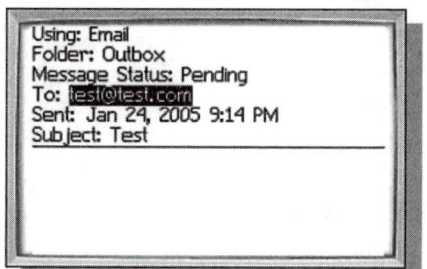

FIGURE 6.5
Viewing the true address of the sender.

CHANGING THE OPENED STATUS OF A MESSAGE

Any time a message arrives to your BlackBerry handheld, it is given a state of unopened, and in the Message list there is a closed envelope icon next to the message. This is to help you notice that a new item has arrived.

You can change the message status directly from within the opened message or in the Message list screen by using the Mark Opened and Mark Unopened pair of menu items. Changing the opened status doesn't change anything about the message other than how it is presented to you in the Message list.

You may want to mark an item as Unopened after opening it, as a reminder to look at it again later. Conversely, you may want to mark many messages as Opened if you've already read them on your PC or otherwise know that the contents aren't relevant to you.

As you would expect, changing the opened status in the View Message screen affects only that message. The menu items to do this are available at any time while viewing a message.

You can also change the status of one or more messages at once from the Message list. To select more than one item, scroll to the first item to select it, then press and hold the Shift key while scrolling the trackwheel to the last item to select. Releasing the Shift key ends the multi-select process. At this point, choosing the Mark Unopened menu item will affect all selected messages (except sent messages and most phone calls—the option to change the status of a missed call is discussed a little later).

If the selected items include both opened and unopened items, you will see both Mark Opened and Mark Unopened menu items. Choosing either menu item will set the appropriate status on all of the selected items. An example of this is shown in Figure 6.6.

FIGURE 6.6
Changing the Opened status on several messages.

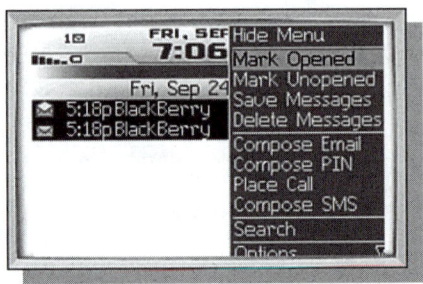

OPENING A CALL MESSAGE

Call messages are really more like call log entries than messages in the traditional sense. I refer to them as Call messages, though, because the BlackBerry software treats creating email, SMS, and calls in much the same way and stores entries about them all together in the Message list. A typical Call message is shown in Figure 6.7.

FIGURE 6.7
A typical Call message.

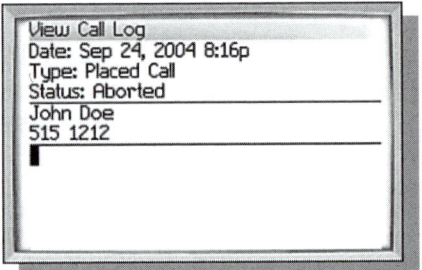

There are three types of call messages—Placed Calls, Received Calls, and Missed Calls. The type of the call is shown in the header along with the date and time of the call. Placed and Received calls have another field for the Duration of the call, but Missed calls do not. Instead, Missed calls have a Status field to show it as Opened or Unopened. Missed calls can have their status changed in the same way as received emails through the Mark Opened and Mark Unopened menu items.

Below the header is the Caller ID information. This will show the phone number on the other end of the connection, regardless of who initiated the call.

ADDING A PHONE NUMBER TO THE ADDRESS BOOK

If there is an entry in your Address Book with a phone number that matches this number, the name from the Address Book entry is displayed in the Caller ID information as well as in the Message list itself. As in the View Message screen, several other menu items are available to initiate new messages to that person and to view the Address Book entry.

If there is not an entry in your Address Book that matches the phone number of the person on the other end of the call, there is an Add to Address Book menu item in case you want to add it. Choosing this menu automatically places the phone number in the Work field and displays an edit screen so you can enter the name of the contact.

ADDING NOTES

One of the most useful features in the Call message is the ability to add additional notes to it. These notes are saved with the message and can be read or edited at a later date—they can even be searched!

To add a note to a Call message, open the message, click the trackwheel, and select the Add Notes menu item. The area under the Caller ID information will become an Edit field that you can enter the notes into, as shown in Figure 6.8. When you are done entering the notes, you must save them using the Save Notes menu item. If you press the Escape key or select the Close menu item, you will be prompted with a dialog box to save or discard changes.

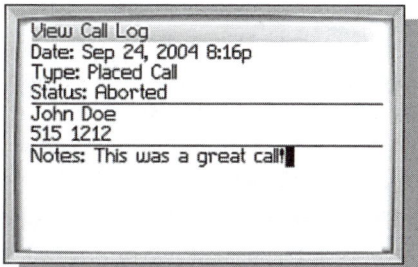

FIGURE 6.8
Adding notes to a Call message.

OPENING AN SMS MESSAGE

Opening an SMS message is a lot like opening an email message. The top of the View SMS Message screen shows the sender, the date and time it was received, and the body of the message. If the address is in an entry in the Address Book, it shows the name in the Address Book. If not, it shows the phone number that sent the SMS message. One thing that is different, however, is a special feature that shows the history of the SMS message as well.

Because a single SMS message is often part of a larger conversation, the context of the conversation can sometimes be important to understanding the message. For this reason, the BlackBerry software automatically shows previous SMS messages sent to and received from the same person. The message history is not part of the SMS message itself. Instead the software automatically searches for SMS messages that were previously received and creates a chain of events that make up the message history. Deleting the original SMS message removes it from the message history and breaks the chain. If you don't want to see the message history, you can also click the Remove History menu item. Be careful, as this is a permanent action, and breaks the chain of messages as well.

ACCESSING OTHER MESSAGES FROM WITHIN A MESSAGE

While viewing any opened message, it's possible to open other messages as well. This allows you to view many messages in succession without going back to the Message list screen each time. You can do this by clicking the Next Item or Previous Item menu items. Clicking the Next Item menu item will open the next or newer message and clicking the Previous Item menu item will open the previous or older message.

When the new message is opened, the appropriate view screen is shown. For example, if you select the Next menu item while viewing an email, and the next message is a call, then the View Call screen will be displayed.

> **note** Navigating through the Message list does not create a history of screens. Clicking the Escape key or clicking the Close menu item displays the Message list once again.

DELETING MESSAGES

After viewing a message, the next thing you are likely to do is delete it (you don't really want hundreds of messages on your handheld, do you?). As I said before, there are nearly always multiple ways to do something. When it comes to deleting messages, there are seven.

When you have a message opened, you can either select the Delete menu item or press the Backspace key. Either action will present you with a dialog asking you to confirm the delete, such as the one shown in Figure 6.9. The dialog appears with the No button pre-selected. This is just in case you get a little click-happy and accidentally select the Delete menu item and immediately click again. Scroll the trackwheel up to select the Yes button and then click the trackwheel again to confirm the delete.

FIGURE 6.9
Confirm deleting a message.

You can also delete a message if you are at the Message list screen. Make sure the message is selected and either select the Delete menu item or press the Backspace key. Again, the confirmation dialog will be shown as before.

DELETING MULTIPLE MESSAGES AT ONE TIME

Sometimes you want to delete more than one message at a time. Like in the morning when you wake up and find you've received 15 pieces of spam email over the night. In this case, you can multi-select the messages to delete by pressing the Cap key while scrolling the trackwheel. Once all the messages are selected, release the CAP key. When you open the menu this time, you will notice that some of the menu items have changed to handle the multi-select while others, which do not apply to multiple items, have been removed. Select the Delete Messages menu item. Again, the confirmation dialog will show up as before. Also as mentioned previously, pressing the Backspace button will also cause the Delete confirmation dialog to appear.

DELETING MESSAGES OLDER THAN A SPECIFIC DATE

Sometimes you get to the point where you want to just purge all of the messages on your handheld that are older than a certain date. Of course, you can just multi-select them all, but there is an easier way. If you select one of the date headers and bring up the menu, there is a Delete Prior menu item. Clicking this menu causes all of the messages of the selected date and older to be deleted, after confirming with the dialog of course.

ORGANIZING EMAIL MESSAGES WITH FOLDERS

Keeping your email messages organized can be a difficult challenge, even if you get as little as a dozen a day. One way to do this is to aggressively delete messages when they are no longer needed. Another way is to organize them into folders.

Your BlackBerry handheld comes with many folders set up automatically. They include folders for Call Logs and Sent Items as well as your main Inbox. There is no way to create new folders from your BlackBerry, however. You must create new folders in your desktop email client first and then they will be synchronized to your handheld.

FILING MESSAGES

Only email messages can be filed into subfolders. Call messages and SMS messages are already automatically filed into special folders. To file an email message, select the message in the Message list and click the File menu item. Or, if the email message is open, select File from the menu. A screen showing the folders on your handheld will appear, and is described in the next section. Select a folder to file the message into and click the File menu item to move the message into the selected folder.

> **caution** If you never delete any messages from your handheld, eventually, the storage space will begin to run out. When this happens, the handheld software will begin to delete messages automatically for you, starting with the oldest messages.

> **note** When multi-selecting messages, selecting the date header as part of the multi-select is okay and has no effect on the delete operation.

CHAPTER 6 MANAGING YOUR MESSAGES

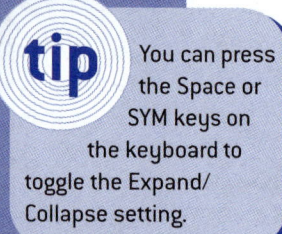

tip You can press the Space or SYM keys on the keyboard to toggle the Expand/Collapse setting.

SELECTING A FOLDER FROM THE FOLDER LIST

The Folder List is a hierarchical list of folders that are organized as a tree—somewhat like you might find in your computer's operating system. Scrolling the trackwheel up or down changes the selected folder. Sometimes, there can be many folders inside of other folders. This is especially true if your company has a large email system. In this case, folders may have to be expanded or collapsed to find the desired folder.

Folders containing other folders have a small circle next to them with either a + or – inside the circle. If the folder is expanded, the circle will have a – inside and the subfolders will be shown. If the folder is collapsed, the circle will have a + inside it.

To expand a collapsed folder, scroll the trackwheel up or down to select it and then click the Expand menu item. To collapse an expanded folder, select it and click the Collapse menu item.

SELECTING A FOLDER TO VIEW

note The View Folder menu is only available when an email message, SMS message, or date header is selected in the message list.

By default, filed messages do not show up in the Message list. If you want to see them again, you have to open the folder they were filed to. Do this by clicking the View Folder menu item.

The Folder List screen is shown again. This time, however, you can see and select folders for different items besides just email. The same instructions for expanding and collapsing folders discussed in the previous section still holds true.

To select the folder to view, simply scroll the trackwheel up or down to the desired folder and click the Select Folder menu item. The handheld may pause a bit as it sorts out the messages, but in a second or two the screen will update to show the contents of that folder. Notice that the title in the header section of the screen is changed to show the name of the folder you are currently viewing.

The functions of the Message list while viewing a folder are the same as those of the unfiltered Message list, and all of the same menus and keyboard shortcuts work here as well. To return to the full Message list, press the Escape button.

note With the 4.0 version of the handheld software, you can view the saved messages by clicking the View Saved Messages menu item from the Message List screen.

SAVING MESSAGES

You may have some messages that you want to keep for a long time, and it's best to keep them separate from the messages in your email system. You keep these messages safe by clicking the Save menu item while the message is selected in the Message list or while the message is opened. You can save any sent or received SMS, PIN, or email messages.

Saving a message does not remove it from the Message list automatically. In fact it doesn't appear or behave differently at all except that the Save menu item is no longer available while the saved message is selected. You can even delete it from the Message list, but don't worry, the message is still saved. To see your saved messages, return to the Home screen and select the Saved Messages icon. This will show you a Message list screen that lists only your saved messages. You can interact with them in the same way as normal messages, but you cannot use this as a way to "undelete" messages and you cannot "unsave" it. Once it's marked as a Saved message, the only thing you can do to change it is to delete it from the handheld.

USING THE SEARCH FUNCTION TO FIND MESSAGES

Sooner or later, there will come a time when you will need to search for a message on your handheld. The BlackBerry software has a thorough search function to help you find the messages you need.

From anywhere in the Message list, click the Search menu item to show the Search screen, shown in Figure 6.10. This screen has many fields to let you search for messages that match the specified criteria. For a message to be shown in the search results, it must match all of the criteria specified, though it does not have to match the case exactly.

note Only one of each search criteria can be entered. For instance, it is not possible to create a search where the subject contains either "assign" or "equals." Putting "assign equals" into the subject field would match any messages with that exact text in the subject.

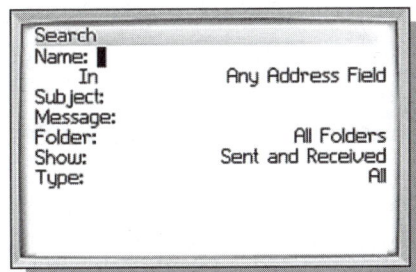

FIGURE 6.10
Entering search criteria into the Search screen.

The Name field is where you enter some part of a friendly name or address that would be found in an address field. The second field, the In field, allows you to specify the type of address field to search.

The Subject field only applies to email and PIN messages, and is only shown if the type is set to Email or All.

The text can be added to the Message field to search the body of PIN, Email, and SMS message types. For Call messages, it searches the Notes field instead.

Finally, there are choice boxes to specify a folder, whether the message was sent or received, and what message types to search. To execute the search, click the Search menu item.

note Even if you set the search type to All, if you enter some criteria to the subject line, only email and PIN Messages will be shown in the search results because the other message types do not have a subject.

 **note** The Search feature cannot be used to search for saved messages.

As with viewing a folder, the Message list will be updated after a short time to show messages matching the search criteria. The title of the Message list changes to Search Results, also. To return to the Message list screen, press the Escape key.

When opening the Search screen, all of the fields default to empty. The Search screen remembers your previous search, however. To see it, click the Last menu item and the criteria from the previous search will be shown in the Search field. To clear all of the fields again, click the New menu item.

CREATING CUSTOM SEARCHES

Custom searching is one of those features that can be very useful, and yet it is tucked away in menus so that many people are not even aware that the feature exists. In fact, you may have used a custom search and not even have known that you were doing it.

From the Search screen, click the Recall menu item to see a list of custom searches that are defined by default for you (see Figure 6.11).

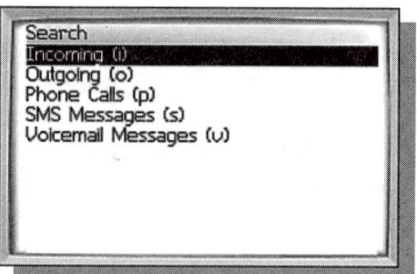

FIGURE 6.11
A list of default custom searches.

The list shows the name of the custom search followed by the hotkey associated with it. For instance, "Incoming (i)" in the list means the search is called Incoming and it is activated by pressing the Alt key and the I key together while viewing the Message list screen. The title of the list changes to Incoming and only received messages are shown. As with other views, pressing the Escape key takes you back to the Message list.

To create your own custom search, return to the Search screen and select the Save menu item. Two new fields are now available, as shown in Figure 6.12. With them, you can specify the title and shortcut key that will be used with the Alt key to activate the search. Once you are done, click the Save menu item to save the search and return to the Message list.

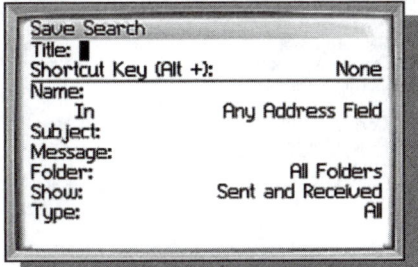

FIGURE 6.12
Creating a custom search.

If you need to modify or delete your custom search, just return to the Search screen and click the Recall menu item to show the list of custom searches. Select the appropriate search and click the Edit Search menu item to edit it, or click the Delete Search menu item to delete it.

SEARCH SUBJECT AND SEARCH SENDER

As powerful as the Search screen is, there are some common searches that can be easier to execute. The software provides these in the form of Search Subject and Search Sender menu items on the Message list menu. These menu items are only available when an email message is selected in the Message list, and they only search other emails, but they make the process of launching the search extremely easy.

To find all of the other messages with the same subject, simply select the message in the Message list, click the trackwheel, and then click the Search Subject menu item. The search results will contain all of the messages with the same subject, including any with additional Re: or Fw: prefixes in the subject.

The Search Sender menu item works in much the same way. The search results will contain all of the messages in which the sender of the selected message is included in an address field. This includes both sent and received messages, as well as those where the person was on the Cc: or Bcc: list.

MESSAGE LIST OPTIONS

There have been a few times when I've said things will work a certain way by default, indicating that the behavior can be changed if you want. This section is where we look at the Message list options and what changing those settings means. To open the Message List Options screen, click the Options menu item while viewing the Message List screen. Figure 6.13 shows an example of this screen.

> **note** In Version 4.0 of the handheld software the options are organized into option groups. The options mentioned here are grouped together into the General Options group.

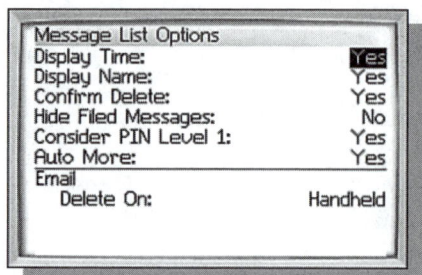

FIGURE 6.13
The Message List Options screen.

CUSTOMIZING THE BEHAVIOR OF MESSAGE LIST

The top portion of the screen contains a number of Yes/No choices that change the way the message looks and behaves in small ways. The following list explains each of them individually.

- **Display Time**—This option specifies whether to display the time of a message in the Message list. The time is either the received time if the message was received, or sent time if it was sent.
- **Display Name**—This option specifies whether to display the name associated with a message on the Message list. The name is the sender's name if the message was received, or the recipient's name if the message was sent.
- **Confirm Delete**—This option specifies whether the Delete Item dialog box is shown each time a message is deleted. If the Option is set to No, the dialog won't be shown. As tempting as this might be, remember that it is also a safety feature to stop you from deleting messages by accident.
- **Hide Filed Messages**—This option specifies whether messages that have been filed into subfolders are shown in the Message list. If the option is set to No, the messages will still be visible in the Message list, but the icon will be changed to look like a folder to indicate that it has been filed.
- **Consider PIN Level 1**—This option specifies whether a new PIN message is considered to be a Level 1 message for notification purposes. In Chapter 4, "Personalizing Your Device," we covered profiles. If you will recall, there is a Notification Type called Level 1 Messages. In Chapter 4 I said that this simply meant PIN messages, and this option is why. If you want to have new PIN messages notify you just like normal email messages, change this option to No.

> **note** A new option in the 4.0 version of the handheld software is the Keep Messages option. This option allows you to specify how long messages are to be kept on the handheld before the software automatically purges them. The default is Forever, which is basically how previous versions of the software operated. If you want the software to automatically delete old messages, change this option to 15 Days, 30 Days, 60 Days, or 90 Days. The software will then automatically delete message that are older than the specified number of days.

- **Auto More**—This option specifies whether the software should automatically request more text of a long message when the least available text is shown. If you recall, we talked about the More and More All menu items in the "Viewing More Text in a Long Email" section earlier in this chapter. At the time I said that if you reach the line that says "More Available: XXXX Bytes" it would automatically request more of the message. This option is why I said that. If you don't want to automatically get more of a message, set this option to No.

> **note** The wireless synchronizations options have been moved into the Email Reconciliation option group in the 4.0 version of the handheld software.

WIRELESS SYNCHRONIZATION RULES FOR MESSAGES

The bottom part of the Message List Options screen allows you to set rules for what happens during a wireless synchronization. The options that are available here will vary depending on how your handheld is set up and whether wireless synchronization is enabled. You should talk to your BlackBerry specialist if you think you need to change them.

EMPTYING THE DELETED ITEMS FOLDER ON YOUR SERVER

If you are set up for wireless synchronization, one function that may be very useful is the ability to empty your Deleted Items folder from your handheld. For those road warriors who don't make it back to their desk, the ability to do this can mean not getting the "your account is over quota" nag emails. From the Message List Options screen, click the Purge Deleted Items menu item to do this. Your handheld will not display a confirmation dialog for this operation.

> **note** The Purge Deleted Items menu item has also been moved into the Email Reconciliation options group.

Chapter 7

MESSAGE ATTACHMENTS

BLACKBERRY BASICS:

- V-Card attachments can be used to share contact information with other BlackBerry users and can be imported into the Address Book easily.

- An Attachment Service can be installed on your BES to enable viewing of common attachment types.

- Attachments cannot be edited.

- Attachments can be viewed in small pieces to minimize bandwidth usage.

Up to now, we've only talked about the basics of working with messages. Now it's time to roll up our sleeves and get into the fun stuff—handling attachments.

Let's face it: We get email messages with attachments all the time, and they are important to us. It's no wonder that people expect to be able to work with attachments on their handheld in much the same way they do on their desktop.

The problem with attachments, though, is that they are generally files that are larger than the handheld can physically store. In addition, there are so many types of files that it is impractical to make a small device such as a BlackBerry have the storage capacity and horsepower to be able to open them all.

WORKING WITH EMAIL ATTACHMENTS

You may recall from Chapter 6, "Managing Messages," that not all the content of an email is sent to the handheld initially. Long email messages are divided into chunks and only the first chunk is sent to the handheld. Attachments are handled in much the same way, where only some of the information is actually delivered to the device. The rest is cached on your BlackBerry Enterprise Server. When a message with an attachment is delivered, only a "stub" or placeholder is provided for the attachment. You can see that the message has an attachment, but most of the time you cannot access the attachment itself.

This is done for the same time and cost reasons that were discussed in the "Viewing More Text in a Long Email" section of Chapter 6. Additionally, there just isn't enough Flash RAM on your device to store attachments locally. With only 8MB of FlashRAM on a 7280, it would take only one really large Word document to use up all the available storage. Some PowerPoint attachments wouldn't be able to fit at all.

CHAPTER 7 MESSAGE ATTACHMENTS

> **note** It is not possible in any way to modify an attachment. All of these features discussed in this chapter are for viewing the data in an attachment only.

V-CARD ATTACHMENTS

V-card attachments (.VCF) are the only kind of attachments delivered to the handheld without plug-ins. (Other attachment types are possible using the BlackBerry Attachment Service; see below for details.) V-cards are allowed because they are generally small and because the BlackBerry client can create messages with attachments using this format for sharing contact information. Figure 7.1 shows a message with a V-card attachment.

When you scroll the trackwheel so that the cursor is on a V-card attachment, the View Attachment item is added to the menu, and selecting it displays a screen listing all of the contact information contained in the V-card.

FIGURE 7.1
A message with a V-card attachment.

The address is not copied to the Address Book automatically. If the Address Book contains an entry whose name matches that of the V-card, an Update Address menu item is available on the View Attachment screen. If not, the Add to Address Book menu item is available. Selecting the appropriate menu item causes the data in the V-card to be updated or inserted into the Address Book.

> **note** We haven't talked about the Address Book in depth yet. To learn more about the Address Book application, see Chapter 10.

If you want to send a V-Card to another person, simply compose an email message to him. Then, before sending the message, click the Attach Address menu item. This will display a screen listing all of the Contacts in your Address Book. Select the proper name in the list and click the Continue menu item. You will be returned to the email you were composing, and now there is an Address Book attachment shown at the bottom of the screen.

OTHER KINDS OF ATTACHMENTS

V-Cards are neat, but you probably don't get them as often as you do other kinds of files. File attachments such as Microsoft Word, Microsoft Excel, and Adobe Acrobat files are far more common. For this, you must have the BlackBerry Attachment Service installed on your BlackBerry Enterprise Server. If you are using the BlackBerry Web Client, your BlackBerry Enterprise Server is operated by your wireless carrier and most likely has the Attachment Service installed. Check with your carrier for more information.

The Attachment Service supports only a few of the most common formats. Table 7.1 lists the file types and the applications that create them.

Table 7.1—Accepted File Formats for Attachments

Application	Extension	Supported Versions
Adobe Acrobat	.pdf	1.1 and later
Microsoft Excel	.xls	97 and later
Microsoft Word	.doc	97 and later
Microsoft PowerPoint	.ppt	97 and later
Corel WordPerfect	.wpd	6.0 to 2000
Compressed Archive	.zip	2.6 and earlier
HTML	.html, .htm	All
ASCII Text	.txt	All

There is really only one way to find out if your handheld is configured to view attachments or not, and that is to try to view one. To start with, you need to receive an email with an attachment. The attachment stub should be shown at the bottom of the message, like the one shown in Figure 7.2. The attachment must be one of the supported types listed in Table 7.1.

FIGURE 7.2
A message with a Microsoft Word document attachment.

Once you have received a message with an attachment, you need to click the trackwheel to display the menu and scroll down to the Open Attachment menu item. If the menu item is not shown then either the attachment is not one of the supported types or the BlackBerry Enterprise Server that your handheld uses does not have the Attachment Service installed.

After clicking the Open Attachment menu item, you are shown a screen that lists all of the files in the message in a tree view. If your message contained more than one attachment, each attachment will be shown in the list, regardless of which attachment stub you selected, assuming they are of the supported types, of course. If the message contained an attachment that is a compressed archive, then the name of each file in that archive is also shown as a node under the name of the archive.

Each file can be opened in two ways. The options are as a Table of Contents or Full Content. These two choices are listed under each filename node in the tree view. This can make for a lot of items in the tree, especially with a compressed archive containing many files. For this reason, the filename nodes of the tree can be collapsed or expanded using the Collapse and Expand menu items to make it easier to see what you are looking for.

If your message has only one attachment in it, then the filename node is expanded by default, but if it has more than one attachment or is a compressed archive, then the nodes will be collapsed by default to make sure as many filenames as possible can be shown.

To open the attachment, select the desired filename node from the tree and click the Expand menu item to display the two ways to view the file. Next, select either Table of Contents or Full Content and click the Retrieve menu item.

Once this is done, the icon next to the open type turns to a clock indicating that you need to wait for it to communicate back to the server and get the data you need. This process can sometimes take a little while, and of course you must be in an area with wireless coverage to do it.

> **note** All the files in a compressed archive are listed, even if the file type is not one of the supported types. You can still attempt to view the attachment, but it will fail to open and will display a red "X" icon next to the open type in the tree.

OPENING AN ATTACHMENT AS A TABLE OF CONTENTS

The idea behind opening an attachment as a table of contents is to deliver an outline of the data that is in the attachment and then retrieve the contents in small chunks. This is good because opening the full content can take more time to process and transmit and uses a lot of the bandwidth, which your calling plan may limit.

Each piece of the outline is shown as a node under the Table of Contents node, and the Table of Contents node itself becomes collapsible and expandable, just like filename node. What exactly goes into the table of contents varies depending on what kind of file it is. Generally speaking, this is the first line of a page of the file. To view a portion of the document, select the outline representing that portion of the document and again select the Retrieve menu item. When that portion of the document is retrieved, it will put a check mark icon next to the node in the tree.

> **note** Retrieving the full content of a document can be good when you know you will want to view the document later and will not be in coverage, such as on an airplane.

OPENING AN ATTACHMENT AS FULL CONTENT

If you know you want to view the entire attachment, opening it using the Full Content menu item is the way to go. Select the Full Content node under the filename node and click the Retrieve menu item. As noted in the previous section, this can take more time, but will ultimately be worth it as you can read the entire document without waiting to retrieve more chunks. Once any portion of a document has been retrieved, a check mark icon is placed next to the Full Content node of the attachment tree.

VIEWING ATTACHMENTS

Once the content of a document is retrieved, it will be viewed automatically, but it will also be stored in the cache so that the next time you want to view it, you do not have to retrieve it again. To view an attachment that has been cached, click the Open Attachment menu item and select either Full Content or a Table of Contents node. An item that has been previously saved to the cache has a check mark icon. This icon indicates that the attachment data has already been retrieved. Then click the View menu item to view the document.

Even though there are some differences in the viewers, all viewers have a Find menu item. You can use this to find text within a document and jump the cursor to the line containing that text. It operates the same way as the Find menu item in the Message viewer. Clicking the menu item displays a dialog where you can enter the text to search for and clicking the trackwheel begins the search. If the text was found, the cursor is placed on the line that contains that text and a new Find Next menu item is enabled. Clicking Find Next allows you to execute the search again from the current position.

VIEWING TEXT DOCUMENTS

All of the attachment types that represent text documents are viewed in the same way. These include Microsoft Word, Adobe Acrobat, Corel WordPerfect, HTML, and ASCII text documents. Viewing one of these types shows you the text portion of the document, including styles such as bold and italic. Other features such as bullets and hyperlinks are also preserved. On handhelds with a color screen, colors are also preserved. Depending on the version of your handheld software, images may also be included.

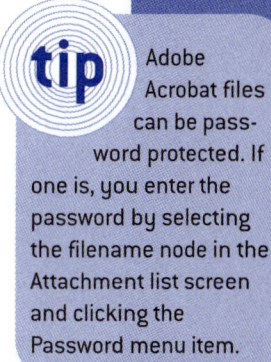

tip Adobe Acrobat files can be password protected. If one is, you enter the password by selecting the filename node in the Attachment list screen and clicking the Password menu item.

There are not many features when viewing text documents. The one thing you can do is click the Select menu item to begin selecting text, which you later copy using the Copy menu item.

VIEWING MICROSOFT EXCEL DOCUMENTS

Microsoft Excel Documents make the most sense when they are displayed in a format with rows and cells like you see using Microsoft Excel on your desktop. When you view the full content of an Excel document, you are shown the first worksheet on the screen. If you retrieve the table of contents instead, you will get the list of worksheets that the document contains.

When viewing a worksheet, you can scroll the cursor around and view the cell contents. To move the cursor up and down, scroll the trackwheel up and down. To move the cursor right and left, press and hold the Shift key while scrolling the trackwheel up and down.

You can also jump to a specific cell by clicking the Go to Cell menu item. A dialog is shown where you can enter the cell index, such as L10. Clicking the trackwheel will cause the screen to be scrolled so that the desired cell is displayed and the cursor will be in the cell.

The height and width of the rows and columns is not preserved when viewing an Excel document on a Blackberry. As a result, sometimes the contents of a cell are bigger than the column width and are not completely visible. You can view the contents of the cell by scrolling to it and selecting the View Cell menu item. The value in the cell will be displayed in a dialog box.

> **note** Viewing a cell means viewing the value in the cell. If a cell was originally a calculation, you will not see the calculation formula, just the resulting value.

You can adjust the width of a column, but not the height of a row. To change the width of a column, scroll the cursor to the column header and click the trackwheel. A menu of sizes will be displayed at the location of the selected column header, not in the normal menu location. Scrolling the thumbwheel up and down changes the menu selection as you would expect, and clicking the trackwheel selects the size. There are four choices: Small, Medium, Large, and Fit. These settings are not saved permanently to the handheld. If you later return to the email message containing the attachment, any changes to the column sizing is lost.

Even if both the full contents and the table of contents are retrieved, you will still see a More menu item when viewing a worksheet. Clicking this menu item will get the list of worksheets and allow some other menu items to be shown. They are the Next Sheet, Prev Sheet, and Select Worksheet menu items. These menu items are used to view other worksheets in the document. Clicking the Next Sheet or Prev Sheet will immediately change the view to the proper worksheet. Clicking the Select Worksheet menu item shows a dialog listing all of the worksheets. Clicking the trackwheel causes the selected worksheet in the dialog to be displayed. Like the column size, the list of worksheets delivered by the More menu item is not saved and will be lost when you return to the message.

When viewing Excel Documents, you can copy the contents of a cell into the clipboard much the same as with a text document. Simply select the cell you want to copy and click the Copy Cell menu item. It is not possible to select or copy more than one cell, however.

VIEWING MICROSOFT POWERPOINT DOCUMENTS

PowerPoint documents receive just a little special treatment. For the most part, they are treated like a collection of text documents—each slide of the presentation is viewed as a text document. Of course, there are no flashy animations, but you can usually still view and understand the presentation without them.

DOCUMENT VIEWING OPTIONS

Lastly, what would any feature be without a set of options that you can change? The Options screen is available when viewing any file. Open the

Viewer Options screen by clicking the Options menu item. The Viewer Options screen displays nine choice fields. Each of these choices can be changed in the standard ways by pressing the Space key or clicking the Change Option menu item.

Because this Options screen is the same for all file types, there may be some that do not apply to the document you are currently viewing. In particular, there are five options relating to how the Excel Worksheet view works. We will look at these options first.

- **Sheet Outline Cells**—Each cell in the worksheet is shown with a rectangle around it if this option is set to Yes. Changing this option to No causes the rectangle to not be shown.
- **Sheet Horizontal Scroll**—If this option is set to Yes, scrolling the cursor horizontally past the last column will cause the cursor to wrap around to the first column on the next row. If this option is set to No, the cursor will remain in the last column and not wrap even if you continue to horizontally scroll.
- **Sheet Vertical Scroll**—This option is the same as the Sheet Horizontal Scroll option, but affects wrapping the cursor when scrolling vertically.
- **Sheet Column Width**—When a worksheet is being viewed, all of the columns are set to this column width by default. Changing this option will change the way all worksheets are viewed and the column width that is used.
- **Sheet Display Labels**—When this option is set to Yes, the column header and row numbers are displayed. These take up some room, obviously, so if you want to hide them, change this option to No.

The other options apply to all attachment viewers.

- **Case Sensitive Search**—Doing a search of the text in an attachment using the Find menu item is not case sensitive if this option is set to No. To enable case sensitive searches, change this option to Yes.
- **Font Family**—Since all of the font information is lost when retrieving the attachment data, the viewer must use its own font settings. This option can be used to select the font family to use when viewing attachments.
- **Font Size**—Like the font family, the size of the font used is set in this option. If you find that you want to see more text on the screen, change this option to a smaller number. If you find that you are unable to read the text on the screen comfortably, make this number larger.
- **Cache Size**—A handheld only has so much storage space available to hold attachments that have been retrieved. If you find that you are hitting the limits of this cache, you may be able to increase its size with this option. On my handheld, the default was already set at the largest value.

Chapter 8

BROWSING THE INTERNET WIRELESSLY

BLACKBERRY BASICS:

- You may have a web browser from your provider, another from your IT staff, or none at all.

- Browsers can be used to view WML or HTML content, though your provider may limit you to one kind.

- If you want to install new ringtones, you must download them through your browser.

- You can clear the local cache your handheld created through the Option menu item.

WEB BROWSERS FOR THE BLACKBERRY

One of the most versatile tools on your handheld is the web browser, but unfortunately not all handhelds have one. A browser is always installed on your handheld, but it requires a special activation to be seen and used. This activation can come from two places, so it's possible to have none, one, or even multiple browsers on your handheld.

The most common way a browser can be activated is from your carrier. Not all carriers offer browser service, but most do. If your browser is activated by your carrier, it will have a name that identifies it with your carrier. For instance, my BlackBerry 7280 has a "Cingular Browser" icon on the home screen.

The other way a browser can be activated is through your corporate IT staff if they have a BES installed with MDS. *MDS* stands for *Mobile Data Services* and is a piece of software that can be installed in addition to the BES. If these are installed, and your IT staff configures your handheld to use a browser, an icon labeled "BlackBerry Browser" will be shown on your home screen.

Another common way is through a service called the BlackBerry Internet Browser Service (BIBS). Many carriers offer this service, though there may be an additional fee. The BIBS is very similar to using an MDS except that the server is not controlled by your IT staff. If your carrier has configured your handheld to use BIBS, an icon labeled "Internet Browser" will be shown on your home screen.

WHAT KIND OF CONTENT CAN YOU GET?

Even if you have a browser icon on your handheld, you may not be able to view every web page out there. This is because there are many kinds of web pages and your browser may not be configured to view them all.

The web content you are most used to seeing on your desktop is content made with Hypertext Markup Language, or HTML. HTML is a feature rich language and is transferred using Hypertext Transfer Protocol (HTTP). Often the rich features of HTML (such as frames and client-side scripting) just don't work well on small devices such as a BlackBerry. To make small devices functional, another web page content type was created called Wireless Markup Language (WML), which is transferred using a subset of HTTP called Wireless Application Protocol (WAP).

The point of all this technical mumbo-jumbo is that your browser may be limited to either WAP or HTTP. Generally a browser offered by your carrier will be configured for WAP content but may allow HTTP as well. However, a browser that has been configured by your IT staff will generally allow both HTTP and WAP content.

> **tip** If you are in a situation where you do not have a web browser on your handheld and want one, you can sign up for browser service from a third-party provider. See Chapter 14, "Finding and Installing Third-Party Applications," for more information on finding third-party software.

WHICH BROWSER SHOULD I USE?

So if you have two browser icons, why does it matter what kind of browser you use? Well, one browser may restrict content, but even if you have two that allow HTTP content, there is an important difference that should be considered. That difference is how the browser traffic gets to the Internet.

With a browser offered by your carrier, the HTTP requests go to your carrier first and then to the Internet through a server in your carrier's office. With a browser that is configured by your IT staff, the requests go to your office first and then to the Internet. This difference may seem insignificant, but having requests go to your office first has some distinct advantages.

First is security. I'm sure you trust your carrier, but the fact is that you just don't know what your carrier might be doing with the data while it is relaying it. Without going into details, we can simply say that using the browser which goes through the servers in your office is more secure.

The second advantage is that by having the browser traffic go to your office first, you can access your company's intranet as well as the Internet. Many companies use an intranet extensively for internal operations of all kinds, so this may be a huge benefit.

> **tip** Pressing the Space key moves the cursor down to the next screenful of data. This can be an easy way to read pages with a lot of content.

SURFING THE WEB WITH YOUR BLACKBERRY

When you launch a web browser you will see either the bookmarks screen or the homepage will be loaded and displayed in the browser screen. Which screen is displayed depends on how your browser was configured. If launching your browser displays your bookmarks, review the upcoming section titled "Using Bookmarks" first so you can load a web page.

Once you have a web page loaded and displayed on your handheld you will need to be able to navigate around it. Figure 8.1 shows the default home page provided by blackberry.com. Each of the links available on the displayed web page are shown in blue text. Regular text is shown in black text. Like an email message, the browser screen has a cursor that can be scrolled around the screen using the trackwheel. The cursor jumps from link to link as you scroll the trackwheel up and down. If there is a section of the web page that has no links, there may be a small black cursor at the end of the line that is scrolled up and down with the trackwheel instead.

To open a link on a web page, first scroll the trackwheel up or down so that the link is selected, then click the Get Link menu item and the new page will start loading—just like a browser on a desktop. Loading the new page will take some time, though. While the page is loading, a small progress bar is shown at the bottom of the screen (see Figure 8.2).

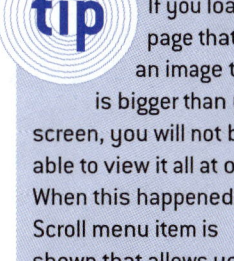

tip If you load a page that has an image that is bigger than your screen, you will not be able to view it all at once. When this happened, a Scroll menu item is shown that allows you to scroll the view instead of the cursor. After clicking the Scroll menu item, scrolling the trackwheel moves the view up and down. Click the Stop Scrolling menu item to exit the scrolling mode.

FIGURE 8.1
Displaying the default home page in the BlackBerry browser.

FIGURE 8.2
The bar at the bottom shows the progress of the page loading.

> **tip** You can also open a link by pressing the Enter key on the keypad.
>
> You can also return to the previous page by clicking the Backspace key on the keypad. Unlike the Escape button, pressing the Backspace key repeatedly will not cause the browser to exit, but simply back up the browser history to the first screen displayed.

If you realize that you opened the wrong page or something is wrong and the page is taking a long time to load, you can stop the loading by clicking the Stop menu item. You can also press the Escape button. Stopping a new page from loading will display the previous page again so you can select a different link.

After opening a link, you often want to go back to the page you came from. You can do this by clicking the Back menu item, or pressing the Escape button.

Each time a page is loaded, it is also added to the cache so that it can be referenced again later. Particularly when you return from a linked page, you may notice that the previous page loaded very quickly. This is because the browser was able to load it from the cache and did not need to retrieve it again over the wireless networks. This is a big time-saver, but unfortunately, clicking the same link again will not reload the page from the cache, even though it is in the link history and was cached.

If you want to return to the page you just came from, you must select it from the link history. Clicking the History menu item displays a dialog, shown in Figure 8.3, that lists all of the web pages you have viewed. The page you are currently viewing is shown in bold in the list. You can scroll to one of the web pages, either above or below your current page, by scrolling the trackwheel up or down. Once a page is selected, clicking the trackwheel displays a dialog asking you to confirm that you would like to go to that link. Click the OK button to confirm and that page will be displayed from the cache.

FIGURE 8.3
The History menu item shows a dialog with the link history.

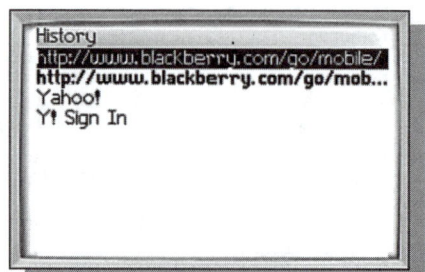

> **note** If you go back to previous pages and then select any link, your forward link history is lost and you will not be able to return to them except by clicking the links as you had originally.

At times you will want to load a page that is not directly linked to your home page. To do this, click the Go To menu item. A dialog will be displayed allowing you to enter the address of the web page (URL) you want to load (see Figure 8.4).

Notice also that the http:// is already entered into the edit box. You can delete it using the Backspace key, but generally you will want it and having it there will be a time-saver. The address in the edit box defaults to the address you entered previously, and often this isn't the desired address. You can quickly clear the edit field by clicking the Clear button on the dialog. If you happen to have the web page copied onto the clipboard, you can paste it into the edit box by clicking the Paste button. Of course, you can type it in manually as well. Pressing the Space key will insert periods into the field, eliminating the need to press the ALT key. Once the address of the web page is entered, click the OK button to load that page.

Sometimes you just want to go all the way back to the beginning, your home page. You can do this at any time by clicking the Home menu item. This is simpler and safer then pressing Escape or Backspace repeatedly most of the time.

Of course you can reload the web page you are currently viewing as well. Do this by clicking the Refresh menu item.

caution If you use the browser a lot, be sure to clear the caches periodically. If the browser cache is not cleaned up, it can use all of the storage space on your handheld and cause messages to be deleted automatically—and frequently—by the handheld software. See the "Clearing the Browser Cache" section later in this chapter.

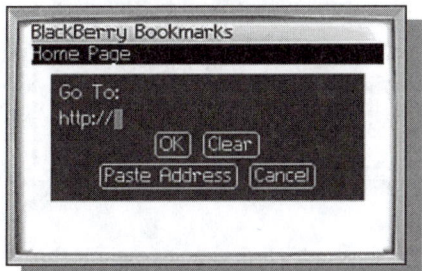

FIGURE 8.4
Enter a web address to visit a site that's not in your bookmarks.

SENDING A LINK AS AN EMAIL MESSAGE

One of the new features in version 4.0 of the handheld software is the ability to send a web page address to someone else in an email message. You could do this in previous versions of the software by manually copying the address to the clipboard, then creating a new message and pasting the link into the body of the message.

With the 4.0 version of the software, however, you can do the same thing by clicking the Send Address menu item while you have a link selected in the browser. This will display the Address Book, where you can select the recipient of the email and then display the Compose Email screen with the web page address already placed into the body of the message. Once you are at the Compose Email screen, you can add more text to the message or edit the web page address before sending the message.

VIEWING WEB PAGE INFORMATION

Occasionally, you might want to see a little more information about the web page you are viewing. This won't happen often, but if it does, you will be glad you know how.

Two of the most common needs are to see the address of the page you are currently viewing or the address of a link on the page you are viewing.

With a browser on your desktop, the web page address is at the top and you can easily see it. With such limited screen space on a handheld, this element had to be removed. You can still view the current page address by clicking the Page Address menu item. This will show a dialog with the page address shown in it and the date and time it was retrieved (see Figure 8.5). Two buttons at the bottom of the dialog can be clicked to close the dialog. If you want to copy the address into the clipboard, click the Copy Address button to copy the address and close the dialog; otherwise, just click the Close button.

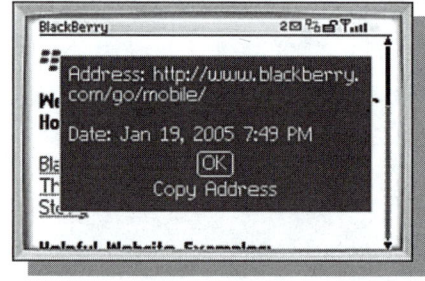

FIGURE 8.5
Viewing the address of the current web page.

> **note**
> With the 4.0 version of the handheld software, there is another button available on these dialogs. The Send Address button can be used to send this web page address to someone in an Email message. Clicking the button works the same as clicking the Send Address menu item discussed in the previous section, "Sending a Link As an Email Message."
>
> The icons at the top of the web page are not selectable in version 4.0 of the handheld software.

Similarly, if a link is selected, you can click the Link Address menu item. The same dialog is shown except the date and time portion is missing because the page has not been retrieved yet.

There are two other ways to view information that is not so obvious and not so commonly used. While you have a web page loaded, scroll the trackwheel up past the top of the web page. There are two icons at the top that the cursor will jump to. These icons look like a padlock and series of squares that are supposed to look like two computers communicating. Clicking the trackwheel will display a small dialog with information about the connection. The first icon, the one that looks like a padlock, is the Security Settings. If you have established a connection to a web server using a secure connection, that information will be displayed in the dialog.

The other icon displays the connection information, including how large the page is and how long it took to load.

Both dialogs contain two buttons. If you want to keep the information presented in either of the two dialogs, you can click the Copy button. This will copy the information in the dialog to the clipboard and close the dialog. To simply close the dialog, click the OK button.

USING BOOKMARKS

Bookmarks are a way of keeping track of some of your commonly visited websites. Keeping them in a separate list allows you to simply select the web page from the list of bookmarks instead of typing the address in and then browsing to that web page each time. To get to the Bookmark list screen, click the Bookmarks menu item. Figure 8.6 shows the default bookmarks screen.

FIGURE 8.6
The bookmarks screen of the BlackBerry browser.

Opening a bookmark is just as simple as opening a link on a web page. Select the bookmark and click the Get Link menu item. You can also press the Enter key while the bookmark is selected.

ADDING A BOOKMARK

You can add a bookmark at the bookmark list screen by clicking the Add Bookmark menu item. The dialog, shown in Figure 8.7, prompts for all of the required information including the address of the page to bookmark and a title that you would like to give it. Although this works, it is not the best way to add a bookmark.

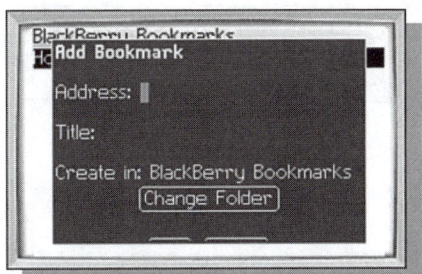

FIGURE 8.7
Adding a bookmark from the bookmark list screen.

Instead, you should use the Go To menu item to actually view the page that you would like to add as a bookmark in the browser first, then click the Add Bookmark menu item. This dialog, shown in Figure 8.8, looks different. The address field is hidden because the browser already knows the address. It also uses the page title as the default bookmark title, further reducing the amount of typing you need to do. It is also a good idea to load the page first to make sure that it will display properly on the handheld before adding the bookmark.

FIGURE 8.8
Adding a bookmark for the current page.

You will also notice a new check box labeled Make Available Offline. Checking this button causes the full data of the bookmarked page to be saved in the cache. Later when you want to view this page, selecting the bookmark will display the saved web page instead of retrieving the page from the Internet again. This is true even if the handheld is out of coverage or the wireless modem is turned off, which can be a very useful at times. The saved content is never updated, however. If the page gets updated and you want to update your bookmark, you will need to delete the bookmark and re-create it with the updated page loaded into the browser. You will find more on deleting bookmarks in the "Managing Bookmarks" section a little later in this chapter.

ORGANIZING BOOKMARKS IN FOLDERS

You probably already noticed that bookmarks could be sorted into folders when we created new bookmarks (shown previously in Figures 8.7 and 8.8). Clicking the Change Folder button on the Add Bookmark dialog displays the folder list shown in Figure 8.9.

FIGURE 8.9
Selecting a bookmark folder.

To add the new bookmark to a folder, scroll the trackwheel up or down until the desired folder is selected and click the Select Folder menu item.

The folder tree only displays two levels of folders at a time, however. If a folder has an icon of a folder with a black up-arrow, a Move Up menu item will be available to move the view up one level to the parent folder. If a folder has an icon of a folder with a plus sign, the folder contains subfolders and will have an Open Folder menu item to move the view down one level to view the subfolders.

You can add a new subfolder by clicking the Add Subfolder menu item. A dialog, shown in Figure 8.10, will be displayed prompting you for the name of the new folder. Clicking the OK button automatically opens the parent folder and selects the new folder in the list.

FIGURE 8.10
Creating a new bookmark folder.

Now you might be wondering how you can get to those bookmarks that are saved in subfolders, because the bookmark list didn't show any folders when we looked at it in Figure 8.6. That's because the Bookmark list screen just shows the contents of one bookmark folder. To select a different bookmark folder to view, click the View Bookmark Subfolders menu item from the Bookmark list screen. This will display the Bookmark selection screen we saw in Figure 8.9. Scroll the selection to the desired Bookmark folder and click the Select Folder menu item again. Now the bookmarks stored in that folder are listed in the Bookmark list screen.

MANAGING BOOKMARKS

Sometimes a bookmark didn't turn out the way you wanted it to and you need to change it. You can do this by scrolling the trackwheel to move the selection to the desired bookmark and clicking the Edit Bookmark menu item. This displays the Edit Bookmark dialog shown in Figure 8.11.

FIGURE 8.11
Editing a bookmark.

In this dialog you can change the name or address of a bookmark. You may need to manually erase the text of the fields by clicking the Backspace key repeatedly. If you have the new text you would like to use in the clipboard, you can paste it by pressing the Shift key while clicking the trackwheel. You can also simply delete the bookmark by selecting it and clicking the Delete Bookmark menu item.

Not all bookmarks can be deleted or have the address changed however. Bookmarks that existed when you received your handheld are created as part of the browser activation and cannot be changed or deleted.

You may also want your bookmarks put into a particular order. You can move a bookmark up or down in the list by clicking the Move Bookmark Up and Move Bookmark Down menu items. These items cause the selected bookmark to swap places with the bookmark above or below it in the list. Of course, if the selected bookmark is already at the top of the list, the Move Bookmark Up menu item will not be shown.

You can also move bookmarks into another folder by clicking the Move Bookmark menu item. This will cause the folder list to be shown. Clicking the Select Folder menu item will then cause the bookmark to be moved into that folder.

INSTALLING A NEW RINGTONE

Installing a new ringtone on your handheld is actually pretty simple once you figure out how to do it and find a source for them. Unfortunately, there is very little guidance on how to install them and most carriers do not include BlackBerry handhelds in their ringtone sections. Also, installing a ringtone requires the use of a web browser, and cannot be done any other way.

BlackBerry ringtones are really just Standard MIDI files. MIDI stands for Musical Instrument Digital Interface and was one of the first standards for making music on the computer. Standard MIDI files play just one note at a time, as opposed to Polyphonic MIDI files, which can play many notes at the same time. MIDI files generally use a. .MID extension.

You need to find a web page that offers links to MIDI files. There are many out there and a search for MIDI should turn up a few, though not all are free. BlackBerry.com offers some as part of a "Browser Demonstration" web page, so this is a good place to start. In your browser, click the Go To menu item to enter the web address of http://mobile.BlackBerry.com. The page offers an interactive way to access many common features such as searches and directories. Select the BlackBerry Extras link in the list and click the Get Link menu item. Next, click the Ringtones link in the list and again click the Get Link menu item. The first time you visit this page you will see a page with a legal disclaimer. Scroll to the bottom (yes, it is a long way down there) and click the I Accept button. The next screen shows a list of ringtones that you can download. Select a ringtone to download and then click the Get Link menu item again.

This actually downloads the ringtone onto your handheld and displays a screen allowing you to save it, shown in Figure 8.12. When the screen is shown, the ringtone automatically starts playing, so don't do this if you are in a meeting! You can stop playing the file by selecting the button with the square on it and clicking the trackwheel. To play the ringtone again, click the button with the triangle on it.

FIGURE 8.12
Playing a downloaded ringtone.

Simply downloading the ringtone does not make it available to be used as a ringtone, however; you must save it first. Do this by clicking the Save button on this screen. When you do this, the screen in Figure 8.13 is shown asking you to name the ringtone. This defaults to the name of the MIDI file you have downloaded, but sometimes this isn't the best name and you can change the name to something easier to read here.

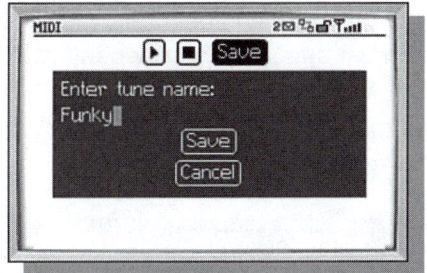

FIGURE 8.13
Naming the ringtone you are saving.

SAVING PICTURES ON YOUR HANDHELD

One of the new features in version 4.0 of the handheld software is the ability to save pictures on your handheld. These pictures can be used as your Home screen image or your Standby screen image if your handheld supports a Standby screen. Sometimes your handheld comes with some pictures already saved into it, but if you want to add more, you have to use the Browser to save them. The process of saving an image is very similar to saving a new ringtone. There are some pictures available on http:\\mobile.blackberry.com under the Wallpapers section of the BlackBerry Extras link. You can save a picture from any web page that has them.

> **note** Most of the time an image displayed on your handheld will be scaled down so that it can fit comfortably on the screen. If you want to see the image full size, click the Full Image menu item. If the image does not fit onto the screen, and it probably will not, you can pan the view sideways by pressing the ALT key while scrolling the trackwheel.

CHAPTER 8 BROWSING THE INTERNET WIRELESSLY

To save an image to your handheld, first scroll the cursor so that the image is selected. Next, click the Save Image menu item. When you do this, you will see a dialog like the one shown in Figure 8.14 with a default name and some buttons. The default name is the name of the file from the web page address. You can change this if you want by scrolling up to the File field and typing a new name in. Clicking the Save button saves the image and closes the dialog. If you want to replace one of the images that you have already saved onto your handheld, click the Select button and choose the name of the image to replace from the list.

FIGURE 8.14
Saving an image from a web page.

> **note**: A third option, Cache Operations, is also available on handhelds with version 4.0 of the handheld software. This section is discussed in more detail later in the section "Clearing the Browser Cache."

CHANGING BROWSER OPTIONS

Like nearly every other BlackBerry application, the browser has its own set of options that can be configured. To access the Browser Options screen, click the Options menu item from a loaded page or the Bookmarks screen. The browser options are divided into two groups called Browser Configuration and General Properties, shown in Figure 8.15.

To open one of the option groups, scroll the trackwheel to the desired group and click the trackwheel.

FIGURE 8.15
Opening the browser options.

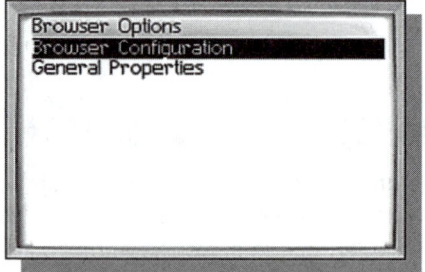

BROWSER CONFIGURATION OPTIONS

This group of options can be rather large and confusing. Some of the options may not be changeable, depending on how your browser was activated.

Most of these options define how your browser works and include addresses and identifiers that should not be changed (see Figure 8.16). I will only mention a few of the more useful options, and the rest you should not change unless told to do so by your wireless carrier or IT staff.

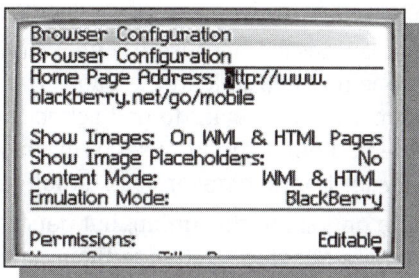

FIGURE 8.16
Viewing the Browser Configuration group of options.

The first option in the list, and the most commonly changed, is the Home Page. The Home Page is the web page that will be loaded when you first open your browser (if you've configured it to do so). It should load fast and be the page you want to use the most often.

The next two options help reduce the amount of data that must be transferred when a page loads. Images are often used in web pages and in order to be displayed properly, they must be downloaded in addition to the web page itself. This sometimes can take a long time on pages with lots of large images and can use up your monthly data faster.

The first option, Show Images, can be set to completely filter out images based on the type of web page being loaded. To not show images at all, change this option to No. Otherwise you can change it to On WML Pages Only or On WML & HTML Pages, depending on what kind of pages you load most often.

If you have the Show Images option set to No, then you will not see any images when you load a web page. However sometimes it is useful to at least know that there was an image there and that it was removed. Changing the Show Image Placeholders option to Yes will do this. With this option set, when a page loads that had an image, the word "[image]" will be shown where the image was.

The Content Mode option lets you specify what kind of content the browser will display. The options are WML Only, WML & HTML, or HTML Only. If you do want to limit the content to just WML or just HTML, you can do it here. Normally, if the content is restricted, it has been configured that way by your provider and you cannot change it.

Next, we will skip several options that are not typically configurable and look at the Start Page option. It is located in the next group of options. The Start Page option lets you specify what page should be displayed when the Browser application is opened.

Like your browser on your PC, you can set the Startup Page option to "Home Page" to have it automatically load the home page when you open the browser. Having the home page load up can be nice, but it can also be frustrating if you don't have good coverage or often want to load a different page. Another common option is the Bookmarks Page. Using this option causes the bookmarks list to be shown when the browser application is opened. This is good when coverage is an issue because the bookmarks are stored locally on the device and there is no need to load the page. The last option, Last Page Loaded, is good when you don't want to go back to the Home Page or Bookmarks each time you enter the Browser. With this option, you can continue to surf the internet from wherever you last left it.

There are many more options in this group, but generally they should not be changed, even if you are allowed to change them, unless instructed to do so by your carrier or IT staff.

GENERAL PROPERTIES OPTIONS

The General Properties option group is very small compared to the Browser Properties option group. This only has two options, neither of which are very complicated (see Figure 8.17).

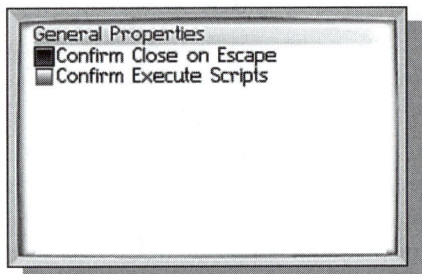

FIGURE 8.17
Viewing the General Properties group of options.

The first option, Confirm Close on Escape, is off by default. If it is checked, the browser will display a prompt asking if you are sure you want to quit the browser when you press the Escape key on the topmost page being viewed.

The other option, Confirm Execute Scripts, is also off by default. With this option off, loading a web page with a script in it will execute the script automatically without prompting the user. This is sometimes viewed as a security risk. Checking this option will cause the browser to display a prompt asking if you want the script to run. Having this option checked impacts the user experience though, and can be annoying.

CLEARING THE BROWSER CACHE

Caching is something that happens automatically to make browsing the web faster for you. As mentioned in a previous section of this chapter, web pages and pictures are stored locally on your handheld so if you request them again they do not have to be retrieved from the Internet each time. Obviously, all these things take up storage space on your handheld.

If you use the browser a lot, you should periodically clear the browser cache so that your handheld does not run out of storage space. The browser cache is cleared when your device is reset, but hopefully this doesn't happen often. Instead, you should use the menu items in the General Properties option group. You can open this group by clicking the Options menu item then selecting the General Properties and clicking the trackwheel again.

There are actually two caches on your handheld, the content cache and the cookie cache. There are three menu items that can be displayed when you display the menu. The menu items to clear the caches are only displayed if the caches contain some data. The Clear Content Caches menu item is used to clear the downloaded content of web pages, including images. This is where the majority of the data is stored. The Clear Cookies Cache menu item is used to clear any cookies that have been received. The last menu item, Clear Raw Data Cache, will clear both the content and cookie caches.

> **note** Cookies are small bits of information that can be sent by a website so when you return to the same website they can read the cookies again. Cookies are generally small and don't take up a lot of storage space.

Version 4.0 of the handheld software makes it easier to clear the caches by adding a new group under the Options screen called Cache Operations. Selecting this option group shows a screen with up to three buttons. The buttons are Clear History, Clear Cookies, and Clear Content Cache, as shown in Figure 8.18. Each button is shown only if the cache contains some data that can be cleared.

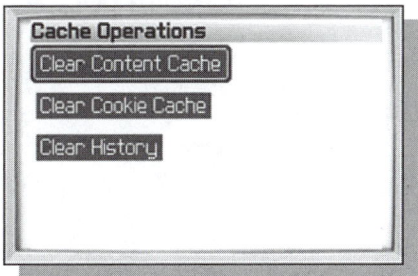

FIGURE 8.18
The new Cache Operations screen where you can clear the caches.

You should clear the caches periodically, especially if you use the browser frequently; every few weeks is a good guideline. However, if you begin to notice messages being deleted automatically, it is time to clear the caches.

Chapter 9

MAKING PHONE CALLS

BLACKBERRY BASICS:

- The Recent Call screen lists all placed and received calls.

- Place and answer calls using the Phone application.

- A Speed Dial feature is available with version 4.0 of the handheld software.

- Manage multiple calls and create conference calls.

- The Phone application includes a variety of options including Call Barring, TTY, and Smart Dialing.

Being able to work with messages and browsing the Internet is great, but sometimes nothing works better than a phone call. For a long time, people have had to carry both a messaging device and a cellular phone to conduct business on the go. I'm sure I am not alone in saying I'm glad that BlackBerry handhelds have both features built in.

> **note** Although the software is the same, some models of BlackBerry handhelds have supported phone calls in different ways. Some have speaker phone capability; others use only an earbud. You should make sure you are familiar with your handheld's phone setup first.

Just like messages, there are several ways to begin a phone call, but the simplest is to open the Phone application from the main screen.

> **tip** Some handheld models (prior to the 7100) also have a Phone button on the top face of the handheld that activates the Phone application at any time without returning to the Home screen.

THE RECENT CALL LIST

The Phone application is sort of a merger between the Address Book and the Messages list. In fact, I think it is more correctly called the Recent Call list because it lists all of the numbers from placed or received calls, with the most recent calls being at the top of the list (this behavior can be changed in a configuration setting, however). Figure 9.1 shows this screen.

FIGURE 9.1
The Recent Call list keeps your most recent communications at your fingertips.

> **tip** You can bring up the One Time Dial dialog by pressing the Space key on the Home screen or the Recent Call list screen as well.
>
> Devices with version 4.0 of the handheld software do not have a [One Time Dial] entry. Instead there is an edit field above the Recent Call list where you can enter the number to call. Figure 9.3 shows an example of this.

This list isn't the same as the Call Logs in the Message list. Only one occurrence of a phone number exists in the list at any time. If the number is not at the top of the list, placing a call to or receiving a call from that number moves it to the top of the list. In this way, the people you communicate the most with are always at the top of the list and easiest to find.

The Recent Call list also integrates with the Address Book as well. If a number matches an entry in the Address Book, that name of that entry shows up in the list instead of just the number. If the Address Book entry contains more than one number, for instance a work and a cell number, the source is also displayed in the list. Placing a call to or receiving a call from either source (in this case work or cell numbers) causes the entry in the Recent Call list to be moved to the top.

ONE TIME DIAL

Like the Address Book, the Recent Call list also contains a special entry called [One Time Dial] that is always at the top of the list. The [One Time Dial] is just like [Use Once], which we saw while composing a message using the Address Book, but behaves just a little differently. Selecting the [One Time Dial] entry and clicking the trackwheel produces a dialog where you can enter the number to use, as shown in Figure 9.2.

FIGURE 9.2
The One Time Dial dialog.

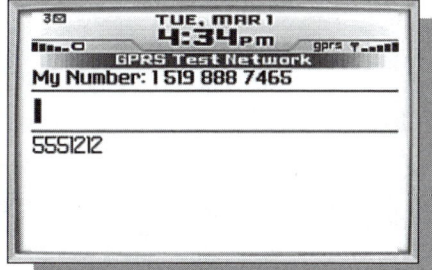

FIGURE 9.3
The Phone application on a handheld with version 4.0 of the handheld software.

Placing a call with this dialog still causes the entry to be added to or moved in the Recent Calls List.

PLACING A CALL FROM THE RECENT CALL LIST

Selecting an item other than [One Time Dial] and clicking the trackwheel displays a menu with many menu items for initiating a message, in much the same way that the Address Book does. Even though this is probably not the preferred screen to use, you can use it to create email, PIN, and SMS messages to people who have entries in your Address Book.

However, unlike the Address Book, this menu shows an item for each phone field in the Address Book entry. If there is only one, it simply says Call Name. If for instance both the Work and Home fields have numbers, the menu items Call Home and Call Work would be shown. The method that was last used to place a call to a contact is set as the default menu item. For instance, if you last called a person at their work number, the Call Work menu item will be defaulted.

USING SPEED DIAL

Version 4.0 of the handheld software adds a speed dial feature. The speed dial feature allows you to map a specific phone number to a key on the keypad. Later, when you want to call that number, all you have to do is press and hold that key and the call will be created to the specified number. The speed dial keys can be used while on the Home screen, Message List screen, and the Recent Call List screen.

VIEWING THE SPEED DIAL LIST

To see the list of keys available for speed dial mappings, click the View Speed Dial List menu item from the Recent Call List screen. The Speed Dial Numbers screen, shown in Figure 9.4, will be shown. The number and actual keys available will be different, depending on the model of handheld you have. On 7100 series handhelds, only the numbers 1–9 can have speed dial entries. On all other handheld models, the keys A–Z can have speed dial entries.

The mapping for each key is shown next to a graphic depicting the key in the list. If the number is part of the Address Book, the name and an indicator of which number it is (home, work, or mobile) is shown as well.

FIGURE 9.4
You can map phone numbers to keys on the keypad that will be used to activate a Speed Dial.

ADDING A SPEED DIAL

You can add a number to the speed dial mapping by clicking the Add Speed Dial menu item while the Speed Dial List screen is open and an empty speed dial entry is selected. Doing this will display the Address Book, from which you can select the contact and number to add.

When you add a number as a speed dial mapping, the Recent Call List changes to reflect the mapping. A small graphic of the key that the number is mapped to is shown on the far right side of the entry in the Recent Call List. This helps to serve as a reminder that the number is a speed dial number.

You can also add a speed dial mapping by selecting the number from the Recent Call List and clicking the Add Speed Dial menu item. This will add the number to the first available entry in the Speed Dial List, but will also start a move so that you can move it to the letter you want.

CHANGING THE SPEED DIAL MAPPING

If you have a speed dial mapping set up, but want to move it to another key, you can do so by selecting the speed dial mapping from the Speed Dial List screen and clicking the Move menu item. Scrolling the trackwheel up or down moves the entry to the next or previous empty entry. Click the trackwheel to select the key and end the move.

REMOVING A SPEED DIAL

Speed dial entries can be removed from the Speed Dial List screen by selecting the entry and clicking the Remove menu item. You can also remove a speed dial mapping by selecting the number with the mapping from the Recent Call List and clicking the Remove Speed Dial menu item.

ACCESSING VOICEMAIL

If you have voicemail service on your calling plan, your carrier should have configured the voicemail access number for you. If so, you can call your voicemail access number by selecting an entry other than One Time Dial and clicking the Call Voicemail menu item. You can also dial your own phone number, and this should connect you to your voicemail access number.

DELETING CALLS FROM THE RECENT CALL LIST

As I've said before, all calls are added to the Recent Call list and moved to the top each time they are used. It might be that you do not want a call to show up in the list for some reason. If so, you can delete a call by scrolling to it in the list and selecting the Delete menu item or pressing the Backspace key. You can also select several calls at once by pressing the Shift key while scrolling and then delete them all with the Delete menu item or Backspace key.

THE CALL SCREEN

Once a call is initiated, the Call screen is displayed to show current information about the call in progress, such as volume level, call duration, and the number of other parties on the call. As you can see in Figure 9.5, the screen clearly indicates that to end the call, you should press the Escape button. Doing so displays a second dialog, further instructing you to press and hold the ESC key to end the call. This was obviously done to prevent accidental disconnects caused by pressing the ESC key inadvertently.

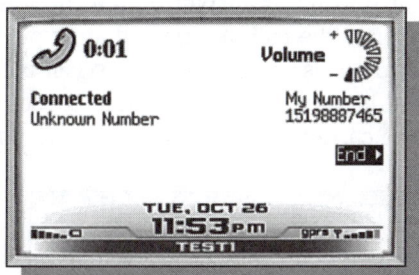

FIGURE 9.5
The Call screen.

While you are making a call, you probably won't be interacting with this screen much. There are a couple of common activities, though, that you will do. One thing that is intuitive, but not obvious, is that you can change the speaker volume by scrolling the thumbwheel up and down. Another is that pressing a number key will create the appropriate tone even after the call is started so that you can interact with phone systems.

This, however, can be one of the weaknesses of using a BlackBerry as a phone. Because of the way the keyboard is arranged, you cannot find a "traditional" telephone alphabet mapping on the numeric keys. For instance on a traditional telephone, the letters ABC are printed above the number 2. Some phone systems utilize this numeric mapping as a way of entering alphabetic information, such as a name, to look up the proper extension of a person.

You can accomplish this on your handheld by pressing the Alt key and then pressing the letter you need. For instance, pressing Alt+A will add an A to the

7100 Pressing the ESC key on 7100 model handhelds displays a dialog asking if you want to go to the Home screen. Clicking the Yes button is the same as clicking the Home Screen menu item.

7100 The 7100 series of handhelds have a special End Call button (the red phone) that you must use instead of pressing the ESC key. On these models, pressing the ESC key presents a dialog asking if you want to go to the Home screen instead. Even pressing and holding the ESC key does not end the call, so if you upgraded from another handheld to a 7100, you may find that clicking the ESC key is a hard habit to break.

telephone number. When the number is dialed, the number 2 will be dialed instead of the A character. Remember there is no number mapping for Q and Z however.

ENDING A CALL

Once you are done with a call, you will of course need to disconnect it. This is done by pressing the Escape key and holding it for a few seconds. Simply pressing the Escape key displays a dialog explaining that you have to hold the escape key to end the call, which is quite helpful to keep you from accidentally disconnecting a call. You can also end the call by clicking the End Call menu item.

RECEIVING CALLS

When a new call is received, your handheld will display a dialog giving you a few choices on what to do, as shown in Figure 9.6. The dialog displays the caller's number if it is known, or, if the number is in the Address Book, the name of the caller. Clicking the Answer button simply answers the call so you can talk. Answer is the default button, so pressing the Enter key will also result in answering the call. Clicking the Answer and Hold button answers the call, but immediately puts it on hold. We'll talk more about putting calls on hold later. The last button is Ignore. This is the equivalent of hanging up on a call and causes the caller to hear a message from the carrier indicating that you are unavailable.

FIGURE 9.6
The options seen here are available on incoming calls.

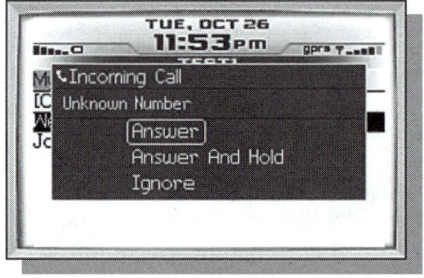

tip Pressing the Space key will silence the audio notification temporarily. When the notification repeats, it will once again be at full volume.

HOLDING CALLS

Being able to put calls on hold is one example of how a BlackBerry handheld is better than many of the traditional phone handsets available now. Oftentimes calls are put on hold automatically when you answer the next call. You can put an active call on hold manually, though, by clicking the Hold Menu Item—as long as another call is not already on hold! The Call screen now shows the status of the call as On Hold, as shown in Figure 9.7.

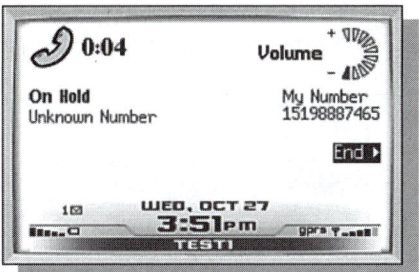

FIGURE 9.7
The Call screen showing a call on hold.

There are two ways to take a call off of hold. If there is only one call active at the moment, you can take a call off of hold by clicking the Resume menu item. However, if there are two calls on the system, you can't resume one without doing something to the other. When this is the case, clicking the Swap menu item causes the two active calls to switch. The current call is placed on hold and the previously held call is resumed.

note Only one call can be on hold at a time. Therefore, the Hold menu item is not shown if another call is already on hold.

MUTING A CALL

Sometimes it is important that the person on a call with you doesn't hear what you are saying. One of the most common times this is desirable is when you are on a conference call and primarily listening. When this is the case, you can mute your call by clicking the Mute menu item. The Call screen now shows the status of the call as Muted, as shown in Figure 9.8. You can take the call off Mute by clicking the Turn Off Mute menu item.

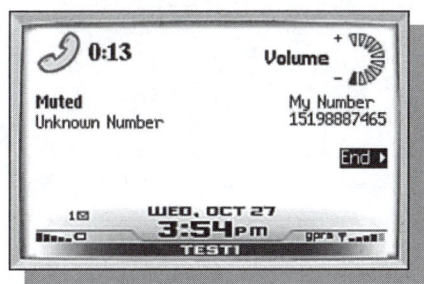

FIGURE 9.8
The Call screen showing a muted call.

RECEIVING ADDITIONAL CALLS

If your wireless service has a call waiting feature, receiving a second call displays a dialog similar to the New Call dialog, shown in Figure 9.9, but with different buttons.

The default button on this dialog is Answer - Drop Current. Clicking this button causes the new phone call to be answered and disconnects the original call at the same time. The other option,

note The audio notification for a second incoming call and the call ending are single beeps of differing tones. These notifications are not configurable.

Answer - Hold Current, causes the current call to be put on hold and answers the new incoming call. When you do this, you will notice that the Call Screen now lists both calls and shows the status of the first call as On Hold.

FIGURE 9.9
When a second incoming call is received, these options are available.

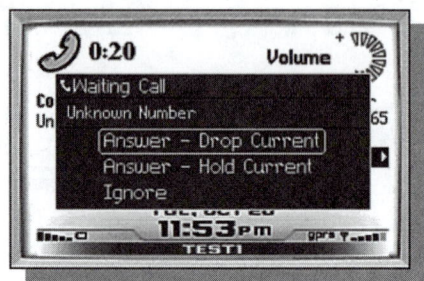

The one held call limit can cause you to make a tough decision if you have two calls already and receive a third. In this case, one of the calls is already on hold and the other is the current call. Receiving a third call in this case displays a New Call dialog similar to the others, as shown in Figure 9.10, but in this case the options force you to drop one of the calls. The default button is Answer - Drop All, which would drop all calls already connected and simply answer the new call. The other option is Answer - Drop Current, which would drop the current call, keep the other call on hold, and answer the new call. If you don't want to answer the call at all, you can just click the Ignore button and the call dialog will disappear.

FIGURE 9.10
When a third incoming call is received, this dialog box appears.

CREATING AN ADDITIONAL CALL

In addition to being able to receive multiple calls, you can also place an outgoing call even when a received call is still active, by using the New Call menu item. Doing this will automatically put the active call on hold, so this menu item is only available if there are no calls already on hold.

Clicking the New Call menu item shows the Address Book, which allows you to select the person you want to call. In addition to all of the normal Address Book menu items (which we will talk about in Chapter 10), there are also menu items to manage the current call such as Hold, Mute, and End Call. The current call is still active until a selection is made. At that point, the current call is put on hold and the new call is started.

With the 7100 series of handhelds, you can also create an additional call by clicking the New Call button (the green phone button) on the keypad.

CONFERENCE CALLS

All GSM (GSM stands for Global System for Mobile communications) phones are capable of creating conference calls, but not all handsets make it easy. Using the BlackBerry to do so is easy and straightforward. If you have two calls already connected (one must be on hold, remember), simply click the Join menu item and the two calls will be joined together into a conference call. The Call Screen is updated to reflect this, as shown in Figure 9.11. The conference call is treated as a single call once again, so you can place or receive an additional call. This additional call can be joined into the conference as well, allowing you to create conferences with many people by repeatedly joining the calls.

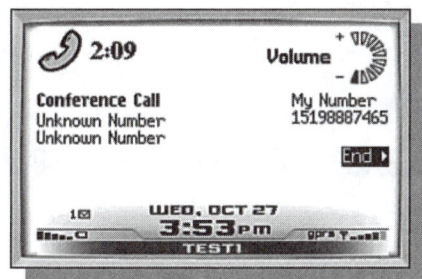

FIGURE 9.11
The Call screen showing a conference call.

If you need to drop a specific call from the conference, you can do this by clicking the Drop Call menu item. This displays a dialog (see Figure 9.12) that lists all of the calls in the conference. Scroll the trackwheel up or down to the appropriate call and click the trackwheel. This will put the call on hold, remove the call from the conference, and then end it. Of course you can press the ESC key to cancel this dialog as well. If there is another call on hold already, the Drop Call menu item is not available.

Splitting a call works in the same way except that it does not end the call afterward. Selecting the Split Call menu item shows the same call selection dialog. After clicking the trackwheel on the selected call, that call is put on hold and removed from the conference.

FIGURE 9.12
Select a call to split or drop.

ADDING NOTES

We already know that you can add notes to a Call History message in the Message list, but why wait until after the call is done to add your notes? You can add notes to an active call by clicking the Notes menu item. This changes the screen to show a smaller header with the call information and adds an Edit field where you can type in the notes (see Figure 9.13). When the call has ended, the notes that you have entered during the call are automatically included in the Call History message when it is created.

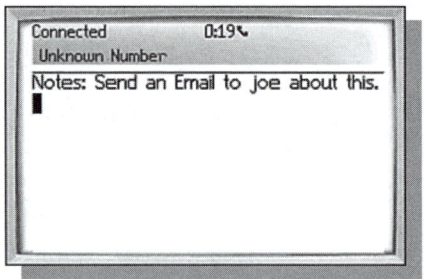

FIGURE 9.13
Add notes during a call.

> **tip**
> You can jump directly to the Home screen, Messages, Phone, or Browser by pressing and holding the Alt key and clicking the ESC button. Then while still holding the Alt key, scroll the thumbwheel to the desired application.

While on the Call Notes screen, you can still manage your calls with the same menu items discussed previously. The one difference is how you can change the call volume. Now, scrolling the trackwheel up or down moves the cursor around in the edit field instead of changing the volume. To change the volume, click the Volume menu item. This will display a small dialog with the graphic for the volume level. While the dialog is displayed, scrolling the trackwheel up or down changes the volume. Clicking the trackwheel dismisses the dialog.

To get back to the original Call screen, click the Hide Notes menu item.

USING YOUR BLACKBERRY WHILE ON THE PHONE

Even though the BlackBerry is being used for a phone call, that doesn't mean that the rest of the functions are unusable. It is true that while you are on a phone call, you cannot send or receive messages, but the rest of the PIM features are available to you. Clicking the Hide Call menu item causes the Home screen to be displayed. From here you can use any application that doesn't use the radio modem for data communications. This basically means that you cannot use a web browser, and don't expect any messages to be sent, although you can compose them and queue them up to be sent when the call is done. You can return to the Call screen by clicking the Phone icon.

> **note**
> On handhelds with version 4.0 of the handheld software, the Hide Call menu item has been changed to the Home Screen menu item. The functionality is the same, however.

PHONE OPTIONS

The Phone application has a lot of options that can change the way your BlackBerry works. From the Recent Call list, click the Options menu item to show the Call Options screen as shown in Figure 9.14. Because there are so many options, they are organized into groups where each group contains a few options that are related. The following sections talk about the options within each group and what they are used for.

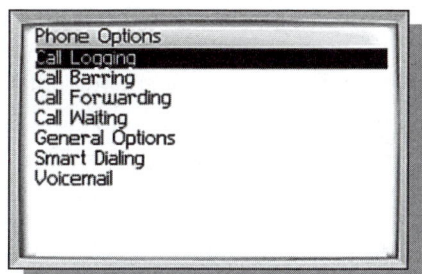

FIGURE 9.14
There are multiple options to configure that affect how the phone features are used.

CALL LOGGING

If you recall Chapter 6, "Managing Messages," we talked about Call History messages. These are the messages that are generated by a phone call of some kind. This option group allows you to manage how those Call History messages are created, as shown in Figure 9.15.

The first option, Show Logs in Message List, determines whether the Call History messages are displayed in the Message list or not. Changing this option to No causes all of the Call History messages to be hidden in the Message list. The Call History messages are still there and will still be generated, but they are simply not shown in the list. You can still find them by using the Search feature of the Message list.

> **note** Some groups, such as Call Forwarding, Call Barring, and Call Waiting, might not be available on your handheld because of your carrier or calling plan features.

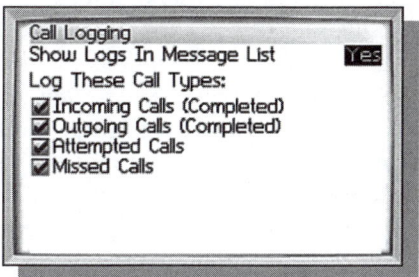

FIGURE 9.15
These options affect how information about call messages are retained.

CHAPTER 9 MAKING PHONE CALLS

The four check boxes at the bottom allow you to specify which kinds of calls generate a Call History message. It may be that you don't want any Call History messages generated for attempted calls. If so, scroll the selection to that check box and press the Space key or click the Change Option menu item to toggle the check box.

> **caution** If call logging is disabled, any notes added to calls of that type will be lost. The software will still allow you to add notes and will give no indication that they are not being saved.

CALL BARRING

If your carrier and wireless plan support call barring, this option group will be available. When you open this option group, a small dialog is displayed that says Waiting for Network. During this time, the option settings are being retrieved from your wireless network carrier. If you are currently not in network coverage, you cannot set any of these options.

The Call Barring configuration screen, seen in Figure 9.16, shows various situations where you can block calls from being completed. The screen is divided into sections—Incoming Calls and Outgoing Calls.

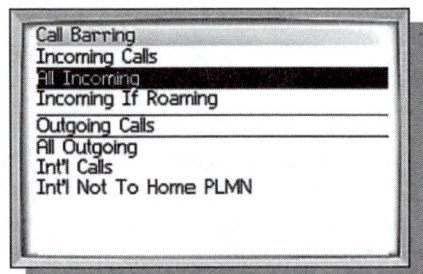

FIGURE 9.16
Blocking certain calls can save you time and money—especially if you are outside your plan's calling area.

In the Incoming Calls section, there are two rules that you can choose from—All Calls and Incoming If Roaming. You can enable either option by clicking the Enable menu item. Enabling the All Calls rule blocks all incoming calls. The other option, Incoming If Roaming, can be used to keep roaming charges under control by only allowing incoming calls if you are currently not roaming.

In the Outgoing Calls section, there are three rules that you can choose from—All Calls, International Calls, and International Calls Not to Home PLNM.

Enabling the All Calls rule restricts the handheld to be used for incoming calls only. Enabling the International Calls rule will prevent the handheld from making calls to other numbers with other country codes, which can help keep your wireless costs under control. The last option will let you make international calls, but only to numbers within your home area. This can be useful when you want to allow international calling, but only so you can call into your company voice mail for instance.

> **note** The Password used in this section is not the same as the handheld security password that is set in the Security Options screen.

These rules can also be password protected to prevent someone from disabling the rules when they shouldn't. Attempting to enable or disable any of these rules while the password is set causes a password verification dialog to be displayed. You can change the password by clicking the Change Password menu item.

CALL FORWARDING

This is another option group that may not be offered, depending on your wireless plan. You will need to be able to communicate with the wireless network in order to change these options.

The screen shown in Figure 9.17 shows two situations when calls may be forwarded. The first is All Calls and means just that: Any call coming to your handheld will be forwarded to another number. The other situation is Unanswered Calls, which will forward calls to another number if you do not answer the call for some reason. Each of these situations can be activated or deactivated with the Enable or Disable menu items respectively. When an option is enabled, it is shown in the list in bold with the word (On) after the name in the list.

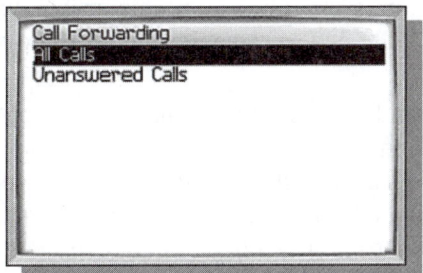

FIGURE 9.17
The Call Forwarding Options screen provides two ways to configure call forwarding.

Each of these options has another screen where the numbers to forward the calls to are entered. Selecting the All Calls option and clicking the Edit menu item shows the screen seen in Figure 9.18. Here you can enter the phone number that all calls should be forwarded to when the Call Forwarding is activated.

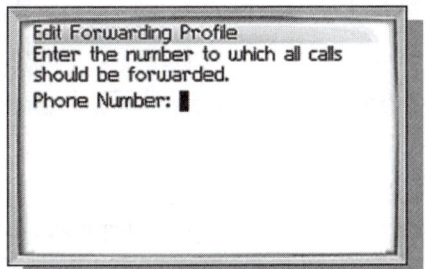

FIGURE 9.18
Forwarding all calls to another number can enable you to finish a task without interruptions.

Similarly, selecting the Unanswered Calls and clicking the Edit menu item shows the screen in Figure 9.19. This screen, however, has three fields where you can enter different phone numbers to forward the calls to, depending on the circumstance of why you did not answer the phone. Even if you want them all to forward to the same number, you must enter the number in each of the three fields.

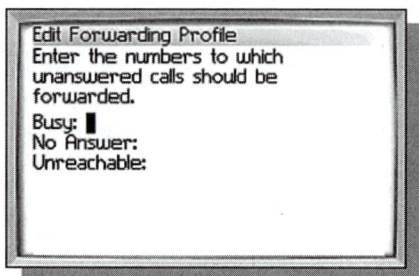

FIGURE 9.19
Forwarding unanswered calls to an assistant or co-worker can help avoid unnecessary "phone tag."

CALL WAITING

This is another option group that may not be visible depending on your wireless plan and that will need to communicate with the wireless network in order to work.

The screen shown in Figure 9.20 contains only one option, Call Waiting Enabled. If this option is set to Yes, receiving a call while already on the phone causes a tone to be played, and the second incoming call dialog that was discussed earlier appears. If the option is set to No, receiving a call while already on the phone generates a busy signal and may trigger Call Forwarding if it has been enabled. You can toggle the option by pressing the Space key or clicking the Change Option menu item.

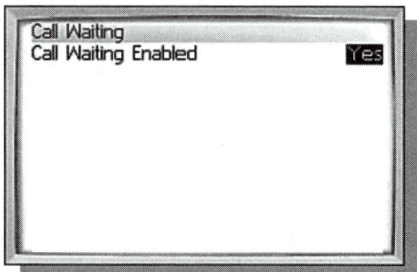

FIGURE 9.20
There is only one option in the Call Waiting group.

GENERAL OPTIONS

Opening the General Options option group displays a screen (see Figure 9.21) with several options. Each of these options can be toggled to another setting by pressing the Space key or clicking the Change Option menu item.

There are two additional options that are not shown in Figure 9.21—Auto Answer and Auto Hangup. Changing Auto Answer to Out of Holster causes the call to be automatically answered when the handheld is removed from the holster. This is defaulted to Never because many people like to see who is calling before deciding to answer it. Auto Hangup is very similar. It defaults to In Holster which causes a call to be ended when the handheld is returned to the holster. The other choice is Never.

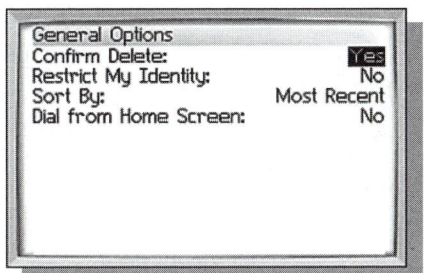

FIGURE 9.21
The General Options offer additional choices for how your device interacts with phone calls.

The next option is Confirm Delete. If this option is set to Yes, a dialog is displayed asking you if you want to delete an item after you click the Delete menu item in the Recent Call list. This option doesn't change the Messages application when deleting Call History Messages, just the recent calls in the Recent Call list.

The Restrict My Identity option determines whether the handheld sends Caller ID information when a call is placed from the handheld. It defaults to No, but if you are concerned about people you call getting your cellular phone number, you can change it to Yes.

Earlier in the chapter we talked about how the Recent Call list is sorted. The Sort By option changes how that list is sorted. The default is Most Recent, which causes any call to a number or person to move that to the top of the list. A count is also kept each time a call is made to a number or person, and the Most Used setting uses this count to keep the calls you make the most often at the top of the list. The third way it can be sorted is by Name, much like the Address Book.

The last option is Dial from Home Screen. In Chapter 2, we talked about the icons on the Home screen and their shortcuts. This option allows you to type a number while the Home screen is displayed and have the One Time Dial dialog box be shown with that typed number already in the edit field. If you type in numbers a lot, this option may be really handy for you.

> **note** Because the number and letter keys are shared, if you enable Dial from Home Screen, all of the Home screen icon shortcuts will be removed. However, disabling this option does not make the shortcuts return immediately. In order to make the shortcuts reappear, the handheld needs to be reset.

SMART DIALING

The smart dialing rules are supposed to clarify the entries that you have made in your Address Book and therefore allow you to not have to enter all of the absolutely necessary information. For instance, you can enter long-distance numbers without the 1 and local numbers without the area code if these options are configured correctly. The screen is divided into three areas and is shown in Figure 9.22.

The top portion allows you to specify characteristics of the numbers in your own country. As mentioned previously, specifying the area code allows you to be able to enter local numbers without it. The National Number Length is used to determine whether a number dialed is an international number or not.

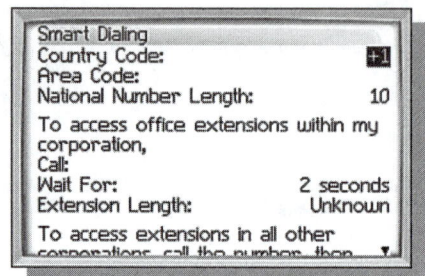

FIGURE 9.22
The Smart Dialing options make it easier to communicate with others in your office, even when you are on the go.

The next two sections define rules for how to handle extensions in the Address Book. The first of these rules is To Access Office Extensions Within My Corporation. This is especially helpful because many corporations have populated their mail servers with only the extension for contacts.

When these contacts are synchronized with your handheld, you can end up with entries where the phone number is simply x202. When this is the case, the smart dialing rule for Accessing Extensions Within My Corporation is used. The Call field is where you put the phone number to call to access your company phone system. The Wait For field allows you to set a timeframe to wait so that the phone system has time to answer the phone. The last field, Extension Length, allows you to specify the extension length for extensions in your company if they are all the same.

The last rule, Access Extensions in All Other Corporations, is used when a number in an Address Book entry has a full phone number in it followed by the extension number, 123-456-7890 x202 for example. The only field associated with this rule is the Wait For field. Just like the other corporate phone system rule, this specifies how long to wait after dialing the number before dialing the extension.

VOICEMAIL

Typically if your handheld has a voicemail service for it, this section will be configured for you. However, if you have a separate voicemail service or use it with your company voicemail, you can configure how to call it in this screen, shown in Figure 9.23.

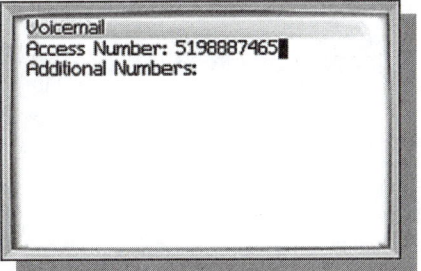

FIGURE 9.23
Set the Voicemail options if they aren't already configured by your carrier or if you use a voicemail system other than your wireless carrier's.

The first field, Access Number, is the phone number that should be called when you want to access voicemail. Only numbers can be entered here. The second field, Additional Numbers, contains any additional numbers that need to be dialed in order to access the voice mail box, such as the box number or a password. In addition to numbers, you can also add waits and pauses with the Add Wait and Add Pause menu items. They are displayed as inverted "w" and "p" characters in the edit field. A pause is a two-second pause and it is used to give the other phone system time to do something. A wait causes a dialog to be displayed prompting you to tell it when to continue, skip this step, or end the call.

TTY

TTY is also known as TDD, which stands for Telecommunications Device for the Deaf. TTY is only supported by some carriers and some networks on BlackBerry handhelds. The TTY option defaults to No, but if you set it to Yes, you can use your handheld to call TTY devices as well as make regular calls. If the handheld detects a TTY, it will disable the speaker and microphone and activate they keyboard. From this point on whatever you type on the keyboard will be displayed on the TTY device at the other end of the call.

PHONE STATUS

One of the things I like to do is keep track of my minutes used as I go through the month so I have an idea of when I'm about to go over my minutes. If you like to do this as well, then the Phone Status screen is going to help you a lot. You can show this screen by clicking the Status menu item from the Recent Call list menu. When you do, a screen is shown that displays the duration of the previous call and a total duration for all of the calls since it was last cleared (see Figure 9.24).

You can clear the saved value for the last call duration by clicking the Clear Timer menu item. Or, clear the total calls duration by clicking the Clear All Timers menu item.

> **note** Of course, as calling plans get more complex with things such as free nights and weekends or free in-network calling, the call statistics are less accurate and therefore less important.

FIGURE 9.24
The Phone Status screen contains several pieces of valuable information.

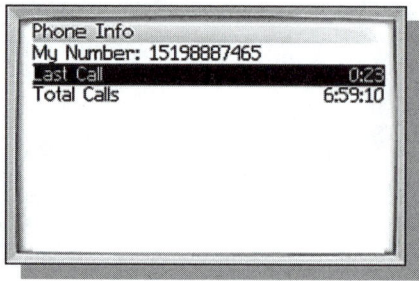

Unfortunately there are no ways to clear these values on a regular schedule; you can only do it manually.

Part IV

BLACKBERRY PIM APPLICATIONS

10 Using the Address Book

11 Using the Calendar

12 Managing Tasks

Chapter 10

USING THE ADDRESS BOOK

BLACKBERRY BASICS:

- The Address Book is used by other applications as the central point for creating messages and calls.

- The Address Book has a nice search feature. To activate it, simply start typing the name you want to search for.

- Menu items allowing you to send messages or create calls are shown only if the address has the proper information to do them.

- Lookups help you find addresses stored in your corporate Address Book if you are using a BES.

- Address entries can be grouped to create a distribution list.

- Categories are used to help organize memos, tasks, and addresses.

The Address Book is integrated tightly with both the Message and the Phone applications. In fact, you've used it already in both Chapter 5, "Composing and Sending Messages," and Chapter 9, "Making Phone Calls," though you may not have realized it. When you compose a message or place a call, the Address Book is used to select the recipient. Up to this point, we have used only the Use Once entry and manually entered the address or phone information. This is fine when you are really using that person's contact information only once, but the Address Book provides you with much more efficient ways to reach your intended recipient.

In addition to using the Address Book simply to select a recipient to communicate with, the Messages and Phone applications also use the Address Book to look up a friendly name for your recipient that is then displayed in the Message list or the Recent Call list to make communicating with that person even easier.

USING THE ADDRESS LIST

To open the Address Book, click the Address Book icon on the Home screen. The screen shown in Figure 10.1 is the Address List screen and is the starting point for anything done in the Address Book.

The Address List screen displays the name and/or company of each contact in the Address Book. If only a name is given, just that name is shown. If only a company is given, then the company name is shown. If both are given, they are both shown with the name first.

Notice the lack of the Use Once entry. This entry is not available when accessing the Address Book directly. It is only shown when the Address Book is opened through the Compose icon or menu items such as Place Call or Compose Email in the Messages application.

FIGURE 10.1
The Address List screen provides access to all contacts saved to your Address Book.

note You can also open the Address Book from the Phone application by clicking the View Address Book menu item.

If you are like most people, you tend to get a lot of addresses in your Address Book, and scrolling through the list one at a time is cumbersome. You can scroll through the list one screenful at a time by pressing the Alt key while scrolling the trackwheel up or down. There is also a Find feature, which we will talk about more later in this chapter in the "Finding Addresses" section.

CREATING A NEW ADDRESS ENTRY

To create a new address in the Address list, click the New Address menu item. This will show the New Address screen, shown in Figure 10.2.

FIGURE 10.2
Creating a new address entry.

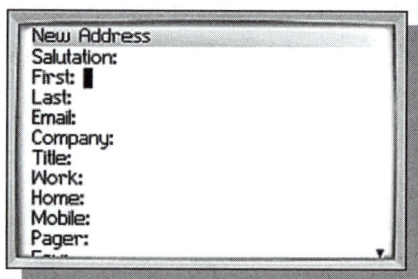

tip When entering a phone number with an extension, the X character may share a key with a number. In this case, the roles are reversed so that pressing the key causes the number to be added to the field and pressing the Alt key then the key causes the X to be added to the field.

This screen is where you can add all of the pertinent information about a person. Every field is optional, but you must at least put something in the First Name, Last Name, or Company field so that a name can be displayed in the Address list.

Some of the fields have special features that make entering the data easier. For instance, there are five fields that store phone numbers. In these fields, pressing a key with a number does not require you to press the Alt key as you normally would. Simply pressing the key enters the number into the field. These fields also allow you to enter characters that are not normally part of a phone number such as parentheses and dashes. You can also enter an X to indicate that the numbers following it are part of an extension.

The Email field also handles keyboard input in a special way. Pressing the Space key causes an @ to be added to the field if you haven't manually typed one. If an @ is already in the field, then pressing the Space key causes a . (period) to be added to the field. Using the Space key allows you to quickly enter an email address without having to use the Alt key to get those special characters.

ADDING MULTIPLE EMAIL ADDRESSES

Some people have more than one email address and you may need to have access to each of them. The New Address screen initially shows only one field for Email; however, there are really three Email fields that you can access. You can add Email fields one at a time by clicking the Add Email Address menu item. If you decide you don't need one of the fields, you can remove it by scrolling to the field you want to delete and then clicking the Delete Field menu item.

CUSTOMIZING ENTRIES WITH USER-DEFINED FIELDS

At the bottom of the screen there are four fields labeled User1 through User4. These are user-defined fields to hold any additional information you might want to keep on a contact. The field name User1 isn't very descriptive, however. Fortunately, you can change these names to something more appropriate. To do this, scroll to the user field you want to change and then open the menu and click the Change Field Name menu item. A dialog appears (see Figure 10.3) with the default field name and a field where you can enter the new field name.

> **caution** These user-defined field names are applied to the Address Book as a whole, so changing the user field name once applies it to all addresses.

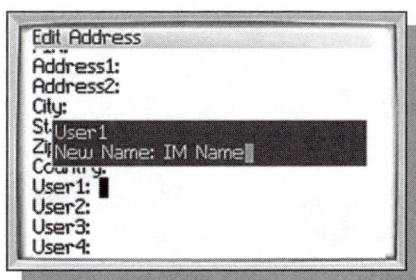

FIGURE 10.3
Change the name of a user-defined field by selecting the Change Field Name menu item.

MANAGING ADDRESSES

Managing the addresses in Address Book is done using the View, Edit, and Delete menu items. It is not possible to multi-select addresses, so each of these operations can be done on only the selected address.

VIEWING AN ADDRESS

Clicking the View menu item displays a screen containing all of the information in that address entry. The field contents cannot be edited while in this screen. Fields that do not contain data are omitted from the screen, so generally all of the contact's information can fit onto one screen.

The information is broken into logical groups that are separated by lines to make the whole screen easier to read.

FIGURE 10.4
Viewing an address entry.

The Edit and Delete menu items are available on this screen, so you have the option to look at an address entry first, and then decide what to do with it. These menu items are discussed in the two sections that follow.

EDITING AN ADDRESS

Clicking the Edit menu item on either the Address List screen or the View Address screen takes you to the Edit Address screen. Here you can add or remove any of the information in any of the fields. You can also rename user-defined fields, and add or remove email address fields. If you make changes you can save those changes by clicking the Save menu item. If you press Escape after making changes, you will see a familiar dialog asking if you want to save or discard your changes.

DELETING AN ADDRESS

To remove an address entry from your Address Book, click the Delete menu item from either the Address List screen or the View Address screen.

By default, choosing to delete an entry results in a dialog asking you to confirm the deletion, but it is possible to disable the confirmation dialog with an option setting. If you've changed this setting, be very sure you want to delete the entry before you click that menu item.

GROUPING MULTIPLE ADDRESSES

A *group* is the BlackBerry name for a distribution list. By creating and populating a group, you create a single address that represents any number of people.

GROUPING MULTIPLE ADDRESSES

Groups can only be used as a recipient for an email message though, so don't expect to be able to create a conference call using a group.

CREATING A NEW GROUP

Click the New Group menu item while viewing the Address List screen to create a new group. The New Group screen shown in Figure 10.5 is displayed. At the top of the New Group screen is an edit field, where you can give the group a name. This name will appear in the Address list along with all of your other Address Book entries.

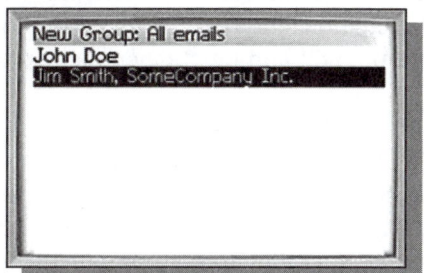

FIGURE 10.5
Creating a new group.

ADDING MEMBERS TO A GROUP

Add addresses to the group by clicking the Add Member menu item. This shows the Address List screen again, but notice now that the title says Select Address. All addresses are shown in this list, even if their Email field is empty. To add an address, select it from the list and click the Continue menu item. If the address does not have an email address in it, the Continue menu item will not be present.

If an address has more then one Email field, a dialog listing all of the email addresses will be shown. To add the address, select the desired email address and click the trackwheel.

Much like the main Address List screen, many menu items are available to help you manage the addresses in the list, such as Edit, New Address, and Delete. Menu items to manage groups are missing, however, because you are already managing a group.

note An Address can only be in a group one time. If an Address entry has multiple email addresses, only one of those email addresses can be used.

DELETING OR CHANGING A MEMBER OF A GROUP

Two menu items that are similar in effect are the Delete Member and Change Member menu items. Both of these menu items can be used to remove the selected member from the list. Using the Change Member menu item causes the Select Address screen to be shown first. Once another address is selected and the Continue menu item clicked, the change takes place—removing the previous member and adding the newly selected member.

tip If a member has more than one email address and you want to change which address is being used, you must delete the member and add it again.

CHANGING HOW THE MEMBER LIST IS DISPLAYED

At any time, you can change the screen to display the email addresses of the members in the group instead of the names. Clicking the Show Email Addresses menu item changes the listing in the group to display the actual email addresses. To change it back to names, click the Show Names menu item.

VIEWING A GROUP

If you want to just see what members are in a group, select the Group in the Address List screen and click the View Group menu item. This shows the same basic screen as the New Group except that the fields are not changeable and the Edit and Delete menu items are not available.

EDITING A GROUP

Clicking the Edit Group menu item from either the Address List screen or the View Group screen causes the New Group screen to be shown again, only this time it is labeled Edit Group. All of the operations that were available when creating the group for the first time are available when editing it.

> **note** Remember, the confirmation dialog can be disabled in the user options. If you have changed your options so that the confirmation dialog is avoided, be sure you have the right group selected before clicking Delete Group.

DELETING A GROUP

Deleting a group works the same way as deleting an address. Selecting the Delete Group menu item while the group is selected in the Address List screen or from the View Group screen displays a confirmation dialog, and deletes the Group when the dialog is confirmed.

UNDERSTANDING CATEGORIES

One of the new features in version 4.0 of the handheld software is the idea of assigning PIM records to one or more categories. The categories themselves can be managed in the PIM applications, and PIM application records can be assigned to one or more categories. These applications include the Address Book, Tasks, and MemoPad applications, but not the Calendar application.

You can create and delete categories from the category list screen. There are several ways to display this screen, but since we need to assign something to a category anyway, let's do this through the Edit Address screen. Remember, though, that you can also use the Edit Memo screen or Edit Task screen.

Select an Address in the Address list and click the Edit menu to edit it. From there, click the Categories menu item to display the Categories List screen, shown in Figure 10.6. The software creates two categories by default, Business and Personal, but you can create your own unique categories and you can delete these default categories if you want.

UNDERSTANDING CATEGORIES 153

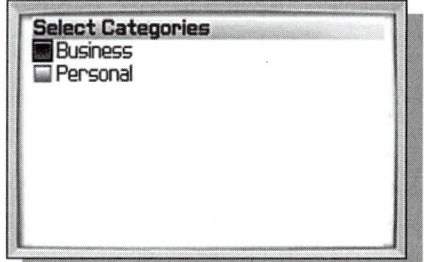

FIGURE 10.6
The Categories List screen showing the default categories.

MANAGING CATEGORIES

Categories themselves do not contain any data. They are nothing more than a name, really. To create a new category, click the New menu item and type the name of the category into the dialog box. Click the trackwheel to complete the process or press the Escape key to cancel it.

Similarly, to delete a category, select it from the list and click the Delete menu item. Because the categories are so simple, there is no way to edit an existing one.

ASSIGNING AN ADDRESS TO A CATEGORY

Next to each category in the list is a check box. These check boxes show which categories a specific address record (or task or memo, whichever is appropriate) is assigned to. So for instance, to assign a record to the Personal category, scroll the selection to the Personal category and check the check box by either pressing the Space key or clicking the Change Option menu item. You can also remove the record from all categories by clicking the Clear Selection menu item.

When you are done assigning categories, click the Save menu item to return to the Edit screen. Clicking the Close menu item will also return you to the Edit screen, but will also display a dialog, if there were changes made, asking what action you want to do with the changes—save them, discard them, or cancel and then close.

note If you delete a category, all of the items that have been assigned to that category will continue to have that category assignment even if the category itself has been removed. Therefore creating a new category with the same name will once more retrieve the records that had previously been assigned to this category.

DISPLAYING ITEMS IN A CATEGORY

Once you have assigned some of the records to categories, you can use this to quickly display the records in a particular category using the Filter menu item. This menu item is available from the Address List screen (or Tasks List or Memo List as appropriate). Clicking the Filter menu item displays the familiar Category List screen. You can still create and delete categories in this screen as before, but now instead of assigning a record to a category, you are selecting a category for which you want to view all of the records. You can select only one category at a time. To select a category, scroll to the desired category and click the Change Option menu item or press the space key.

As soon as a category is selected, the Category List screen disappears and the Address List (or Memo List or Task List) screen is shown and only those records in the selected category are displayed in the list. All of the normal operations can be done; the only difference is not all of the records are shown in the list.

To stop filtering the list, click the Filter menu item once again and click the Clear Selection menu item. This will immediately return you to the List screen and display all of the records once more.

FINDING AN ADDRESS

One thing you may have noticed earlier is that the title of the Address List screen was unusual. Instead of saying something descriptive like Address Book, its title is Find. This is because the Find feature is always active and the title of the screen is used to display the search criteria you enter. Initially, there is no search criterion and as a result all of the addresses in your Address Book are shown.

When you type a character, that character is added to the search criteria and is displayed in the screen title. So pressing the letter J causes the title to be updated to show Find: J (see Figure 10.7). This also reduces the Address list to only those Address Book entries that match the search criteria. Typing additional characters adds them to the title in the same way and also further reduces the Address list based on the new criteria.

The Find feature of the Address list attempts to match the search criteria to the First Name, Last Name, and Company fields separately. If a value in any of these fields begins with the search criteria, it will be shown in the Address list.

note You can use the Backspace key to remove characters from the search criteria in case you made a mistake or if you want to broaden the list of addresses shown. For Example, if you don't find the contact you are looking for after typing in "johnson" you can broaden the search by removing some characters until your search is just "johns" and thus be able to find the contact under "johnsen."

FIGURE 10.7
Entering search criteria.

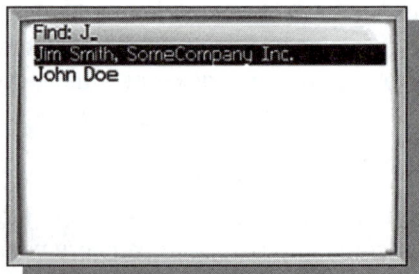

After the search criteria has been entered, there are two ways to return to the full Address Book list. The first is to use the Backspace key to erase the characters in the search criteria one at a time. The other way is to press the Escape key. This will cause the search criteria to be removed completely.

USING LOOKUPS ON BES

Lookups are a special feature available to users who are configured to use a corporate email server using the BlackBerry Enterprise Server (BES). Lookups allow you to enter search criteria that will search the Global Address List (GAL) on the email server and return the matches to your handheld. From here, you can look at the results and work with the addresses in the lookup just like they were part of your Address Book on your handheld. Lookups are not permanent, however. If your handheld is reset, all lookups are lost.

CREATING A LOOKUP

If the feature is available to you, there will be a Lookup menu item available from the Address List screen. Clicking this menu item shows a small dialog where you can enter the search criteria to be used in this lookup. Click the trackwheel to dismiss the dialog.

Once a lookup has been created, it is displayed in the Address List with square brackets around it. The text of the entry changes to reflect the state of the lookup. For this example, let's say you entered the character K in the Lookup dialog. At first it will display [Looking up: K] while the lookup is sent to and resolved on the email server. Once the lookup results are returned, the entry will display [No Matches: K] if there were no matches, [2 Matches: K] if there were two matches, or [*Name*] if there is only one match.

> **note** Because the lookup needs to be resolved on the email server, you must be in your wireless coverage area to create a lookup.

VIEWING LOOKUP RESULTS

Once a lookup is resolved, you can view the results by scrolling to Lookup and clicking the View Lookup menu item. This will display another Address List screen that contains just the results of the lookup. This list has many of the same features that the main Address list does, including Search, View, and Edit menu items and the appropriate Call Name, Email Name, SMS Name, and PIN Name menu items to contact that person. There are also several menu items enabling you to manage the lookup.

ADDING LOOKUP RESULTS TO THE ADDRESS BOOK

One of the most common things you will want to do is permanently add an address returned by the lookup to your Address Book. You can do this by clicking the Add menu item. When this is done, the address that was selected is copied into your Address Book and then deleted from the lookup results. If that was the only entry in the results, the lookup is automatically deleted and you will be shown the Address List screen again. If you want to add all of the matches, click the Add All menu item. This will also delete the lookup and return you to the Address List screen.

> **note** The Edit menu will allow you to modify and save changes to an entry returned in the Lookup. However, these changes are not returned to the email server and if the lookup is deleted, these changes will be lost.

MANAGING LOOKUP RESULTS

Sometimes the results returned by a lookup are larger than you want because the search criteria are applied to the First Name, Last Name, and Company fields. You can modify the search criteria and resubmit the lookup by clicking the Lookup menu item in the View Lookup screen. This is basically the same procedure as deleting the current lookup and creating a new one based on the new search criteria.

If there are just a few entries in the lookup that you don't want, you can select them individually and click the Delete menu item to remove them. This just removes them from the current lookup results and doesn't modify other lookup results or your main Address Book.

DELETING A LOOKUP

Once you are done with a lookup, you can remove it with the Delete Lookup menu item from either the Address List screen or the View Lookup screen.

RESOLVING A LOOKUP

One menu item on the View Lookup screen that may not be obvious is the Resolve menu item. I know when I saw it, I didn't know what it meant or would do. It's really quite simple, however. When a lookup has more then one match, the Address List screen is unable to show the Call Name, Email Name, and other menu items to contact a person because the lookup contains more than one entry. Resolving a lookup is simply selecting one entry from the lookup results to use for this purpose. Resolved lookups change the entry in the Address list from [Matches: 2] to [*Name*]. When a lookup that has been resolved is selected on the Address List screen, it is treated like the address that it was resolved to. For example, if a lookup is resolved to John Smith, then selecting the lookup in the Address List screen results in all of the menu items being enabled as if the entry for John Smith were selected. Of course, you can still click the View Lookup menu item to open up the lookup as before.

CONTACTING AN ADDRESS

The thing you will do most often is use the Address Book to contact someone. This is handled with a few menu items that we've seen and talked about before. When you click the trackwheel to display the menu, either on the Address List screen or the View Address screen, several menu items may be displayed depending on the Address that has been selected.

The four menu items Call *Name*, Email *Name*, SMS *Name* and PIN *Name* (where *Name* is the name of the selected contact) allow you to contact the person using the specified method (see Figure 10.8).

ADDRESS BOOK OPTIONS

FIGURE 10.8
An address entry with contact information allowing all four menu items to become available.

Each of the menu items is only displayed if the address has the information needed to contact the person in that manner. If the address entry has something in the Email field, then the Email *Name* menu item will be available. Phone *Name* and SMS *Name* both are shown if there is something in any of the phone fields, Home, Work, Mobile, or Pager. The PIN *Name* menu item is available if the PIN field of the entry has something in it.

If the address entry has more than one Email field or information in more than one of the phone fields, then you will also need to choose which field it should use. When this happens, a dialog, shown in Figure 10.9, is displayed listing all of the possibilities. Choose the one you want to use by scrolling the trackwheel to the desired button and clicking the trackwheel or pressing the Enter key.

FIGURE 10.9
Choosing which email to use when an address has more than one entry.

ADDRESS BOOK OPTIONS

Like most other applications on the handheld, the Address Book has several options that can change the way you interact with it. You can get to the Address Book Options screen by clicking the Options menu item from the Address list (see Figure 10.10).

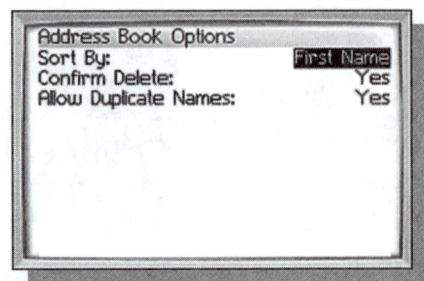

FIGURE 10.10
The Address Book Options screen offers three options you can configure.

> **tip** If you run into a situation where you have two people in your Address Book with identical names, you will either have to disable duplicate name filtering, or add something to one of the names to allow it pass the filter. For example, if you have two entries for "John Smith," simply add a middle initial to one, or add some other character to the first or last name to make it unique.

- **Sort By**—The first option allows you to change how the Address list is sorted when it is displayed. You can change this option to First Name, Last Name, or Company by pressing the Space key or clicking the Change Option menu item.

- **Confirm Delete**—The second option allows you disable the confirmation dialog when you delete an address. Change the option to No to disable the dialog. If you choose to disable the confirm dialog, be very careful to select the item you want to get rid of before clicking the Delete menu item. You cannot undo a Delete operation.

- **Allow Duplicate Names**—The last option allows you to have the software allow or disallow entries that have the same name. Since multiple entries for the same contact can be confusing, it is probably a good idea to change the default Yes setting to No. Only the first and last names are used to check for duplicates. When you save an entry, the first and last names are checked. If there is a duplicate, a dialog is shown telling you that a duplicate already exists in the Address Book and the entry is not saved.

ACCESSING THE SIM PHONE BOOK

The SIM card can store more than just your carrier and provisioning information. Another thing it stores is a phone book so that if you transfer your SIM card to another device, your phone book information travels with it. This phone book is not the same as your BlackBerry Address Book, though. The SIM Phone Book is where traditional handsets store the phone book information they use. Generally you won't use the SIM Phone Book for your daily address book. Instead, if you had previously used another handset, you will use these screens to copy the phone book data into your new BlackBerry.

To open the phone book on your SIM card, click the SIM Phone Book menu item from the Address List screen. A progress bar will display briefly as your handheld accesses the information on your SIM card.

ACCESSING THE SIM PHONE BOOK

The phone book on your SIM card is much more narrowly focused than the BlackBerry Address Book and stores only a phone number and a name. Even so, you can use this screen to place calls or send SMS messages to entries in your phone book by clicking the Call *Name* or SMS *Name* menu items in the same way that you can call or SMS someone in your Address Book. You can create new entries by clicking the New menu item and entering the name and number into the new phone book entry, but keep in mind that these new entries are going into your phone book, not your Address Book.

The Address Book is integrated into this screen as well. If it can find a matching phone number in the Address Book for the selected entry in the phone book, the View Contact menu item will be available. Clicking this menu item shows the View Address screen that best matches the number in your phone book. If it cannot find a match however, the menu item Add to Address Book will then be available. Clicking this menu item shows the New Address screen and automatically copies the data from the phone book into fields in the Address. All phone numbers are automatically entered into the Work field.

Chapter 11

USING THE CALENDAR

BLACKBERRY BASICS:

- The Calendar application is used to keep track of your appointments. You can view your appointments in four different ways—Monthly, Weekly, Daily, and as an Agenda.

- Appointments that happen repeatedly can be entered once as a Recurring Appointment.

- You can delete all of the past appointments using the Delete Prior menu item available in Agenda view.

The Calendar is another important application in the Personal Information Management set of applications. You use it to keep track of meetings, appointments, and other important events. This isn't the same thing as your To-Do list, however. The Tasks application is used for traditional to-do lists. We will discuss the Tasks application in the next chapter.

In addition to just setting up meetings and appointments, you can create appointments that automatically recur in your calendar without any input from you. You can customize how Calendar works, including choosing the view that Calendar displays its content in, which is the first topic we'll look at in this chapter.

WORKING WITH CALENDAR VIEWS

When you open the Calendar application for the first time, you are presented with a screen that looks like a standard wall calendar, which shows one month at a time. This may be useful sometimes, but other times you really need to look at the calendar in a different way. Calendar offers four different ways of viewing information. They are

- Monthly
- Weekly
- Daily
- Agenda

The next few sections explain each view in more detail.

MONTHLY VIEW

This is the default view for the Calendar application. The Monthly view shows you an entire month at a time in a way that is similar to a wall calendar. Each day is given a small square to display the appointments in that day. Obviously, the space is too small for any kind of text that describes your appointments. To let you know what days have appointments, a small bar inside the box is filled up proportionally to the time and duration of an appointment. Appointments marked as All Day appointments show the numeric date in the box as bolded. This view is generally good for people who do not use the Calendar heavily. Figure 11.1 shows an example of the Monthly view.

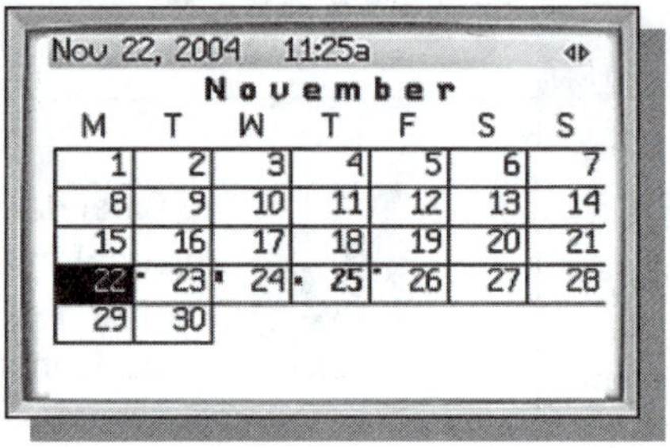

FIGURE 11.1
Looking at the calendar with the Monthly view, you get a snapshot of the days that you have appointments and a graphical representation of the length of each appointment.

> **note** Because the selection is one whole day, it's not possible to view a specific appointment from this view. Instead, you must first change the view to a Daily view by clicking the View Appts menu item or the View Day menu item. The difference between the two menu items is that clicking the View Appts menu item and then pressing the Escape key returns you to the previous view. Clicking the View Day menu item and then pressing the Escape key exits the Calendar Application and returns you to the Main Screen.

Scrolling the trackwheel up or down moves the selection box forward or backward one day at a time. You can move the selection box forward or backward one week at a time by pressing and holding the Alt key while scrolling the trackwheel up or down.

WEEKLY VIEW

Sometimes you can only think about things one week at a time and the Weekly view is there to show you your week at a glance. The days of the week, Sunday through Saturday, and the numeric dates for each day are displayed at the top. Along the side, the hours of a typical workday are listed from 9 a.m. to 5 p.m. Again, there isn't enough room for any description of the appointments, but the duration of each appointment is blocked out appropriately. Figure 11.2 shows an example of the Weekly view.

Scrolling the trackwheel up or down moves the selection box up or down one hour at a time. You can move the selection box forward or backward one day at a time by pressing and holding the Alt key while scrolling the trackwheel up or down.

DAILY VIEW

Daily view is used to see the details of appointments for a given day. Similar to Weekly view, the times of a typical workday are listed down the side. Next to the times the description of each appointment is shown and a square bracket is used to show the duration of an appointment. If there are any overlapping appointments, the screen shifts slightly and a second square bracket is shown for the other appointment. At the top of the screen, a series of boxes show the days of the week. The solid block indicates the day of the week being viewed. Figure 11.3 shows an example of Daily view.

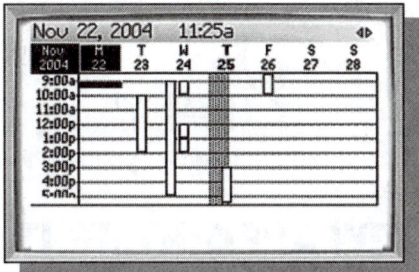

FIGURE 11.2
Looking at the calendar with the Weekly view provides a more detailed view than Monthly view, while still showing multiple days at once.

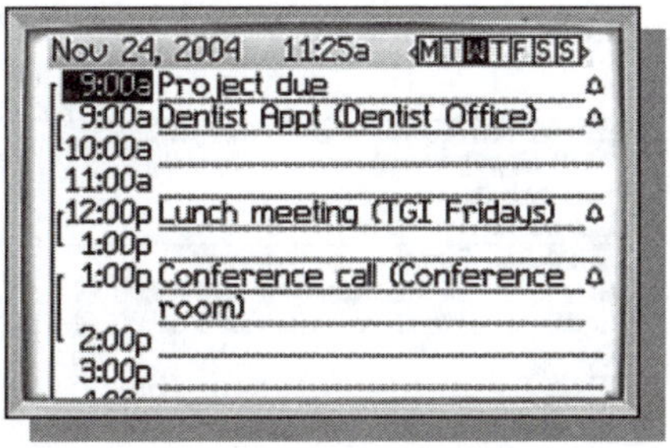

FIGURE 11.3
Looking at the calendar with the Daily view gives you a clear picture of what is scheduled on any given day.

Scrolling the trackwheel up or down moves the selection box up or down one hour at a time. You can move the selection box to another date by pressing and holding the Alt button while scrolling the trackwheel up or down as well. If you scroll up past the beginning of the day, the selection box moves to the day of the week box at the top of the screen. Clicking the trackwheel on a day of the week moves the Daily view to that day. On either side of the day of the week box are small arrows that can also be selected. Clicking the trackwheel on one of the arrows moves the selected day forward or backward appropriately. If you scroll up more, the selection moves to the date in the title as well. Clicking while any part of the date is selected is the same as clicking the Go To Date menu item, which we will talk about more later.

AGENDA VIEW

Maybe your schedule isn't so busy that you need to worry about seeing your appointments on a daily or weekly basis. Agenda view is probably more well suited for you because it shows each appointment in a list, regardless of how much time may be between them. Similar to the Message List screen, appointments are grouped under a date header and each line shows the start time and subject of the appointment (see Figure 11.4).

FIGURE 11.4
Looking at the calendar with Agenda view gives you a concise glimpse at your scheduled appointments for each day.

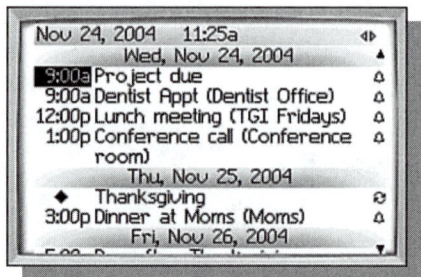

CREATING A NEW APPOINTMENT

You can create a new appointment from any view by clicking the New menu item. This will show the New Appointment screen, which allows you to enter all the details of the new appointment (see Figure 11.5).

FIGURE 11.5
The New Appointment screen is where all the action takes place for setting up a new appointment.

There are also ways to create new appointments utilizing shortcuts on each of the other views:

- **Weekly**—Shift scrolling the trackwheel selects a block of time. Pressing the Enter key shows the New Appointment screen with the appointment time and duration set to the selected block.

- **Daily**—Shift scrolling the trackwheel selects a block of time. Pressing the Enter key changes the description field on the Daily view into a text entry block where you can type in the subject of the appointment. Scrolling the trackwheel changes the duration and pressing the Alt key while scrolling the trackwheel changes the start time. Clicking the trackwheel will create the new appointment using this shortcut.

- **Agenda**—Pressing the Enter key on a date header shows the New Appointment screen with the appointment date.

When creating a new appointment, there are two portions of the screen that you will be using most often. In the top portion of the New Appointment screen are the Subject and Location fields. The text of these fields is shown in the Daily and Agenda views, so make sure that you put something appropriate here. If there is an entry in the Location field, it is shown in parentheses after the Subject.

The other portion of the screen that is used most often contains the time information of the appointment. The Start and End fields allow you to set both a date and time. The Duration field shows the duration of the appointment in hours and minutes. Although you can determine the duration yourself, having it as a separate field is very nice and saves time.

It seems pretty straightforward; however, not all of these options work the way you would expect them to. The following sections detail the options in the New Appointment screen.

SETTING AND CHANGING THE START, END, AND DURATION FIELDS

The Start, End, and Duration fields are linked together, and changing the entry in one field causes the other fields to change accordingly. For example, if you change the time in the End field, the Duration field changes to reflect the new duration of the appointment. One important thing to note here is that changing the Start field does not change the duration. Instead, it causes the End field to change so that the time reflected in the Duration field remains the same. For example, changing the start of a 1-hour meeting from 9 a.m. to 8 a.m. causes the end to change from 10 a.m. to 9 a.m. In addition, you can change the duration directly as well. Changing the duration causes the End field to change accordingly.

Although generally just the time portion of the Start and End fields is used, having a date and time means that you can block out time for marathon, 36-hour appointments. Most appointments that last a whole day or more should use the All Day Event check box, however, because it more accurately represents how the time is being used and is easier to enter. This check box is discussed in the next section.

SETTING AN ALL DAY EVENT

Checking the All Day Event check box causes the New Appointment screen to change slightly. Now, the Start and End fields show only the date and the Duration field counts the time of the appointment in days instead of hours (see Figure 11.6). Appointments with the All Day Event check box checked are displayed differently in all of the views to indicate that the entire day is used up. Even if you have several appointments that together utilize all of the time in the day, they will not look the same as appointments with the All Day Event check box checked.

FIGURE 11.6
The New Appointment screen with the All Day Event checked gives you slightly different options than those seen in Figure 11.5.

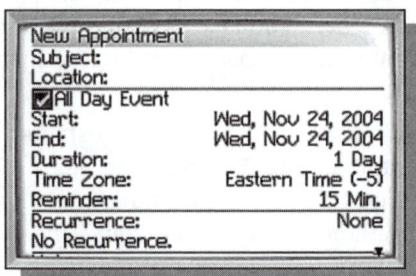

USING THE TIME ZONE FIELD

Sometimes someone will arrange an appointment and tell you the time in terms of their local time zone, which might be different from yours. If this happens, you can avoid the problems of manually converting the time to your time zone by simply changing the time zone of the appointment. If you are asked to be on a conference call at 12 p.m. Pacific and you are on Eastern time, simply change the time zone to Pacific and make the start time 12 p.m. The software will automatically make the time zone adjustment and block out the correct time in the time zone that you have set for the handheld. Be aware that if the time zone of your handheld is not set correctly to where you are located, this field won't be of much use to you.

SETTING REMINDER NOTIFICATIONS

> **note** Only one reminder is allowed for each Appointment. There is no way to add an additional reminder and there is no "snooze" feature as on an alarm clock.

The Reminder is a notification of your upcoming appointment at a set time before the appointment is to begin. The default is 15 minutes, but you can change it from 0 Minutes to 1 Week or disable it totally. To disable the reminder for an appointment, simply select None in the Reminder field.

The way that the notification alerts you is defined by the profile that you have selected. A dialog will always be shown as well; an example of this is shown in Figure 11.7. The dialog has two buttons. Clicking the Open button will cause the appointment to be opened so you can see the details of it. To dismiss the reminder, simply dismiss the dialog.

FIGURE 11.7
This dialog is shown when a reminder is activated. Click the trackwheel on Dismiss to close the dialog and dismiss the reminder.

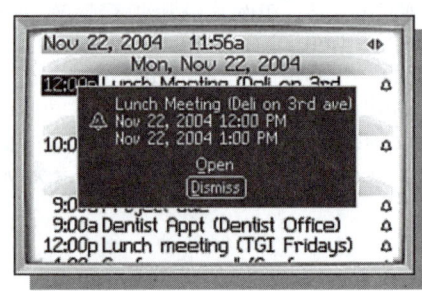

MARKING AN APPOINTMENT AS PRIVATE

One of the new features in the 4.0 version of the handheld software is the Mark As Private field for appointments. When this field is checked, the appointment will be considered private and the details of the appointment will not be visible to other people.

This doesn't really mean anything on the handheld, but when the record is synchronized with your desktop calendar system it can be beneficial. Many calendar systems, such as Lotus Notes and Microsoft Exchange, allow calendar appointments to be shared with other people in the company. You may want to experiment with this feature to determine whether your system supports private appointments.

USING THE NOTES FIELD

The final portion of the screen is for the Notes field. The Notes field is not displayed in any of the views, but is a place where you can enter additional textual information about this appointment. This is a good place to take notes during an appointment, or if you know you will need some information, such as driving directions, for an appointment, you can enter it here.

CREATING RECURRING APPOINTMENTS

There is one portion of the New Appointment screen that was not touched on in the previous sections. The third section of that screen is devoted to creating recurring appointments. Recurring Appointments are appointments that happen over and over again on a regular schedule. This could be a birthday you want to remember, a regular monthly breakfast, or even a reminder for the time of your favorite television show.

An appointment is not recurring by default. To designate an appointment as recurring, change the Recurrence field to something other than None. There are four types of Recurring Appointments based on how often they reoccur: Daily, Weekly, Monthly, and Yearly.

> **note** Directly under the Recurrence field is a field with text that begins "Occurs every...." This field is not selectable or changeable, and is there to provide a simple description of how the recurrence will work.

DAILY RECURRING APPOINTMENTS

A daily recurrence is the simplest recurrence because the amount of time between occurrences is the smallest. When creating a daily recurrence, there are only two new fields. An example of creating a daily recurring appointment is shown in Figure 11.8.

The first field in the Recurrence area is the Every field. This field is a number and is used to say each occurrence of the appointment happens every X number of days. Changing the value of the Every field to 2 changes the Recurrence description to "Occurs every other day." Changing the field to 3, makes the description say "Occurs every 3 days." If you have a regular 8 a.m. meeting every day as part of your job, this would be a good way to add those meetings to your calendar.

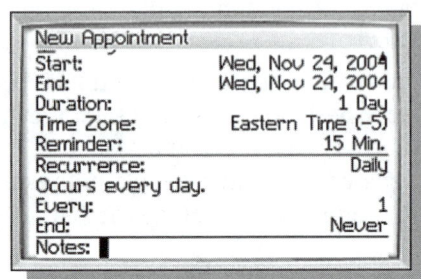

FIGURE 11.8
Adding a daily recurring appointment requires you to set the number of occurrences and how many days there are between occurrences.

The other Recurrence field is the End field. This isn't the same as the End field in the other part of the New Appointment screen, however. This End field is used to tell when the recurring appointments are supposed to end. It defaults to Never, but changing the field to Date (the only other available option) displays a new field below it where the end date can be set. Notice also that the description of the Recurrence has changed as well to specify the date. Setting an end date is useful for those appointments that occur regularly, but only for a little while. An example of this may be if you are working on a special project and your boss wants a meeting every day for the duration of the project. The End date is the last day of this recurring meeting. From that day forward, the meeting will no longer be entered into your calendar (unless you do it manually, of course).

WEEKLY RECURRING APPOINTMENTS

A daily recurring appointment will create appointments on Saturdays and Sundays if the End date is beyond a standard work week, and often this isn't desirable.

A weekly recurring appointment adds a new field called Days to the screen. Using the Days field, you can specify which days of the week the appointments should occur on. Each day of the week is selectable using the Change Option menu item or by pressing the Space key in much the same way a check box works. When a day is selected, the letter is shown in bold font (see Figure 11.9).

Looking at the previous example where you want an appointment every day for two weeks, the weekly recurring appointment is really much better suited. Selecting M, T, W, T, and F from the Days ensures that your appointment is scheduled to occur on each work day of the week, but not on the weekend.

FIGURE 11.9
Adding a weekly recurring appointment gives you the option of choosing the day that the appointment occurs on.

MONTHLY RECURRING APPOINTMENTS

Changing the recurrence type to Monthly changes the screen yet again. The Days field is removed and a Relative Date check box is shown. The Relative Date check box is used when an appointment happens every month, but not necessarily on the same date each month. An example of this would be a monthly bridge game on the second Tuesday of the month. The appointment may be on the tenth one month and the twelfth the next.

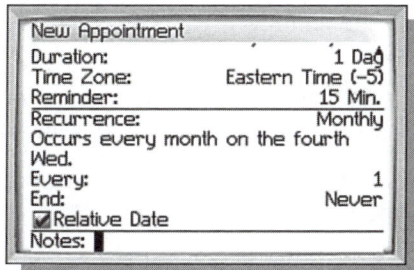

FIGURE 11.10
Adding a monthly recurring appointment gives you the flexibility to choose a day of the month rather than a specific date.

Notice that checking the Relative Date check box changes the recurrence description to reflect the relative date that it occurs. In the example given previously, it should read "Occurs every month on the second Tue." You may be wondering how it knew that since you did not pick the day and the Days field is missing. The start date is used to calculate that information. In this case, the start date would have to be on the second Tuesday.

YEARLY RECURRING APPOINTMENTS

The last recurrence type is Yearly. When selecting this recurrence type, the Every field is removed, leaving only Ends and Relative Date. Both of these fields work in the same way as described previously. The only thing to note is that when the Relative Date check

> **tip**
> Yearly recurring appointments are a great way to remember those special birthdays and anniversaries. Be sure to give yourself a reminder early enough to get a gift or make plans! If you are like me and very forgetful of such things, use more than one appointment so you get lots of reminders days or even weeks ahead of time.

box is checked, the description also includes the month that the appointment recurs, such as "Occurs every year on the fourth Thu in Nov.," which would be the U.S. holiday of Thanksgiving (see Figure 11.11). Because the Every field is missing, it is not possible to set a yearly recurring appointment that happens less frequently than once a year.

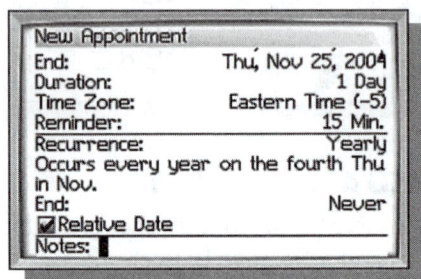

FIGURE 11.11
Adding a yearly recurring appointment.

MANAGING APPOINTMENTS

To interact with any existing appointments, you must be in the Weekly, Daily, or Agenda view. The Monthly view is a nice way to look at your schedule at a glance, but it doesn't provide any ways to directly select a specific appointment.

You can edit appointments, including recurring appointments, as well as delete appointments from the calendar. The following sections detail the specifics of these tasks.

EDITING AN APPOINTMENT

To edit an existing appointment, first scroll the trackwheel until the cursor is on an appointment, then click the Open menu item. The Appointment Details screen appears, which is essentially the same as the New Appointment screen. Many of the details can be edited in the same way as you could when entering a new appointment. When the edits are done, you can save them by clicking the Save menu item.

If the appointment is part of a recurring series of appointments, selecting Open will first display a dialog asking whether you want to edit that specific occurrence, or the entire series of occurrences (see Figure 11.12).

Opening the occurrence allows you to change the details of that specific occurrence and does not affect the rest of the appointments in the series. Opening the occurrence does not show any of the recurrence information in the Appointment Details screen, even though it is part of a recurring appointment.

Opening the series allows you to change the details of all of the appointments in the series. This is the only way you can change the recurrence information, such as if your meeting moved from Tuesdays to Thursdays.

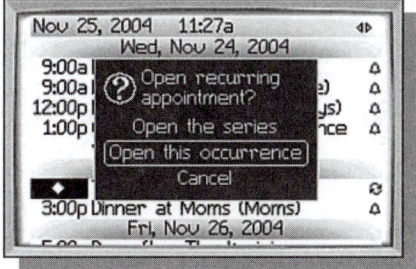

FIGURE 11.12
Dialog shown when opening a recurring appointment.

DELETING AN APPOINTMENT

Deleting an appointment works in much the same way as opening an appointment. First select the appointment to delete by scrolling the trackwheel to move the cursor to it, then select the Delete menu item. You can also delete an appointment that is open by clicking the Delete menu item from the Appointment Details screen. In either case a confirmation dialog is shown, though this behavior is configurable. (See the upcoming section "Setting Calendar Options" for more details.) Clicking the Delete button finishes the operation and deletes the appointment.

Appointments that are part of a recurring series will first show a dialog similar to Figure 11.12 asking if you want to delete the entire series or this specific occurrence of the appointment. Deleting one occurrence of the series does not affect the rest of the appointments in the series.

DELETING PRIOR APPOINTMENTS

After a while you will get a lot of appointments that have already happened. Unless you need to know what you did last month, you probably do not need all of these records taking up memory in your handheld. In that case you can delete them all with one click using the Delete Prior menu item. The trick is that this menu item is hidden very well and you may not have ever stumbled upon it even if you've used the calendar application for some time already.

To get to this menu item, you must first change the calendar to the Agenda view. Then scroll the trackwheel to move the cursor to one of the date headers, not an appointment. The Delete Prior menu item is now available on the menu. Clicking it will delete all of the appointments prior to the selected date.

SETTING CALENDAR OPTIONS

Like most of the applications on your BlackBerry, the Calendar application has some options you can configure. Click the Options menu item to display the Options screen, shown in Figure 11.13.

FIGURE 11.13
The Calendar Options screen offers a few ways to customize Calendar to work the way you want it to.

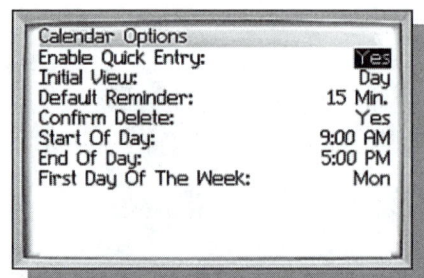

The first option on the screen is Enable Quick Entry. This option only affects the Daily view and the New Appointment shortcut we talked about earlier. If you recall, you can create a new appointment by simply typing in the subject of the appointment on the Daily view. Changing the Enable Quick Entry option to No disables this functionality.

The next option allows you to specify the view that you want to see first when opening the Calendar application. It defaults to the Monthly View, but if you would like to be in the Daily view whenever you open the calendar, change this option to Daily, or whatever view best suits your needs.

The Default Reminder option allows you to specify the reminder time that is set for any new appointment. The default 15 Minutes is usually a good amount of time, but if you typically require additional time, to allow time for driving for example, a default of 30 Minutes may be better.

When you delete an appointment, a confirmation dialog is usually shown. If you find that dialog annoying, you can disable it by changing the Confirm Delete option to No.

The next three options adjust how the Weekly and Daily views look. The first two, Start of Day and End of Day, change the times that are displayed down the left side of the Weekly and Daily views. Not all people work a 9 a.m.–5 p.m. day. If this is you, you should change these to match your typical workday.

The last option changes which day of the week is shown in the first column of the Weekly view. Some people may simply prefer to see Saturday and Sunday together at the end of the week. Others may have a non-traditional workweek. In either case, you can change the day that shows up in the first column with this option.

Chapter 12

MANAGING TASKS

BLACKBERRY BASICS:

- The Tasks application is used to store your to-do list items.

- The status, priority, and name are shown in the Tasks List.

- You can change the sort order of the Tasks List in the Options screen.

- You can delete all completed tasks by clicking the Delete Completed menu item.

The Tasks application is the "to-do" list portion of the standard Personal Information Management software suite. Tasks are more than just simple to-do items, though. They have helpful features such as a due date, and several different statuses that can be applied. The Tasks application is probably the least complex of the applications in your BlackBerry arsenal, however you'll find that you can hardly manage to get through a day without it.

USING THE TASKS LIST

When you open the Tasks application, the first screen you will see is the Tasks List. The Tasks List shows you all the tasks that have been created and displays some basic information about each of them, as shown in Figure 12.1. The largest portion of the list is given to the task name, but there are also two columns to the left of the task name that show the priority and status of the task.

FIGURE 12.1
A sample of the Tasks List screen.

If no tasks have been created yet, the Tasks List screen indicates this with a single line that cannot be selected.

CHAPTER 12 MANAGING TASKS

CREATING A NEW TASK

Creating a task begins by clicking the New menu item. Enter information about the task on the next screen (see Figure 12.2). A name, which is entered into the Task field, is the only piece of information required in order to save the task.

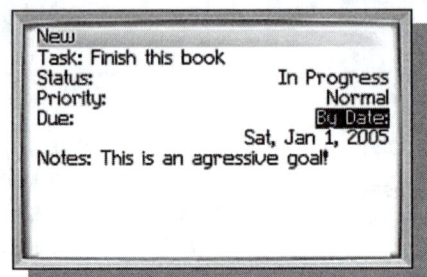

FIGURE 12.2
Creating a new task.

SETTING A DUE DATE

Each task can have a due date given to it as well. A due date is not the same as creating an appointment for it. A due date is not able to specify a completion time and does not generate a reminder. Because of these things, it may be desirable to create both an appointment and a task so that the due date appears on your Calendar.

The due date is not shown in the Tasks List at all, but the Tasks List can be set to sort the tasks by due date. This is typically the only situation where the due date is useful.

TASK STATUS

There are five possible statuses that a task can have:

- Not Started
- In Progress
- Completed
- Waiting
- Deferred

The Tasks List shows the status of each task in the second column in the list. You'll notice that some of these statuses are displayed in the same way, which reduces their usefulness. Also it is possible to change the status of a task in the Tasks List as well, but only two statuses are supported with this. Because of these limitations, the only two statuses most people worry about are In Progress and Completed.

Not Started and In Progress are both shown in the Tasks List as an empty square. Waiting and Deferred are both shown in the Tasks List as a small clock. The Completed status is shown in the Tasks List as a square with a check mark in it.

If a task does not have the Completed status, clicking the Mark Completed menu item or pressing the Space key will change the status of the selected task to Completed. Conversely, if the status is Completed, clicking the Mark In Progress menu item or pressing the Space key will return the status of the selected Task to In Progress.

TASK PRIORITY

Each task can be given a priority as well—High, Normal, or Low. Tasks with a High priority are shown in the Tasks List with an exclamation point in the first column. Tasks with a Low priority are shown in the Tasks List with a down arrow. Normal priority Tasks have no icon in the first column of the list.

SETTING A CATEGORY

Tasks can also be assigned and sorted into categories in version 4.0 of the handheld software. It works in exactly the same way for tasks as it does for addresses. If you have not yet read about it, see the section titled "Understanding Categories" in Chapter 10 for more information.

EDITING A TASK

As we discussed already, the status of a task can be changed from the Tasks List, but anything else needing to be changed must be done from the Edit Task screen. To edit a task, simply select the task from the Tasks List and click the Open menu item (or press the Enter key). The Edit Task screen is the same as the New Task screen, and any of the fields can be changed. Clicking the Save menu item saves any changes and returns you to the Tasks List screen.

DELETING A TASK

You can delete a task from either the Tasks List or the Edit Task screen. To delete a task from the Tasks List, select the task to delete and click the Delete menu item. To delete a task from the Edit Task screen, open the task and then click the Delete menu item. In both cases, a confirmation dialog will be shown before the deletion is performed.

DELETING COMPLETED TASKS

I'm always a fan of making things easier and one of the things I hate more than anything is having to delete a lot of things one at a time. It can be gratifying to see how many things on your to-do list you've gotten done, but at some point it gets to be too much to sift through. Fortunately the Tasks List screen has a Delete Completed menu item. This menu item is available at any time and clicking it will delete all of the tasks that have a status of Completed.

After a task has been deleted it cannot be recovered without completely re-creating it.

FINDING A TASK

You might have noticed that the title of the Tasks List looks very similar to the title of the Address Book. This is because the Tasks application has a find feature that works very similarly to the Address Book find feature.

To find a task, just begin typing the Name of the task. Each letter appears in the title and each task is examined to find a match. If any word in the Name field matches the search text, the task is displayed in the updated list. Those tasks that do not match are hidden from view.

Pressing the Escape key will remove all of the search criteria and display the entire Tasks List again.

TASK OPTIONS

Even a simple Application such as Tasks still has some options that can be configured. To view these options, click the Options menu item from the Tasks List screen (see Figure 12.3).

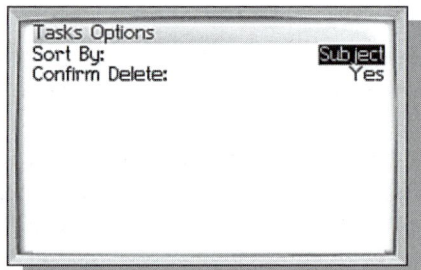

FIGURE 12.3
A sample of the Tasks List screen.

> **note** Sorting by due date may be useful, but there is no way to differentiate the tasks with a due date and those without.

The Tasks application only has two options available. Like every other application, you can disable the confirmation dialog that is shown when deleting items. Do this by changing the Confirm Delete option to No.

The other configurable option is the Sort By option. This option changes the order that tasks are shown in the Tasks List. The four choices correspond to the field that is used to do the sorting. They are Subject (also called Name), Priority, Due Date, and Status. The way each task is displayed in the list doesn't change, just the way they are sorted.

Part V
ADVANCED TOPICS

13 Other Applications on Your BlackBerry

14 Finding and Installing Third-Party Applications

Chapter 13

OTHER APPLICATIONS ON YOUR BLACKBERRY

BLACKBERRY BASICS:

- The MemoPad is a great place to store notes that don't really belong anyplace else, such as driving directions, recipes, and more.

- The Alarm application is better than a normal alarm clock, and it travels well.

- The Calculator can take a bit of getting used to, but considering you always have it with you, it's definitely worth getting to know. Its conversion functions can be a great timesaver if you need them.

- Password Keeper is a great new feature in the 4.0 system software.

- BrickBreaker is a fun game that you can use to pass the time.

WHY USE MEMOPAD?

MemoPad is a general use application for entering notes or memos of whatever kind you may need. Each memo has a title and a body for entering free-form text, much like an email message. The body of the memo can be quite long, up to 32,000 characters.

Many other applications have places where you can enter notes of various kinds. You can enter notes during a call, as part of addresses or appointments, and even tasks have their own notes fields, so why do we need MemoPad? The simple answer is that it is used in all those situations that you run across where you can't or don't want to put notes in these other areas.

I've used memos to store driving directions, timesheet information, expenses, access codes, gift lists, and even recipes. I'm sure everyone has their own ways of using it as well, and over time I'm sure you will too.

MANAGING MEMOS

Of course, when you open MemoPad for the first time you will have no memos created and will need to create one. You can do this by clicking the New menu item. This will display the Edit Memo screen, shown in Figure 13.1, where you can enter the title and body of the memo. A title is the only piece of information that is required and you will not be allowed to save the memo without one.

When you are done creating the memo, clicking the Save menu item will save it and return you to the Memo List screen. Like most screens pressing the Escape key will exit the screen without saving. If you happen to have made changes, it will display a dialog asking if you want to save or discard the changes.

FIGURE 13.1
Creating a new memo.

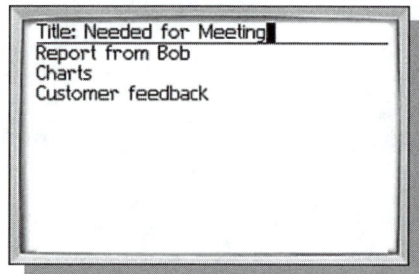

Now when you open the MemoPad application you will see the Memo List screen that lists the memos that have been created (see Figure 13.2).

FIGURE 13.2
The Memo List screen is similar in look and function to the Message List screen. You can search the list, select memos to view or edit, and delete memos.

If you do have a memo already created, you can edit it by scrolling the selection cursor in the Memo List screen to the memo you want to edit and clicking the Edit menu item to display the Edit Memo screen.

Memos can be deleted from the Memo List screen by scrolling the selection cursor to the memo and clicking the Delete menu item. Unlike many of the other applications, you can only delete memos from the Memo List screen and not in the Edit Memo screen.

You might have noticed the title of the Memo List screen is Find. That is because the MemoPad application has the same fast searching capabilities that the Address Book and Tasks applications do. Pressing a key causes the Memo List to hide all of the memos that do not have a word in the title that begins with that character or characters you typed. For instance pressing the letter T will show the memos "My Time" and "Tim's wish list," but hide "Matt's wish list." Like the other applications, pressing the Backspace key erases the search criteria one letter at a time, and pressing the Escape key removes the search criteria altogether.

Most of the time a memo will be small, at most one screen's worth of information. It is certainly possible to hold more information, however, and if you do make large memos, there will likely be a time when you want to search them.

Unfortunately, it is not possible to search all of the memos for some text in the body of a memo. It is only possible to search the body of a single memo. To do this, select the memo from the Memo List screen and open it by clicking the View menu item. Once the memo is open, click the Find menu item and enter the text to find into the Search For dialog, shown in Figure 13.3. Click the trackwheel to start the search.

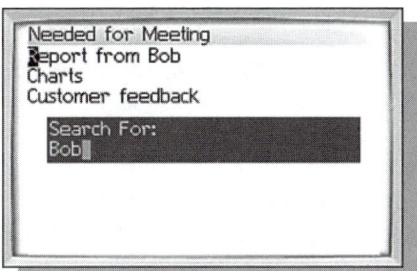

FIGURE 13.3
Searching a memo for text can only be done within a single memo, not the entire Memo List.

If the search criteria is found, the cursor will be placed at the beginning of the text on the screen. If the text is not visible already, the screen will be scrolled so that it is visible. You can continue searching by clicking the Find Next menu item again and again until no more occurrences of the text can be found. When this happens, a dialog box is shown briefly with the words "Not Found."

> **note** It is not possible to search a memo while the memo is being edited. The Find menu item is only available by selecting the memo and clicking the View menu item.

SETTING A CATEGORY

Memos can also be assigned and sorted into categories in version 4.0 of the handheld software. It works in exactly the same way for memos as it does for addresses. If you have not yet read about it, see the section titled "Understanding Categories" in Chapter 10 for more information.

MEMOPAD OPTIONS

Like most applications, MemoPad also has its own set of options that can be changed by opening the MemoPad Options screen. You can view this screen by clicking the Options menu item from the Memo List screen, as shown in Figure 13.4.

The only option available in this application is the Confirm Delete option. Like many of the other applications, deleting a memo causes a confirmation dialog to be shown if this option is set to Yes, which is the default. Changing this option to No will cause the confirmation dialog to not be shown when a memo is deleted.

FIGURE 13.4
The MemoPad options are pretty limited—there is only one choice.

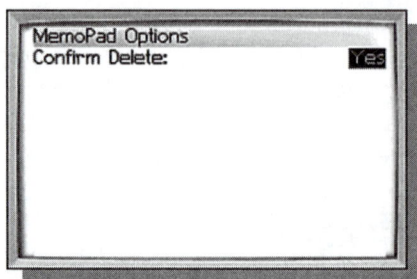

SETTING AN ALARM

The Alarm application is there in case you don't have or don't want to use an alarm clock for whatever reason. It essentially allows you to set an alarm to alert you at the same time every day. This application has some distinct advantages over a more traditional alarm clock that you may find in your hotel room or bedroom that can make this simple application really useful.

Opening the Alarm application shows the Alarm Configuration screen for configuring the Alarm (see Figure 13.5). The first field, Daily Alarm, is the On/Off button for the alarm. Changing this option to On causes the alarm to alert you when the next field, Time, is met. This, of course, is the time of the day when the alarm is supposed to go off. When the alarm goes off, you may have the option to Snooze it, meaning to silence the alarm for a short period of time and have it alert you again afterward. You can set a snooze time of 5 Minutes, 10 Minutes, 15 Minutes, or Off. This last option is something that makes this application smarter then almost any other alarm clock out there: If the Active on Weekends field is set to No, the daily alarm will not activate if the day is a Saturday or Sunday. I know none of the alarm clocks in my house can do this.

FIGURE 13.5
Setting the daily alarm can help keep you on time, and is even smart enough not to bother you on the weekend.

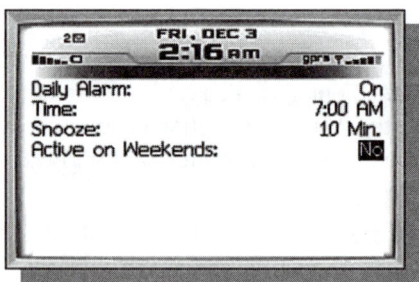

When the alarm goes off, its notification type is based on the profile you have set. So, for example, if you have the Default profile activated with the default settings, your alarm will vibrate and then play a tone when the time you set it for arrives. It also displays a dialog, shown in Figure 13.6, which requires you to dismiss it. If the snooze is set to something other than Off, there will also be a Snooze button. Clicking the Snooze button dismisses the dialog and causes the alarm to be reset to go off again in that amount of time.

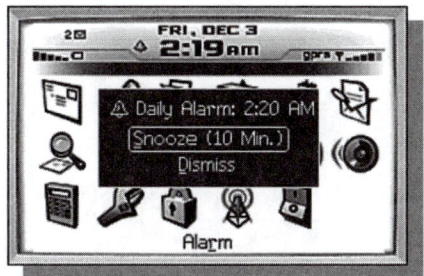

FIGURE 13.6
Click in the dialog to have the alarm let you roll over and snooze another 10 minutes (or whatever time you've set it for) before you hear from it again.

The current date and time is shown at the top of the Alarm Configuration screen so you can make sure the local time of the handheld is correct. It doesn't do any good to set the alarm when the time of the handheld is incorrect! If this is the case, you can jump directly to the Date/Time settings screen by clicking the Change Date/Time menu item. When that is done, you will once again see the Alarm Configuration screen.

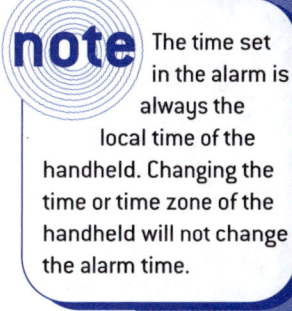

note The time set in the alarm is always the local time of the handheld. Changing the time or time zone of the handheld will not change the alarm time.

When the daily alarm is set, a small bell icon is added to the header of the main screen to indicate that it is set (see Figure 13.7).

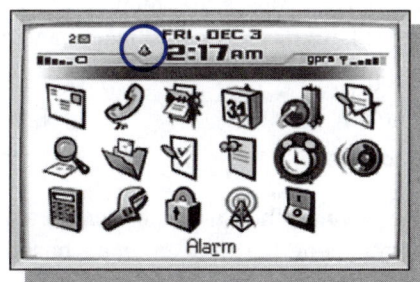

FIGURE 13.7
The bell icon indicates the alarm has been set.

USING THE CALCULATOR

The Calculator application is another one of those very simple and incredibly useful applications. It definitely takes some getting used to, but once you do, you will find yourself using it a lot. More than anything, it is just so handy to have it always on your hip.

If there is any application that doesn't look and feel like a BlackBerry application, this is it. Most of the other applications that we've looked at so far are text based and the screens are usually a collection of fields that display and collect text data. The Calculator application is mostly graphical however, and therefore most of the conventions we've seen so far do not apply here.

When you open the Calculator application, you see the screen, shown in Figure 13.8, with graphics and buttons that resemble a calculator like you might see on your desk.

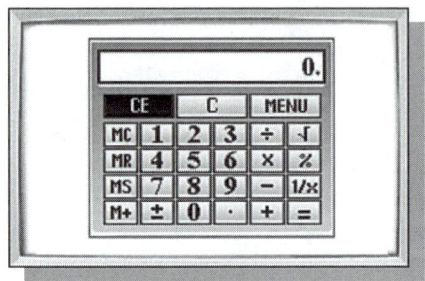

FIGURE 13.8
Here's a look at the Calculator application.

Notice that one of the buttons is shown in reversed colored text. This is the current selection cursor like we have seen before. Scrolling the trackwheel up and down moves the section cursor from one button to the next. Clicking the trackwheel causes the button to be pressed and whatever action on it to be taken.

For instance, if the 1 button is selected, clicking the trackwheel causes a 1 to be added to the display screen of the calculator.

Scrolling the trackwheel around to press buttons is time consuming and annoying. For this reason, each key on the calculator has a corresponding key on the keypad that will trigger the button. Of course pressing one of the keys with a number on it causes that number key to be pressed on the calculator. A few other keys have standard mappings that can be listed as well.

- \+ for addition
- – for subtraction
- * for multiplication
- / for division
- Enter for equals
- . for decimal point

> **tip**
> Although there is not a backspace button on the calculator screen, pressing the Backspace key causes the number in the rightmost position on the display to be erased.

Most of the other keys on the Calculator screen also have keys on the keypad that trigger them, but they can vary based on the devices. Below is a listing for the 7200 series of devices.

- T key for Clear/Erase
- Y key for Clear
- H key for Memory Clear
- J key for Memory Remember
- K key for Memory Set
- L key for Memory +
- B key for percent
- V key for square root
- Q key for sign change (+/–)

> **7100** Because of the smaller keyboard, only the shortcuts using the asterisk, period, and Enter keys work on the 7100 series handhelds. The others must be selected by moving the cursor to the button on the screen and clicking the trackwheel.

Because the trackwheel needs to be clicked to activate any of the buttons on the calculator, the standard mechanisms of clicking the trackwheel to display a menu cannot be done. Instead, there is a MENU button on the calculator and clicking the trackwheel while this button is selected causes the menu to be displayed.

KEEPING PASSWORDS SAFE WITH PASSWORD KEEPER

A large set of conversion operations are available through the menu to convert to and from English and Metric systems of measurement. These operations are done just like any other operation is done on the calculator in that you must first enter the number to work with, and then select the operation. For instance, in order to convert 5 inches to centimeters, you would first click the 5 button, then the MENU button to display the menu. Click the To Metric menu item to display another menu of operations that convert from English to Metric, then click the in->cm menu item. Notice that the number in the calculator display has changed to 12.7, indicating that 5 inches is about equal to 12.7 centimeters.

> **note** Unfortunately, there is no keypad key that is the same as pressing the MENU button on the calculator. You must scroll the trackwheel to it each time.

KEEPING PASSWORDS SAFE WITH PASSWORD KEEPER

Password Keeper is a new application that comes with version 4.0 of the handheld software. It provides a place to securely store the passwords that you use in your everyday activities.

When you first open the Password Keeper application, you must set a password that you will use to open the application later. Figure 13.9 shows the dialog used to enter the initial password. As with many password creation screens, you must enter the new password twice in order to protect against misspellings. Click the OK button to set the password.

FIGURE 13.9
When you first open Password Keeper, you must enter a password.

From then on out, when you launch the Password Keeper application, you must enter that same password into the dialog that appears and click the OK button to open the application. If you want to change the main password to Password Keeper again, you can do so by clicking the Change Password menu item from the Password List screen.

Once you get past the password prompt, you will see the Password List screen. This screen lists the records that store the passwords you have created. Figure 13.10 shows an example with two entries that have been created.

FIGURE 13.10
The Password List screen shows the passwords you are storing.

CREATING A NEW PASSWORD RECORD

When you create a new password record for Password Keeper to store, there are several fields of information available. To create a new password record, click the New menu item from the Password List screen and you will see the screen shown in Figure 13.11.

FIGURE 13.11
Creating a new password record.

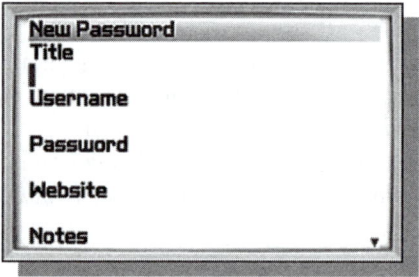

> **tip** Storing records with blank Password fields kind of defeats the purpose of the Password Keeper application, so even if you do have accounts with a blank password, take this opportunity to change them and store the passwords in the Password Keeper.

Most of these fields are optional and are for your reference only. In fact, the only required field is Title, because the title is what is shown in the Password List screen. This means that you can have a record with a blank password.

The Username field is only for your reference, but sometimes remembering your username is as hard as remembering your password, so it is a good idea to enter it as well.

The Password field is where you can enter the password you want to store. Oftentimes we choose passwords that are easy to remember, and these are usually also not very secure passwords. Another common behavior is to use the same password on many different accounts, and this is also not very secure.

Password Keeper has the ability to create random passwords that are more secure than ones you might choose on your own. These random passwords are often hard to remember, but then that is the benefit to using the Password Keeper application in the first place. If you want to create a random password, click the Random Password menu item. This will create a new random password and replace any password you may have in the Password field. If you create a new random password for each system you have an account on, your accounts on those systems will be very well protected. Be sure that you change the password at the site where the account is held as well!

The last two fields are also there just for your own reference. If you do enter a website into the Website field, though, scrolling to that field will enable a Get Link menu item that will launch your default browser and go to that website.

USING PASSWORD KEEPER TO HELP YOU LOG IN

If you access password-protected websites using your handheld, Password Keeper can help you login to those websites by copying your password to the clipboard. Then when you launch the browser, you simply have to paste the contents of the clipboard into the password field of the login and you don't have to worry about trying to type in those long random passwords. To do this, scroll to the desired password record and click the Copy To Clipboard menu item.

PASSWORD KEEPER OPTIONS

Password Keeper has quite a few options that you can change to configure how the application works. To change them, click the Option menu item from the Password List screen and you will see the screen in Figure 13.12.

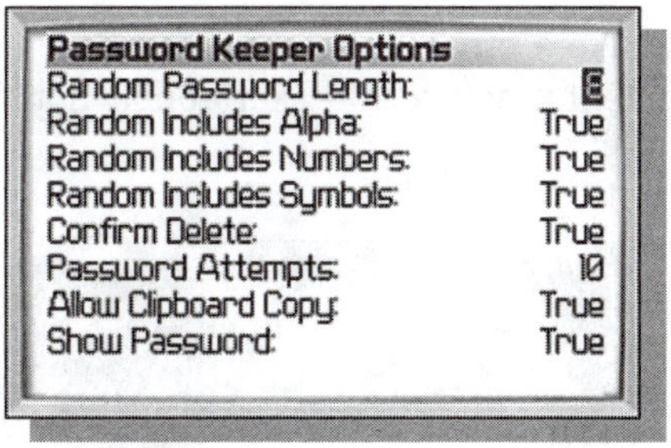

caution Because your passwords can be saved to the clipboard, you could inadvertently paste that password anywhere, including an email message. One thing you can do to protect yourself is to go back into Password Keeper and click the Clear Clipboard menu item. This will clear the password from the clipboard and help to prevent that from happening.

FIGURE 13.12
Password Keeper options.

The first four options define how the random passwords are created when you use the Random Password menu item. The first option is the length of the new password. You can have as few as 4 characters and as many as 16. Most systems require at least 6 characters to use be used, but longer passwords are always more secure.

The next three options determine what kinds of characters are used to make a new password. If you want random passwords to include alphabetic characters (A–Z), the Random Includes Alpha option should be True. If you want random passwords to include numbers as well, the Random Includes Numbers option should be True. Lastly, if you want random passwords to include symbols (such as #, !, %, and others) the Random Includes Symbols option should be True. As a general rule, the more varied your selection of characters is in your password, the more secure it will be.

As with many other applications, if you do not want to be prompted when you delete a record, change the Confirm Delete option to be False.

The Password Attempts field lets you specify how many times you can enter a wrong password when you open the Password Keeper application. If you enter the password incorrectly the maximum number of times, the password database will be erased. 10 is probably a good number, but you may want to set it to as low as 3.

The last two options affect features that I've already discussed. Copying the password to the clipboard can make things easier if you are using the browser on the handheld to access a web page. It also is a security weakness that you may not want to allow. If you don't want to allow it, change the Allow Clipboard Copy option to be False.

Similarly, viewing or editing a password record shows the password on those screens. Other people may be able to see your password by looking over your shoulder, and thus showing the password on the screen is a security weakness. If you want to mask the password with stars, change the Show Password option to False.

PLAYING BRICKBREAKER

Everyone needs to take a break every now and then to relax with a little mindless entertainment. The BrickBreaker application fills this need well (see Figure 13.13).

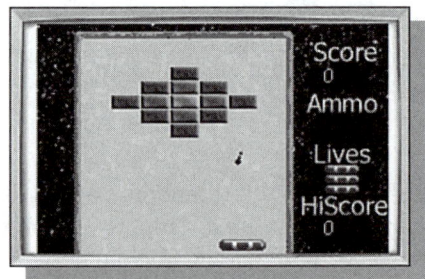

FIGURE 13.13
Playing BrickBreaker can be addictive—watch out.

The goal of BrickBreaker is to clear the bricks from each level by breaking them with a small ball that bounces around the screen. Over time, the ball will move faster and faster, making the game more challenging the longer you go at it. At the bottom of the screen is a paddle that you use to keep the ball from falling off the screen. You can control the ball somewhat by making the ball hit the paddle in different places. When the ball hits closer to the edge of the paddle, it will bounce with a shallower angle and go faster. When the ball hits closer to the center of the paddle, it will bounce with a steeper angle and slow down.

Some bricks require multiple hits before they are broken, and in higher levels, some bricks cannot be broken at all. Fortunately there are some power-ups that will help you out along the way. These power-ups fall from predetermined bricks when they are broken. Generally only one power-up can be active at one time, but there are a few that work in addition to any existing power-up effects. Below is a list of the power-ups that are available.

- **Slow**—This is the most common power-up. It reduces the ball speed to its slowest speed. This power-up does not remove the effects of the currently active power-up.
- **Multi**—This power-up causes the ball to break into four balls. This is nice for clearing an area of bricks, if you can keep them all in the air. This power-up does not remove the effects of the currently active power-up.
- **Laser**—The Laser power-up adds two laser cannons to the paddle that you can fire by pressing the Space key. Two laser hits are the same as one hit by the ball.
- **Gun**—This power-up adds a missile launcher to the paddle and gives you three missiles to shoot. You can shoot a missile by pressing the Space key. When a missile hits, it completely destroys the brick, no matter how many hits are required. A missile will even destroy a brick that cannot otherwise be destroyed by the ball.
- **Long**—The Long power-up causes your paddle to become extra long, making it easier to make sure it is under the ball. The Long paddle is exceptionally helpful when you have the Multi power-up active.
- **Flip**—The Flip power-up causes the paddle to move in the opposite direction than it had previously. This power-up tends to be more harmful then helpful.
- **Catch**—This power-up causes the ball to get stuck to the paddle for a short period of time each time it hits. This allows you time to move the paddle to a position that may be more beneficial once the ball is released. You can release the ball by pressing the Space key.
- **1-Up**—This power-up gives you an extra life. This power-up removes any existing power-up effects, but is always worth it.

- **Wrap**—This power-up is new to version 4.0 of the handheld software. Normally the paddle will not move past the wall, but with this power-up, moving past the wall causes the paddle to wrap around to the other side of the screen.

- **Bomb**—This power-up is new to version 4.0 of the handheld software. It turns the ball into a bomb that will explode when it hits a brick. When the bomb explodes, it counts as a "hit" to each of the surrounding bricks as well as the brick that the ball actually hit.

There are many more games and utility applications available from third-party vendors. See Chapter 13, "Other Applications on Your BlackBerry," for more details on how to do this and where to find them.

Chapter 14

FINDING AND INSTALLING THIRD-PARTY APPLICATIONS

BLACKBERRY BASICS:
- Add third-party applications to your handheld to make it an even more useful tool for you.
- Applications can be small productivity applications and games, but also can be enterprisewide applications that integrate with your current enterprise systems.
- Make your own applications using a free tool and the Java programming language.
- www.Handango.com, www.PDATopSoft.com, and www.RimRoad.com are three of the best websites for finding applications.

Now that you've had a chance to learn about all the applications that come with your handheld, you might be surprised to learn that you can add applications that other people have written. These are collectively called third-party applications because they have been written by someone other than Research In Motion (RIM), the company that makes the BlackBerry.

WHAT KIND OF APPLICATIONS RUN ON A BLACKBERRY?

Now you can't go downloading just any ol' application and think it will install on a BlackBerry. The fact is that only special applications can be loaded and run on your handheld.

You may have seen the acronym J2ME used somewhere in conjunction with BlackBerry before. J2ME stands for Java 2 Micro Edition. It is a standard for Java that is focused on being able to create applications for devices that have small screens, slow processors, and small amounts of memory—such as handhelds, cell phones, and embedded processors. Basically stuff that's not a full personal computer.

Within the J2ME specification, there are several profiles defined that further refine the specification to a specific class of devices. One of the most common profiles is *MIDP*, which stands for *Mobile Information Device Profile*.

BlackBerry handhelds can run applications written with J2ME for MIDP, or midlets as they are commonly called. However a conversion process is required. The conversion process requires a developer tool or help from your BlackBerry Enterprise Server administrator. For these reasons, I will not go over the specifics in this book.

Unfortunately, J2ME and MIDP just don't provide enough details to make the complex applications that many people want. Because of this, Research In Motion (RIM) created a set of BlackBerry-specific extensions to J2ME that provides more functionality and better integration to enable these complex applications. However, applications that use these extensions cannot be used on any other devices. These are true BlackBerry applications because they are written and designed specifically for BlackBerry handhelds.

Generally, you will find that BlackBerry applications are more useful and better looking than pure midlets. There are a lot more midlets than BlackBerry applications though, so a midlet may be the only way to get that specific functionality you are looking for.

FINDING THIRD-PARTY APPLICATIONS

When it comes to finding third-party applications, the best place to start is on the BlackBerry.com website at https://www.blackberry.com/ThirdParty/search.jsp. This page allows you to search for applications written by BlackBerry Alliance Partners—companies that have signed up as partners with RIM.

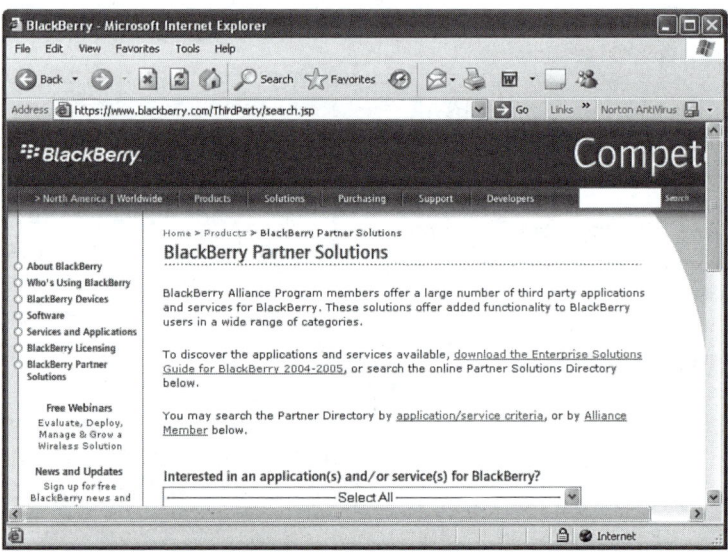

FIGURE 14.1
The BlackBerry.com website is the place to start when looking for applications.

At this site you can search for applications in a specific industry or vertical market. The applications and providers listed here will be those that are focused on providing a solution to your enterprise in some area, such as improving field service support by allowing field service workers to view trouble tickets remotely for instance.

There are many other applications and developers that are not listed on this page though, and these are the ones that are more difficult to find. The next two sections list some websites where you can find them.

WEBSITES OFFERING BLACKBERRY APPLICATIONS

There are just a few websites that have good selections of applications for BlackBerry handhelds. This is because there are proportionally fewer BlackBerry handhelds out there, compared to other classes of handheld devices, and proportionally fewer developers for it.

My favorite website for BlackBerry applications is www.Handango.com. Handango offers applications for a wide variety of handheld devices, and powers the search engines behind several other websites such as tucows, Dell, and Compaq. When it comes to BlackBerry applications, their listings detail which handheld models are supported by each application, which can be a real benefit for those users who aren't very experienced with finding applications that work for them. Because Handango.com has a storefront, it is the only place where you can find certain applications that require payment to register them.

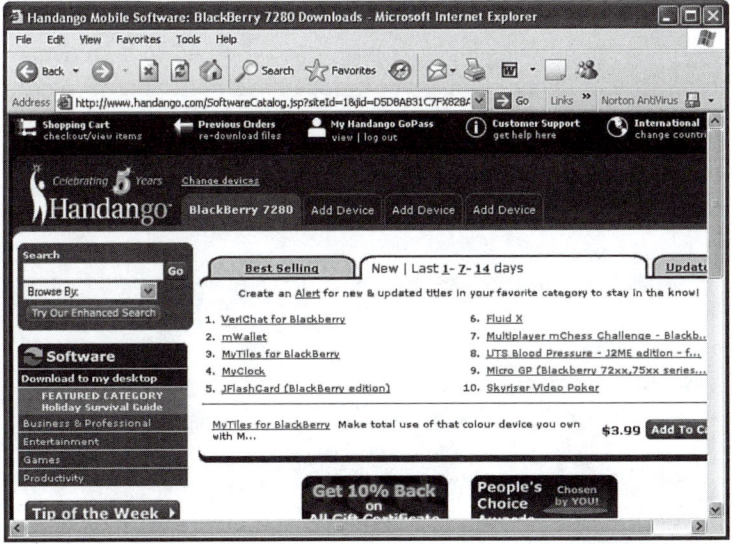

FIGURE 14.2
The Handango.com website.

A great website offering software for a variety of handhelds, including BlackBerry, is www.PDATopSoft.com. Like Handango, it sorts applications based on handheld model, though some are listed under different names and therefore are not grouped together in the list. PDATopSoft is newer to the BlackBerry market than Handango, so its selection is smaller and less cluttered.

FIGURE 14.3
The PDATopSoft.com website.

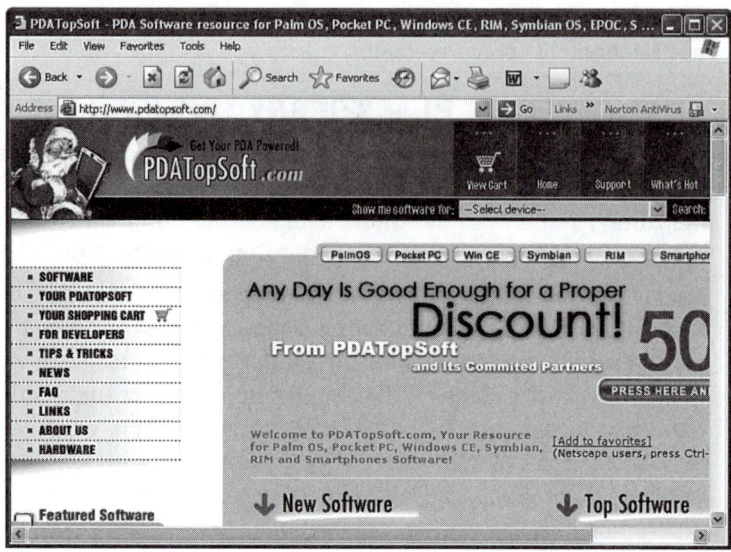

Another nice website is RIMRoad.com. RIMRoad is the BlackBerry arm of the PDAStreet.com network of websites. It is primarily intended to be a community website with news and lively forums, but it does have a section devoted to free downloads that is up-to-date and well-stocked. Be sure to look at the New Software list because this website does not sort the downloads for each device and some of the entries are old enough that they will not work on most current devices.

FIGURE 14.4
The RIMRoad.com website.

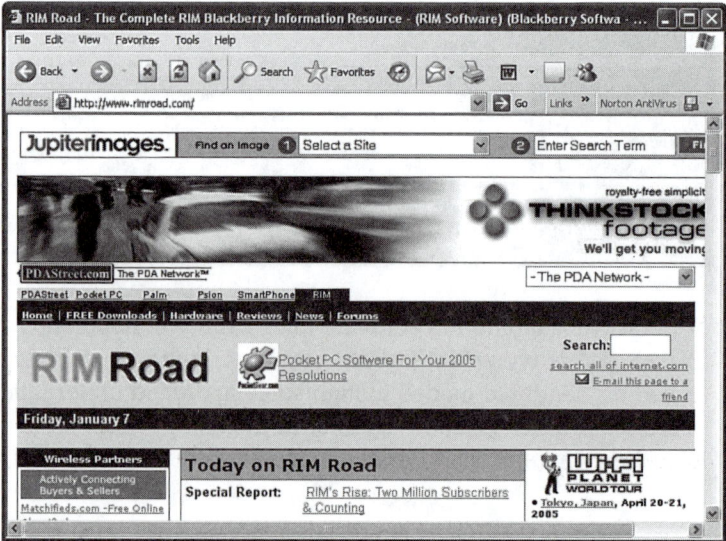

Of course many applications are listed at all three of these sites, but it is definitely worth it to check out all of them and to check back frequently to see what's new.

HELPFUL THIRD-PARTY APPLICATIONS

There are really two kinds of applications that you might want to install on your handheld—productivity applications that help you do something better, and games that help you get through that two-hour layover at the airport. Personally, I like games, but I have to admit that the productivity applications do some pretty neat things. Besides, if you wanted a gaming system you would have bought a GameBoy Advanced and not a BlackBerry.

PRODUCTIVITY APPLICATIONS

The following sections describe a few productivity applications that I find to be interesting and useful. They aren't in any particular order.

POCKETMAC FOR BLACKBERRY

If you use an Apple Macintosh, you have probably already noticed the lack of any Mac support on the BlackBerry CD. Without a Mac version of the Desktop Manager, you are already at a disadvantage when it comes to setting up your handheld. One application is there to help you out. PocketMac for BlackBerry can synchronize your Address Book, Calendar, and other PIM information as well as do backups and restores for the Mac user.

URL: http://www.pocketmac.net/products/pmblackberry/indexrim.html

Price: $29.95

Trial: No

REQWIRELESS WEBVIEWER

We've already gone over using the web browser that comes with your handheld in a previous chapter. If your handheld isn't able to browse HTML-based pages, you may want to look at this software. The Reqwireless WebViewer is a bigger, better web browser that supports HTML pages, cookies, JavaScript, and nearly everything else you would expect from a desktop browser. If you need more from a web browser, this is your answer.

URL: http://www.reqwireless.com/webviewer.html

Price: $29.99

Trial: Yes

> **note** Once you have an application downloaded, you will likely find that it has been packaged and compressed. If this is the case, you will need to uncompress it first. When it is uncompressed you should see at least two files, one with a .ALX extension and one with a .COD extension. These two file work together to describe the application for the Desktop Manager. The .ALX file is a small text file that describes the .COD file, which is the file that will eventually be loaded onto your handheld. Some of the software comes with an installer executable. In cases like this, the installer usually takes care of registering the application with the Desktop Manager Application Loader, a process which is described in a section later in this chapter titled "Installing a Third-Party Application."

IM+ MOBILE INSTANT MESSENGER FOR BLACKBERRY

For all you instant messaging addicts out there, now you can take your IMs with you as you travel. IM+ works with all the major instant messaging services such as AOL, MSN, and Yahoo!, as well as others.

URL: http://www.shapeservices.com/eng/im/implus.php

Price: $44.95

Trial: No

IDOKORRO MOBILE SSH FOR BLACKBERRY

If your job is to administer networked computers, then SSH needs no introduction, and you probably spend a good deal of time in your SSH client. Idokorro Mobile SSH is an SSH client for your handheld that connects directly to SSH and Telnet servers and provides vt100 terminal emulation. It is somewhat slow, as you might expect from a device with such small bandwidth, but quite usable.

URL: http://www.idokorro.com/imssh.html

Price: $195

Trial: No

MYTIP 2.0

This handy little utility can be used to compute tax, tip, and to split the bill at the restaurant. Great for those on the go!

URL: http://www.pdatopsoft.com/software/item.php?pid=4617&

Price: $3.99

Trial: No

ENGLISH DICTIONARY FOR BLACKBERRY

Whether you need a pure dictionary, or one that converts to various languages (including Spanish, French, and German), Beiks is the place to go. They also have several professional and religious reference books as well!

URL: http://www.beiks.com/rim/showprod.asp?prodid=494

Price: $19.95

Trial: No

EXPENSEMINDER

Keeping track of expenses is always a chore, but this application lets you enter your expense items into your handheld as you go. It shows a running total and can email the reports to you as an attachment that can be opened in Excel.

URL: http://www.handango.com/PlatformProductDetail.jsp?productId=119517

Price: $20

Trial: Yes

GAMES FOR YOUR BLACKBERRY

Here is the fun part. Everyone needs a good selection of games on their handheld for those rare moments when you don't have, or want, anything to do.

WHITE NINJA

Now you might expect to get some sort of ninja fighting game with a title like White Ninja. No, this game looks and feels just like Pac-Man except the guy is collecting gemstones and wearing a red headband. The graphics here are very nice and the controls are pretty easy to use, though nothing beats a joystick.

URL: http://www.berrygames.net/blackberry_games.html

Price: $9.95

Trial: Yes

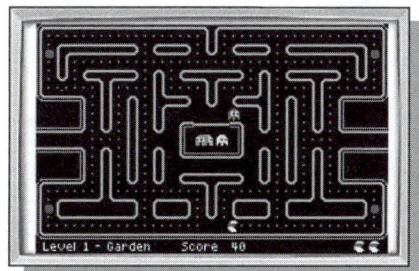

FIGURE 14.5
White Ninja—a Pac-Man throwback for your BlackBerry.

STREET RACER

Here is another game with great graphics. You are a car thief running from the cops through the streets of LA. If one catches you, your car stealing days are over! This game uses the thumbwheel to steer the car across the lanes as you dodge cars and other emergency vehicles. The load time is a bit rough, but the game looks very nice.

URL: http://www.pdatopsoft.com/RIM/StreetRacer

Price: $6.99

Trial: Yes

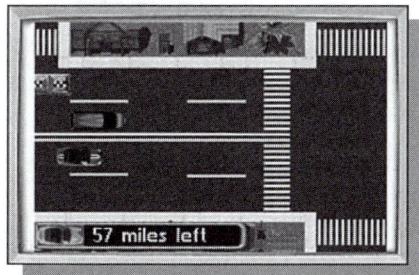

FIGURE 14.6
Street Racer—not quite Grand Theft Auto, but it'll get you where you want to go.

LINKS SCORECARD

Not all entertainment happens on your handheld. For you golf enthusiasts out there, this golf scorecard application will be a great addition to your handheld. In addition to keeping track of the score for a game, you can chart how well you are doing over time.

URL: http://www.concretesoftware.com/product/linksscorecard.shtml

Price: $9.99

Trial: No

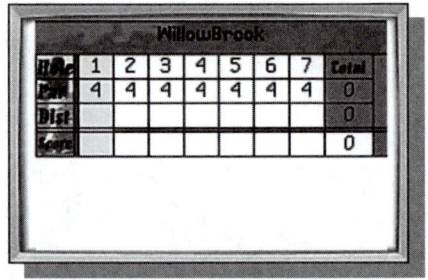

FIGURE 14.7
Links Scorecard.

OUTROAD

If you prefer to race on a track and take the corners at high speed, then OutRoad is for you. Its smooth graphics and sharp color make it stand out. While you race the clock on one of several tracks, you also have to dodge other cars and still keep your car on the track—not an easy feat!

URL: http://www.handango.com/PlatformProductDetail.jsp?productId=140306

Price: $9.95

Trial: No

FIGURE 14.8
Just try to beat the clock as you dodge cars and take sharp corners in OutRoad.

CARD GAMES PACK ONE

Card Games has five popular Vegas style card games in one Application—Blackjack, Poker, Solitaire, Red Dog, and HiLo. The graphics and animations are nice and it's easy to use.

HELPFUL THIRD-PARTY APPLICATIONS

URL: http://www.javatekmedia.com/cardPackOne.jsp
Price: $19.99
Trial: No

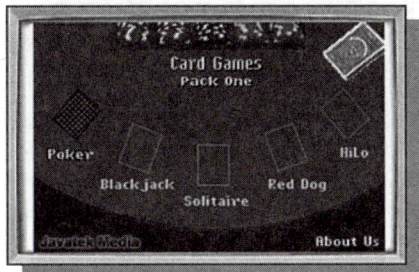

FIGURE 14.9
Card Game Pack One is perfect for you card game lovers.

ACES TEXAS HOLD'EM—NO LIMIT

If you are into Texas Hold'em poker, this is the game for you. Play against five other computer controlled players where the sky's the limit on the bets. The options and extras include changing out the computer players' skill and tracking your success over time, making this game a sure bet.

URL: http://www.concretesoftware.com/product/athnolimit.shtml
Price: $9.99
Trial: No

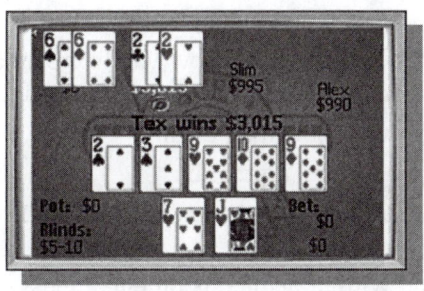

FIGURE 14.10
Compete against five computer players in Aces Texas Hold'em—No Limit to be the poker champion.

KARPOV X3D CHESS

For all you chess enthusiasts out there, you will be glad to know that you can play while on the go. You can play against the computer, or play against another person by sharing your handheld. The view changes for each player as you pass it back and forth.

URL: http://www.miforum.com/3dchess.asp
Price: $9.95
Trial: No

FIGURE 14.11
Take your love for chess on the road with Karpov X3D Chess.

CREATING YOUR OWN APPLICATIONS

If the idea of creating your own applications for the BlackBerry is appealing to you, then this section is for you. How to develop applications for a BlackBerry is a book topic all by itself; this section is simply to provide a few pointers to let you know what to do to get started.

TOOLS YOU NEED TO DOWNLOAD

The first thing to do is to visit the BlackBerry Developers site at http://www.blackberry.com/developers/index.shtml. There you can find instructions on how to download and install the BlackBerry Java Development Environment (JDE). The JDE is a Java-based Interactive Development Environment (IDE) similar to Microsoft Developer Studio. With it, you can create and package applications for the BlackBerry. Of course you have to know the Java programming language to do so.

The latest versions of the JDE allow you to create applications that do a lot of different things. Some of the most interesting ones are

- Interacting with incoming email.
- Sending email from a program.
- Accessing data in the Address Book, Calendar, and Tasks applications.
- Interacting with attachments on email messages including providing a viewer.
- Sending and receiving wireless communication via HTTP or sockets.

note It is also possible to download an application *over the air (OTA)*. That is to say that the application is installed onto your handheld wirelessly. Some websites offer OTA downloading, or you can also use the BES to install the application OTA. In either case, you do not need to connect the handheld to your desktop computer nor do you have to run the Desktop Manager.

INSTALLING A THIRD-PARTY APPLICATION

After you download one of these nifty applications, you need to get it onto your device. Fortunately, this is easily done through the Desktop Manager.

When the Desktop Manager is launched, you are shown a screen with icons at the bottom that each represent different operations. This screen is shown in Figure 14.12. One of these icons is the Application Loader, and as the name implies, double-clicking this icon launches a wizard that will help you load a new application onto your handheld.

FIGURE 14.12
You can launch the Desktop Manager by clicking its icon in the BlackBerry group of your Start menu.

The first step in the wizard is a welcome screen, shown in Figure 14.13. One of the important things on this screen is a reminder to make sure your handheld is plugged into the computer through the serial or USB cable that came with your device. Click the Next button to continue.

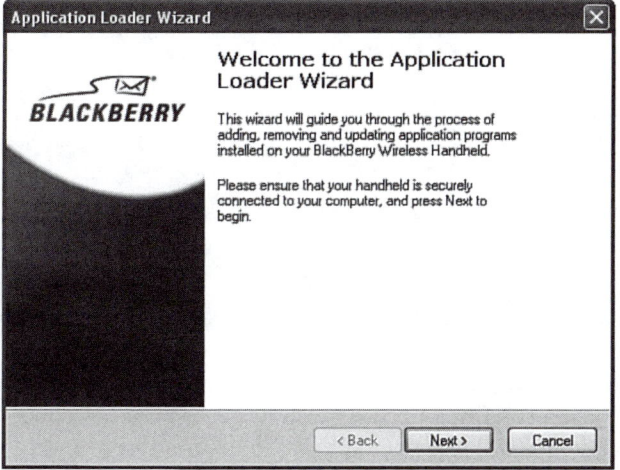

FIGURE 14.13
The first step of the Application Loader wizard is simply a reminder to connect your device.

The next screen should be shown only briefly. This screen, shown in Figure 14.14, is shown while the Desktop Manager is communicating with your handheld. During this time, the Desktop Manager is finding out what applications are already loaded onto your handheld. Click the Next button to continue.

After the Desktop Manager has successfully communicated with your handheld, the wizard displays a screen that lists all of the applications on your handheld (see Figure 14.15). Most likely, if you don't have any other applications already loaded, the list will be empty.

FIGURE 14.14
The communicating phase of the Application Loader wizard.

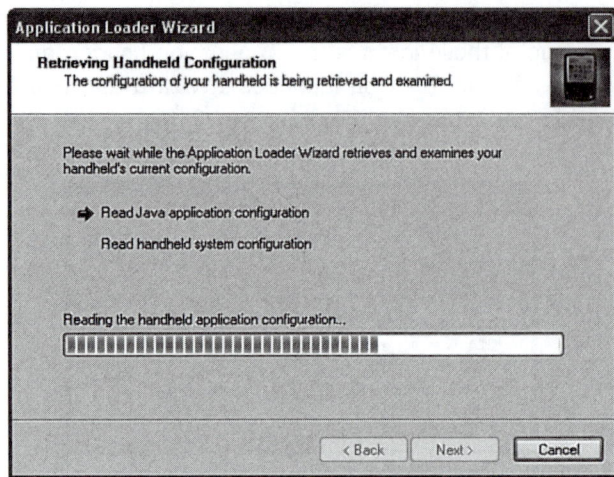

FIGURE 14.15
This screen of the Application Loader wizard will show any applications you've previously installed.

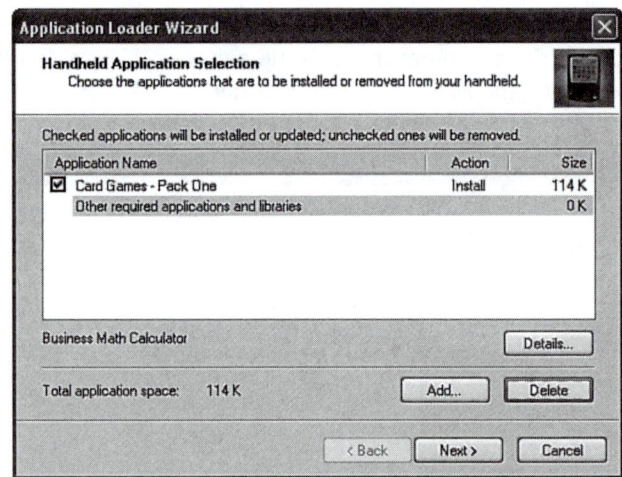

> **note** There is only one install of the Desktop Manager software for all models of handhelds. Because of this, you do not have a copy of the BlackBerry software that is already installed on your handheld also installed on your computer. The Desktop Manager will still load other applications, but it also displays the message that "No system software is found for your handheld" in the Application List.

To add other applications to this Application List, click the Add button and choose the .ALX file for the application using the file chooser dialog. The Application List dialog should now be updated to include the file. The Action column for the selected application now contains the phrase "Install" to indicate that it will be installed.

Later on, if you want to remove this application from your handheld, all you have to do it run the Application Loader wizard again and at this step uncheck the check box next to the application you wish to remove. Click the Next button to continue.

The next screen is a confirmation screen that outlines in simple terms the actions that will be performed if you continue (see Figure 14.16). Click the Finish button to start the loading process.

INSTALLING A THIRD-PARTY APPLICATION 203

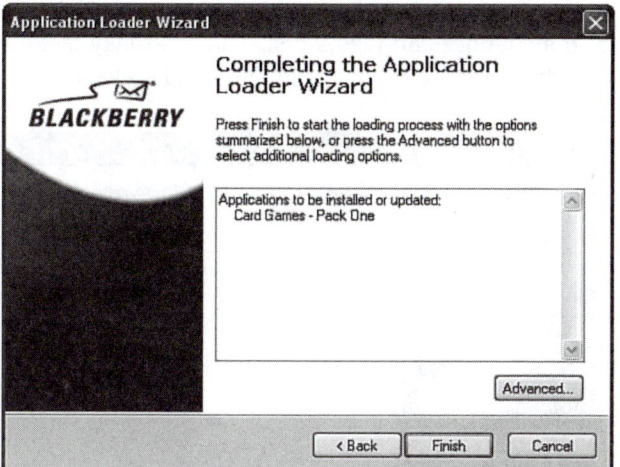

FIGURE 14.16
The confirmation phase of the Application Loader wizard.

The loading screen should display only briefly while the Desktop Manager communicates with your handheld and loads the new application onto it (see Figure 14.17).

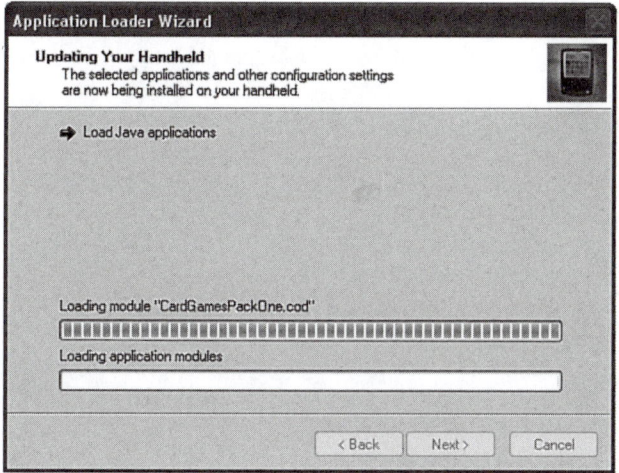

FIGURE 14.17
The loading phase of the Application Loader wizard.

If the application fails to load at this point, you'll receive a message saying "No Additional Applications found for your handheld." You most likely have an older version of the Desktop Manager that requires the BlackBerry Software be installed, and most likely you do not have that software installed.

If this is the case, the best thing to do is to download and install the latest version of the Desktop Manager. At the time of this writing, it is version 3.6 Service Pack 3, and it can be downloaded by clicking the Service Packs link on the web page at http://www.blackberry.com/support/index.shtml.

Finally, the confirmation screen is shown to let you know that everything was installed correctly, as shown in Figure 14.18. At this time the handheld will be reset so that the changes can take effect. The reset may last a minute or so, but when it is done, the new application should be available.

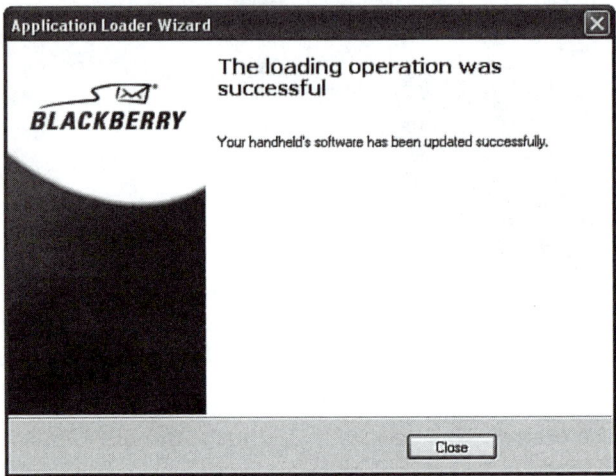

FIGURE 14.18
Confirmation is given when the installation is completed.

Part VI
APPENDIXES

A Considering an Upgrade?

B BlackBerry Behind the Scenes

Appendix A

CONSIDERING AN UPGRADE?

This section is for everyone out there who currently has a BlackBerry handheld and is thinking of upgrading to one of the new 7100 models. You may be asking yourself if there are enough differences to make it worthwhile, or you may be asking yourself if you will like the new form factor. Of course, I can't completely answer those questions for you, but I will share my observations, thoughts, and concerns.

I've had a 7280 for more than a year. Like many people, I wondered whether I would like a 7100 and whether I should upgrade or not. Luckily, I've had an opportunity to use a 7100v for a couple of weeks to get a feel for how they work, and while I have not yet decided whether to upgrade, I do have a better feeling for how I might like the 7100.

COMPARING THE DEVICES AS PHONES

Chances are that you have a 7200, 7500, or 7700 model handheld. There are a lot of different specific models in each of these series of handhelds, but generally the differences are on the inside in terms of the wireless networks that they support.

These devices were designed to be like a PDA that happens to also have a phone in it. As a result, they are wide, have a larger screen, and have a keypad with keys for every letter of the alphabet. Because of this, however, using the phone is awkward at first. You generally get used to it, but if you have ever passed your handheld to someone else to use the phone, you've seen their puzzled looks as they try to figure out how to place a call or even how to end a call.

The 7100 models take the opposite approach. They look and feel like phones that also happen to have PDA functionality. Using the phone is much more intuitive and doesn't feel as awkward when you hold it to your ear. It has a few more keys than a traditional cell phone, but these don't confuse a new user and the use of the common Begin Call and End Call buttons make it much easier for a new user to use. Of course, as a person used to the older style, I still find myself pushing the ESC button to end the call instead of pressing the End Call button.

Of course, it is also worth noting that the 7100 series handhelds are the only handhelds that support all four mobile phone bands used commonly in the world. If you need a BlackBerry that can work in this way, then the 7100 is the only real choice.

COMPARING THE DEVICES AS PDAS

The software on both devices is basically the same, if not exactly the same. If you already have the 4.0 software on your handheld, you won't notice any differences. If you are still using an older version of the handheld software, you will notice a few differences, but they are minor and don't really factor into a comparison of the handhelds. Of course, using a PDA depends very much on entering data, which is different and will be discussed separately.

LET'S TALK ABOUT FORM FACTOR

The biggest difference is the size and shape of the new 7100 handhelds compared to the other models mentioned previously. As I said, the 7100s are slimmer, about 2/3 as wide as my 7280, but just as tall and just as thick. That small change, however, is noticeable in both appearance and feel. Figure A.1 shows how the devices differ in size.

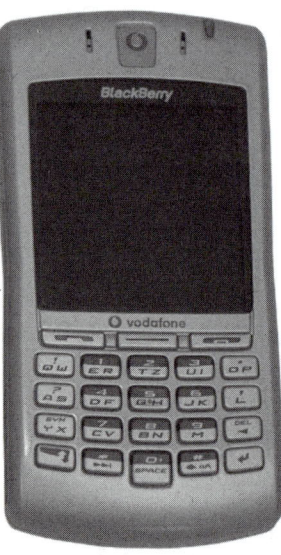

FIGURE A.1
A 7280 and 7100v side by side to show the size difference.

I've always felt sort of awkward using my 7280 as a phone. Because of its wide size it just didn't feel right as a phone. I also felt like people had to look twice when they saw me using it because it looks look like I'm talking into my shoe or something equally unusual. Of course, I got used to it and I think they did too as more and more people use BlackBerry handhelds, but I could never quite shake the feeling that it just wasn't a phone.

The 7100 changes this. It looks like a phone. It feels like a phone. In fact, unless you look closely, you barely notice that it is more than just a phone. Of course, that ruins the "Hey look at me! I'm cool and use a BlackBerry" aspect of it, but I don't think people will mind.

In general, I like how the 7100 feels in my hand. It's easier to hold and more comfortable than my 7280. I also don't feel like it will slip out of my hand as easily.

One thing I do notice, however, is that the trackwheel and the ESC button are positioned lower on the side, and this bothers me. On my 7280, my thumb could rest against the side and not have to be bent in order to use the trackwheel, and the ESC button was just under the joint in my thumb making it easy to press. Figure A.2 shows the slight difference in position of the trackwheel and Escape button.

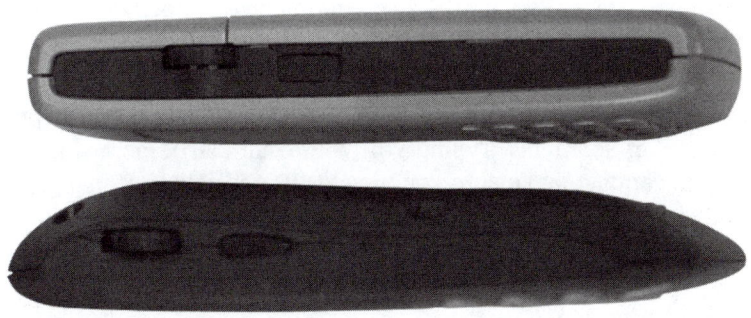

FIGURE A.2
A 7280 and 7100v side by side to show the position of the trackwheel.

The trackwheel is also slightly depressed into the side and this makes it harder to click because my thumb is pressing against the side of the handheld as well as the trackwheel. As a result, I feel like I have to use the tip of my thumb to click the trackwheel. Because of this, and because it is lower on the side, it is not as comfortable to me.

JUST HOW HARD IS IT TO USE THAT KEYPAD?

The new smaller keypad is the single biggest difference and the thing that made me wonder if I would like using a 7100. I read the literature about how there was this software called SureType that was there to figure out what you really meant when you typed something. My reaction was "Yeah, I saw that five years ago and it didn't work so well."

Well, now I've had a chance to use it, and I have to say that it really does work pretty well. There are a few more keys on the keypad than those phones had five years ago, which means there are only two letters per key instead of three. This helps reduce the set of possible matches which makes the guesses more accurate.

The letters are still organized in the traditional QWERTY arrangement, so it is still easy to find the keys as well. On the phones five years ago, the letters were arranged using the telephone style, which was alphabetically ordered and that made it a lot harder to type.

There are still times when the software doesn't guess correctly, however. Usually simply erasing the word to the point where the guess was incorrect will cause it to guess again using the other possible letters and fix the problem. You always have to be on alert, however, and check to make sure it has guessed your word correctly and I find this to be annoying. Of course, you can choose MultiTap and disable the software, but I think this is annoying as well.

I've noticed that when you are using common words, the guesses are normally correct. The longer the word, the better your chances are of having the correct guess. I don't think I've ever had an incorrect guess for a word more than six characters long, but small words are guessed wrong often enough that you really have to be careful. For instance, typing PAT might guess PAY or typing NUT will likely guess BUT. The software does learn, though, which is nice. It only took one time of me correcting BULL to BILL for the software to guess correctly from then on out. The internal dictionary also takes into account the Address Book, so the names of people in your Address Book will usually be guessed correctly.

The one area where the software doesn't work so well is when you are typing slang, abbreviations, or acronyms. Typing YUR will result in TIE most of the time. Of course you can just make sure you type YOUR and this is probably better anyway, but you get the point.

The last area where things can really go awry is when you have some kind of typo. Accidentally pressing the keys out of order or accidentally not pressing a key will often cause the software to make some pretty odd guesses. Lets face it: We all make typos and half the time we don't fix them because the intended word is still clear. Saying "We ned some hep" is still pretty clear, but when using a 7100, that would turn into "We bed some gro," which is not only not clear, it is also changes the meaning of the sentence.

BLUETOOTH SUPPORT

This is really a no brainer. None of the other models have Bluetooth support, so if you want it you need to upgrade. I love the idea of using a wireless earbud, but I have not been able to try it out myself. An earbud is the only thing that is supported, however, so don't expect to be able to use Bluetooth to allow your laptop to be able to surf the net while sitting on a park bench. I was told that you can write programs to use the Bluetooth capability to communicate with other hardware, but it can't do that out of the box.

Appendix B

BLACKBERRY BEHIND THE SCENES

Anyone who spends a little time thinking about how email actually gets from your email server to your handheld must realize that there are other steps in the middle that make the whole process possible. We've already mentioned the BlackBerry Enterprise Server, and this is certainly one important component, but there are other components that play an important role as well. Let's look at that process starting with when you get a new email.

FROM SERVER TO HANDHELD

The process begins when a piece of software detects that there is a new email in your email account. This software can be either the Desktop Redirector or the BlackBerry Enterprise Server. While there are many differences between the Desktop Redirector and the server, in this regard they have the same function—to get the new email message from your account and begin the process of sending it to your handheld.

Processing begins by first removing any attachments that are part of the email message. The attachments are replaced with a stub that will let you know the attachments were there, but not actually sent to the handheld. The stubs also help the Attachment Service to find the attachment if you later want to view the attachment.

Next, the email is broken into chunks. Normally there is only one chunk because most emails are small enough to not need more than one chunk. However, if an email is large enough, the first chunk is separated out. Later, if you make requests for more chunks of an email message, those requests come back to your server and the next chunk is sent out in the same manner as the first.

The last thing that happens is that the message chunk is encrypted. The encryption is done using the encryption key you created in the Desktop Manager when you first set up your handheld.

At this point, the encrypted message chunk leaves your computer and travels over the Internet to something called the BlackBerry Network Operations Center (NOC). The BlackBerry NOC is an important step in the process of delivering your messages, but is also seldom mentioned.

When an encrypted message chunk is sent out, it contains only one piece of information, a PIN number that is the address of the device to receive the chunk. The BlackBerry NOC is essentially a proxy server whose job is to direct the encrypted message chunks to the appropriate carrier. To accomplish this, the BlackBerry NOC has direct connections to each wireless carrier so that this communication happens as fast as possible.

As part of the job of directing the encrypted message chunk to the appropriate carrier, the BlackBerry NOC must also convert the PIN into an address that the carrier can use to deliver the chunk to the handheld. This conversion happens transparently to us because we never have to configure the Desktop Manager with this information. Each time a handheld enters an area with coverage, it communicates with the NOC and tells the NOC what its address is so that the NOC can deliver future messages to the handheld.

Now of course a device is not in coverage areas all the time or is sometimes turned off. When this happens, the NOC saves the encrypted message chunks until the handheld communicates with it again. Once the registration is done, the stored chunks are delivered to the handheld one by one in the order they were received.

Once the encrypted message chunk is on the handheld, there is still one last step that needs to be done. The encrypted message chunk is decrypted using the same encryption key that the Desktop Redirector or BlackBerry Enterprise Server used originally. If there is a problem and the decryption fails, the message chunk is simply discarded. If everything goes well, however, the chunk is processed, the handheld alerts you, and the new message appears in your Message List screen on your handheld. For those of you who like pictures, Figure B.1 shows how all of the components work together to get your email to your handheld.

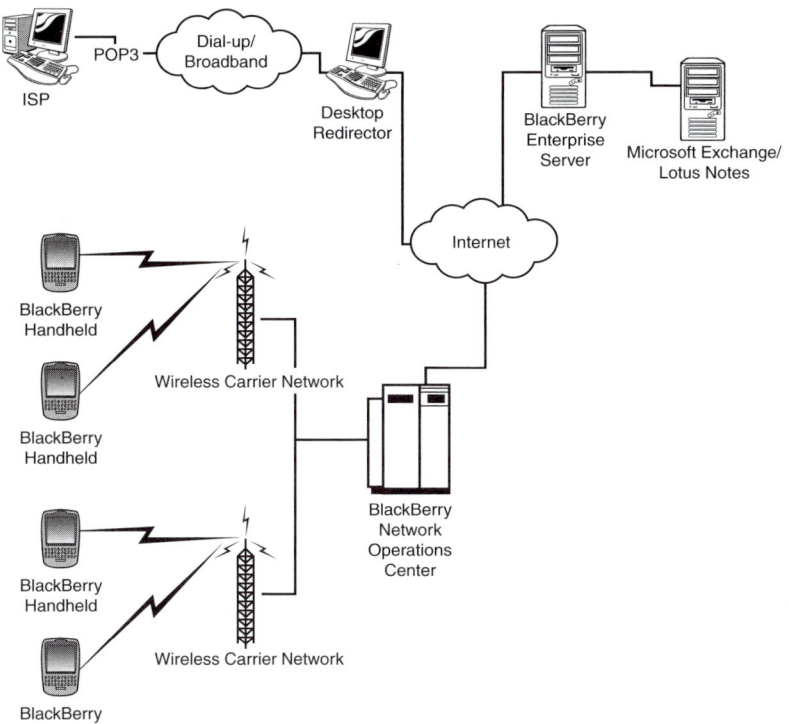

FIGURE B.1
How a message gets from your server to your handheld.

FROM HANDHELD TO SERVER

The same basic communication happens any time you send a message from your handheld, but in reverse. Your handheld breaks up a message into chunks, encrypts each chunk, and sends them to the NOC. Once again, the PIN is used to find the address of your Desktop Redirector or server and the message chunks are sent through the Internet to your server. The chunks are decrypted and reassembled into a message, which is then sent to your email server as an outgoing message.

It might seem like an awful lot of work, but the whole process takes just a few seconds and is repeated over and over every day.

Index

SYMBOLS

7100 series handhelds
    applications, selecting, 16
    BlueTooth support, 210
    End Call button, 132
    Escape key, 131
    icons
        Help, 18
        Password Keeper, 17
        Pictures, 18
        shortcuts, non-use of, 17
    keyboard layout, 12
    New Call button, 134
    power button location, 6
    QWERTY keyboard, 14
    screen savers, lack of, 63
    text edit fields
        MultiTap feature, 24-25
        SureType feature, 23-24
    themes, 17
    thumb typing difficulties, 9
    versus other models
        keyboard usage, 209-210
        PDA capabilities, 208
        phone capabilities, 207-208
        size differences, 208-209

7200 series handhelds versus 7100 series handhelds, 207-210

7500 series handhelds versus 7100 series handhelds, 207-210

7700 series handhelds versus 7100 series handhelds, 207-210

A

accessing
    battery, 8
    messages from within other messages, 94
    SIM card, 8
    SIM Phone Book, 158-159
    voicemail (Phone application), 130

Aces Texas Hold'em – No Limit game, 199

activating buttons, 20

add-ins, synchronization settings, configuring (IntelliSync applet), 45

Address Book
    addresses
        contacting, 156-157
        deleting, 150
        editing, 150
        groups, creating, 151
        groups, deleting, 152
        groups, member modification, 151
        groups, viewing, 152
        searching, 154
        viewing, 150
    categories
        Business, 152
        entries, assigning, 153
        Personal, 152
    duplicate names, filtering options, 158
    messages, compose options, 75
    multiple email addresses, adding, 149
    new entries, creating, 148-149
    opening, 147-148
    Options menu, 157-158
    phone numbers, adding from call messages, 92-93
    smart dialing rules, 141-142
    user-defined fields, custom entries, 149

Address List screen (Address Book), 147-148
    contacts
        adding, 148-149
        multiple email addresses, 149
        user-defined fields, 149
    Find feature, 154

addresses (Address Book)
    deleting, 150
    editing, 150
    email messages, friendly, 90-91
    groups
        creating, 151
        deleting, 152
        member deletion, 151
        member modification, 151

ADDRESSES

new member additions, 151
viewing, 152
searching, 154
viewing, 150
addresses (email)
    attaching, 78-79
    Redirector Settings applet (Desktop Manager), configuring, 52
Adobe Acrobat, file attachments, 104-105
Agenda view (Calendar), appointment creation, 163-164
Alarm application
    notification options, setting, 182-183
    R icon shortcut, 17
    setting, 183
    small bell icon, 183
    snooze settings, 182-183
    time options, setting, 182
    versus traditional alarm clock, 182
alerts (Profiles application), setting, 60
all day events (Calendar), 165-166
Alt key, 13-14
    list items, scrolling one at a time, 20
answering phone calls (Call Waiting Options screen), 140
applets (Desktop Manager), 37
    Application Loader, 38
    Backup/Restore, 38-39
        backups, data restoration, 39
        backups, performing, 39
        backups, specific databases only, 39-40
        time interval settings, 40-41
    IntelliSync, 41
        configuring synchronization, 43-46
        data synchronization with PCs, 42
    Redirector Settings, configuring synchronization, 47-53
application icons, highlighting via trackwheel, 16
Application Loader applet (Desktop Manager), 38
    third-party applications, installing, 201-204
applications
    buttons, clicking via trackwheel, 20
    choice fields, 20-22
    components overview, 18
    development tools, Java Development Environment (JDE), 200
    edit fields
        data entry, 22-23
        text entry, 22-23
    games, 197-199
    Home screen, organizing, 65-66
    icon shortcuts, 16-17
    J2ME requirements
        Mobile Information Device Profile (MIDP), 191
        RIM (Research In Motion) extensions, 192
    launching while on the phone, 136
    list items, selecting, 19-20
    menus, 18-19
    moving on Home screen, 65
    OTA (over the air) downloading, 200
    selecting, 16
    third-party, 195-196
        installing, 200-204
        locating, 192-194
        packages, installing, 195
appointments (Calendar)
    Agenda view
        creating, 164-165
        viewing, 163-164
    all day events, 165-166
    Daily view
        creating, 164
        viewing, 162-163
    deleting, 171
    duration times, setting, 165
    editing, 170
    end times, setting, 165
    Monthly view, viewing, 161-162
    notes, adding, 167
    prior, deleting, 171
    privacy options, setting, 167
    recurring
        daily, 167-168
        monthly, 169
        weekly, 168
        yearly, 169-170
    reminder notifications, setting, 166
    start times, setting, 165
    time zone conversions, 166
    Weekly view
        creating, 164
        viewing, 162
ASCII file attachments, 104-105
assigning addresses to categories (Address Book), 153
attachments (email), 103-104
    addresses, 78-79
    Adobe Acrobat (.pdf), 104-105
    ASCII text, 104-105
    Corel WordPerfect (.wpd), 104-105
    HTML, 104-105
    Microsoft Excel (.xls), 104-105
    Microsoft PowerPoint (.ppt), 104-105
    Microsoft Word (.doc), 104-105
    opening, 106
    V-card (.VCF), 104
    Viewer Options screen (Excel Worksheet view), 108-109

viewing, 105-107
 text documents, 107-109
 ZIP archives, 104-105
Auto Answer option (Phone application), 140
Auto Hangup option (Phone application), 140
Auto More option (Message list), 101
Auto-start synchronization settings, configuring (IntelliSync applet), 46
AutoText
 rules
  deleting, 83
  list, opening, 82
  new, creating, 82-83
 typos, fixing, 82

B

backlight feature, 6
Backup/Restore applet (Desktop Manager), 38-39
 backups, performing, 39
 data restoration, 39
 specific databases only, 39-40
 time interval settings, 40-41
battery
 accessing, 8
 owner information, placing, 56
 performance, extending, 59
 recharging via connection ports, 8
Bcc (Blind carbon copy) recipients, 77
Begin Call Key (7100 series), 14
Beiks.com website, 196
BerryGames.net website, 197
BIBS (BlackBerry Internet Browser Service), 111
BlackBerry Enterprise Server (BES)
 email lookups
  adding results to Address Book, 155
  creating, 155
  deleting from Address Book, 156
  resolving multiple matches, 156
  viewing results, 155
 email messages, redirecting, 29-30
BlackBerry Internet Browser Service (BIBS), 111
BlackBerry web client, email message redirection, 30
BlackBerry.com website
 ringtones, downloading, 120-121
 third-party applications, 192-193
 wallpaper downloads, 121-122
blocking phone calls (Call Barring screen), 138
BlueTooth, 7100 series support, 210

Bomb power-up effect (BrickBreaker application), 190
bookmarks
 adding, 117-118
 editing, 119-120
 folders, organizing, 118-119
 moving order of, 120
 opening, 117
 removing, 120
BrickBreaker application
 goal of, 188-189
 power-up effects, 189-190
Browser application, B icon shortcut, 17
Browser Key (7100 series), 14
Browser Options screen, 122-124
Business category (Address Book), 152
buttons (application component), 18
 clicking via trackwheel, 20

C

Cache Operations screen, clearing options, 125
caches
 types, 125
 web browsers, clearing, 125
 web pages
  adding to, 114
  clearing, 115
Calculator application
 buttons, trackwheel navigation, 184
 conversion operations, 185
 keypad mappings, 184-185
 moving, 65
 screen appearance, 183-184
 U icon shortcut, 17
Calendar application
 appointments
  all day events, 165-166
  creating, 164-165
  deleting, 171
  duration times, 165
  editing, 170
  end times, 165
  marking as private, 167
  notes entry, 167
  prior, deleting, 171
  recurring, daily type, 167-168
  recurring, monthly type, 169
  recurring, weekly type, 168
  recurring, yearly type, 169-170
  reminder notifications, 166
  start times, 165
  time zone conversions, 166
 C icon shortcut, 17

configuration options, 171
    Confirm Delete, 172
    Daily View, 172
    Default Reminder, 172
    Enable Quick Entry, 172
    Weekly View, 172
view options, 161
    Agenda, 163-164
    Daily, 162-163
    Monthly, 161-162
    Weekly, 162

Call Barring screen (Phone application), 138

Call Forwarding Options screen (Phone application), 139-140

Call History messages (Phone application), 138

Call Logs folder (email), 95

call messages
    forwarding, 85
    Missed Calls, 92
    notes, adding, 93
    opening (View Email screen), 92
    phone numbers, adding to Address Book, 92-93
    Placed Calls, 92
    Received Calls, 92

Call screen (Phone application)
    conference calls
        creating, 135
        dropping specific calls, 135
        splitting, 135
    information display, 131
    numeric-alphabetic mapping, 131-132
    phone calls
        call waiting settings, 133-134
        creating additional, 134
        ending, 131
        holding, 132-133
        muting, 133
        note additions, 136
        receiving, 132
    volume controls, 131

Call Waiting Options screen (Phone application), 140

calls
    additional, creating (Call screen), 134
    call waiting settings (Call screen), 133-134
    conference
        creating (Call screen), 135
        dropping specific calls (Call screen), 135
        splitting (Call screen), 135
    deleting (Recent Call list), 131
    ending (Call screen), 131
    ending (Phone application), 132
    holding (Call screen), 132-133
    muting (Call screen), 133

    note additions (Call screen), 136
    placing (Recent Call list), 129
    receiving (Call screen), 132

canceling email messages while in progress, 80

Cap key function, 13

Catch power-up effect (BrickBreaker application), 189

categories
    Address Book
        assigning entries, 153
        Business, 152
        Personal, 152
    list screen
        creating, 152-153
        deleting, 152-153
        filtering, 153-154
    memos, assigning (MemoPad application), 181
    records, viewing, 153-154
    supported applications, 152
    tasks, assigning (Tasks application), 175

Cc (carbon copy) recipients, 77

choice fields (application component), 18
    value selections, 20-22

clearing caches from web browsers, 125

clicking trackwheel, 16

communication port, configuring (Desktop Manager), 33-34

completed tasks, deleting (Tasks application), 174-175

Compose application, 74-76

composing
    email, 76
        additional recipients, 77-78
        addresses, attaching, 78-79
        canceling, 80
        priority levels, setting, 78
        saving in progress, 79
    PIN messages, 76
    SMS messages, 81

ConcreteSoftware.com website, 198-199

conference calls (Call screen)
    dropping certain calls, 135
    splitting, 135

configuring
    data synchronization
        IntelliSync applet (Desktop Manager), 43-46
        Redirector Settings applet (Desktop Manager), 47-53
    Desktop Manager
        Application Data folder location, 35
        communication port settings, 33-34
        email system connections, 34

icons, 35
IntelliSync file location, 35
MemoPad application, 181
Password Keeper application, 187-188
Phone application options, 137
Tasks application, 176
web browsers, 122-124
Confirm Delete option (Calendar), 172
Confirm Delete option (Message list), 100
Confirm Delete option (Phone application), 141
connection ports, 8
Consider PIN Level 1 option (Message list), 100
contacts (Address Book), 156-157
adding, 148-149
address groups
creating, 151
deleting, 152
member deletion, 151
member modification, 151
new member additions, 151
viewing, 152
addresses
deleting, 150
searching, 154
viewing, 150
multiple email addresses, adding, 149
user-defined fields, 149
content cache in web browsers, clearing, 125
cookies in web browsers, clearing, 125
copying
text to edit fields (applications), 22-23
URLs into web browsers, 116
Corel WordPerfect, file attachments, 104-105
custom searches of messages, creating (Search screen), 98-99
custom user-defined fields (Address Book entries), 149

D

daily recurring appointments, setting (Calendar), 167-168
Daily view (Calendar), 162-163, 172
appointments, creating, 164
data, password-protection, 57, 60
data entry, edit fields (applications), 22-23
databases, backing up (Backup/Restore applet), 39-40
dates
messages, deleting by age, 95
setting, 55-56
deaf communication (TTY) configuration, 143

default home pages, sample, 112-113
Default profile, changing, 60-61
Default Reminder option (Calendar), 172
Deferred status (Tasks application), 174-175
deleting
addresses (Address Book), 150
appointments (Calendar), 171
memos (MemoPad application), 180
messages, 94-95
by date criteria, 95
multiple, 95
from servers wirelessly, 101
phone calls (Recent Call list), 131
prior appointments (Calendar), 171
rules (AutoText), 83
tasks (Tasks application), 175
Desktop Manager
applets, 37
Application Loader, 38
Backup/Restore, 38-41
IntelliSync, 41-46
Redirector Settings, 47-53
configuration options
Application Data folder location, 35
communications port settings, 33-34
email system connections, 34
icons, 35
IntelliSync file location, 35
installing, 31-33
primary function of, 29
Service Packs, downloading, 203
software
new installations, 36-37
upgrading, 36-37
third-party applications, installing, 200-204
Desktop Redirector
email messages, redirecting, 30
message statistics, 35
Options menu, 36
primary function of, 35
development tools (applications), Java Development Environment (JDE), 200
device locking (SIM cards), 9
Dial from Home Screen option (Phone application), 141
disabling password security settings, 58
discarding email messages while in progress, 80
Display Name option (Message list), 100
display options (screen)
changing, 63-65
font settings, 64
keyboard settings, 64-65
screen saver activation, 63-64
trackwheel, navigating, 7
varieties, 6

DISPLAY TIME OPTION

Display Time option (Message list), 100
Do Not Disturb rule, alerts (notification types), 62-63
downloading ringtones (BlackBerry.com), 120-121
dropping callers from conference calls (Call screen), 135
due dates (Tasks application), 174-176
duration of appointments, setting (Calendar), 165

E

earbud connector, location of, 8
edit fields (application component), 18
    data entry, copying and pasting, 22-23
edit fields (text entry)
    7100 series handhelds
        MultiTap feature, 24-25
        SureType feature, 23-24
    copying and pasting, 22-23
email
    attachments, 103-104
        ASCII text, 104-105
        HTML, 104-105
        opening as full content, 106
        opening as table of contents, 106
        V-card (.VCF), 104
        viewing, 105-109
        ZIP archives, 104-105
    composing, 76
        additional recipients, 77-78
        addresses, attaching, 78-79
        canceling, 80
        priority levels, setting, 78
        saving in progress, 79
    Folder List, expanding/collapsing views, 96
    folders
        Call Logs, 95
        default views from Folder List, 96
        filing, 95
        organizing, 95
        selecting from Folder List, 96
        Sent Items, 95
    forwarding, 84
    header information
        friendly names/addresses (View Email screen), 90-91
        viewing (View Email screen), 89-90
    long text views (View Email screen), 88-89
    lookups (BlackBerry Enterprise Server)
        adding results to Address Book, 155
        creating, 155
        deleting from Address Book, 156
        function of, 155
        managing, 156
        resolving multiple matches, 156
        viewing results, 155
    message chunks, 211-212
    multiple addresses, adding (Address Book), 149
    opened status, changing (View Email screen), 91-92
    opening (View Email screen), 88
    recipient types, 77
    replying, 83-84
    senders, searching by, 99
    sending, 80-81
    servers, connecting (Desktop Manager), 34
    subjects, searching by, 99
    synchronization settings, configuring (IntelliSync applet), 43-44
    text, searching (View Email screen), 89
    transmission process
        handheld to server, 213
        server to handheld, 211-212
    web page links, sending in messages, 115
emergency number (GSM), 58
Enable Quick Entry option (Calendar), 172
encryption of email, message chunks, 211-212
End Call button (7100 series handhelds), 14, 132
end times of appointments, setting (Calendar), 165
ending phone calls (Phone application), 132
English Dictionary for BlackBerry application, 196
escape key, 7100 series handhelds, 131
ExpenseMinder application, 196
extending battery life, On/Off behavior, 59

F

filters
    Redirector Settings applet (Desktop Manager)
        configuring, 48-50
        creating, 49-50
    lists in categories, 153-154
Find feature (Address List screen), 154
Flip power-up effect (BrickBreaker application), 189
Folder List views, 96
folders
    bookmarks, creating, 118-119
    email messages
        Call Logs, 95
        default views (Folder List), 96
        expanding/collapsing views (Folder List), 96
        filing, 95

organizing, 95
selecting (Folder List), 96
Sent Items, 95

fonts, screen display, changing, 64

Forever option (Message list), 100

forwarding
Call messages, 85
email, 84
messages, SMS (Short Message Service) type, 84
phone calls (Call Forwarding Options screen), 139-140
PIN messages, 84

friendly names/addresses, email messages, viewing (View Email screen), 90-91

Full Content node (outlines), opening file attachments, 106

G

games
BrickBreaker application
goal of, 188-189
power-up effects, 189-190
third-party
Aces Texas Hold'em – No Limit, 199
Card Games Pack One, 198
Karpov X3D Chess, 199
Links Scorecard, 198
OutRoad, 198
Street Racer, 197
White Ninja, 197

General Options screen (Phone application), 140-141

groups (Address Book)
creating, 151
deleting, 152
member deletion, 151
new member additions, 151
viewing, 152

GSM (Global System for Mobile Communications) devices, 135
device locking features, 9
SIM cards, function of, 9
standard emergency number, 58

Gun power-up effect (BrickBreaker application), 189

H

Handango.com website, 196-198
third-party applications, 193

headers in email messages, viewing (View Email screen), 89-90

Help icon (7100 series handhelds), 18

help topics, 69

Hide Filed Messages option (Message list), 100

Hide Menu item, 19

holding phone calls, 132-133

holsters
function of, 9
security protections, 57

Home screen
applications, moving, 65
customizing, 65-66
organization of, 65-66
Profiles icon
hiding, 65
unhiding, 66
version 4.0, setting, 68

HTML (Hypertext Markup Language)
email messages, inability to view, 88
file attachments, 104-105
page content limitations with smaller devices, 112

I

icons
7100 series handhelds, 17-18
application list, 16
screen display, 15-16
shortcuts, 16-17
view options, configuring (Desktop Manager), 35

identification, owner information (Options application), 56

Idokorro Mobile SSH for BlackBerry application, 196

IM+ Mobile Messenger for BlackBerry application, 196

images
saving, 121-122
web pages, viewing via scrolling, 113

In Holster rule, notification types for profiles, 61-62

In Progress status (Tasks application), 174-175

installing
Desktop Manager, 31-33
new software (Desktop Manager), 36-37
third-party applications, 195, 200-204

IntelliSync applet (Desktop Manager), 41
data synchronization with PC, 42
file location, setting (Desktop Manager), 35
synchronization, configuring, 43-46

J - K

J2ME (Java 2 Micro Edition)
    application requirements, 191
    Mobile Information Device Profile (MIDP), 191
    RIM (Research In Motion), 192
Java 2 Micro Edition. *See* J2ME
Java Development Environment (JDE), application development, 200
JavatekMedia.com website, 198

Karpov X3D Chess game, 199
keyboard (QWERTY)
    7100 series handhelds, 14
        ease of use versus other models, 209-210
        layout of, 12
    advantages, 6-7
    Alt key, 13-14
    behavior, setting, 64-65
    Cap keys function, 13
    navigation overview, 12
    phone numbers, alphabetic-numeric mapping, 131-132
    Symbol Key, 14
    thumb typing, 9-10
    typos, fixing (AutoText), 82
    uses, 6-7
Keyboard Lock application, K icon shortcut, 17

L

Laser power-up effect (BrickBreaker application), 189
Level 1 messages, 61
links
    bookmarks
        adding, 117-118
        editing, 119-120
        folder organization, 118-119
        function of, 117
        moving order of, 120
        removing, 120
    web pages
        opening, 113-114
        refreshing, 115
        sending in email messages, 115
        viewing history of, 114
Links Scorecard game, 198
lists (application component), 18
    Alt key function, 20
    items, selecting, 19-20

locating
    addresses (Address Book), 154
    tasks (Tasks application), 176
    third-party applications, 192-194
locked screens, appearance of, 57
lockouts, incorrect password entry, 58
logging phone calls (Call History screen), 138
logins for websites (Password Keeper application), 187
long email messages, viewing (View Email screen), 88-89
Long power-up effect (BrickBreaker application), 189
lookups (email)
    creating, 155
    deleting from Address Book, 156
    resolving multiple matches, 156
    results
        adding to Address Book, 155
        managing, 156
        viewing, 155

M

MemoPad application
    configuration options, setting, 181
    D icon shortcut, 17
    function of, 179
    memos
        category assignments, 181
        creating, 179
        deleting, 180
        searching, 180-181
    uses, 179
memos (MemoPad application)
    categories, assigning, 181
    creating, 179
    deleting, 180
    searching, 180-181
menus (application component), 18-19
Message application, notification types, 61
    In Holster rule, 61-62
    Out of Holster rule, 61-62
Message list
    behaviors, 100-101
    date header, 87
    options, 99-101
    screen appearance, 87
    viewing, 87-88
Message screen, message types, selecting, 74-75
Message Viewer, inability to view HTML content, 88

messages. *See also* messages (email)
  accessing from within other messages, 94
  call
    note additions, 93
    opening (View Email screen), 92
    phone number additions to Address Book, 92-93
  Call type, forwarding, 85
  composing (Compose application), 74-76
  custom searches, creating (Search screen), 98-99
  deleting by date criteria, 95
  HTML, inability to view, 88
  Message list options, 100-101
  multiple deletion, 95
  phone calls, placing, 81
  PIN
    forwarding, 84
    opening (View Email screen), 88
    text searches (View Email screen), 89
  saving, 96
  searching (Search screen), 97-99
  SMS (Short Message Service)
    composing, 81
    forwarding, 84
    opening, 93-94
    recipients, changing, 81
  subjects, searching (Search screen), 99
  types
    email, 74
    phone calls, 73
    PIN, 74
    SMS (Short Message Service), 73
  viewing (Message list), 88
  wireless synchronization, 101
messages (email)
  adding more recipients, 77-78
  address attachments, 78-79
  attachments, 103-105
    ASCII text, 104-105
    HTML, 104-105
    opening as full content, 106
    opening as table of contents, 106
    V-card (.VCF), 104
    viewing, 105-109
    ZIP archives, 104-105
  changing opened status of (View Email screen), 91-92
  chunks, 211-212
  composing, 76-80
  discarding during composing, 80
  filing, 95
  folders, 95-96
  forwarding, 84
  friendly names/addresses (View Email screen), 90-91
  header information (View Email screen), 89-90
  long text views (View Email screen), 88-89
  opening (View Email screen), 88
  priority levels, 78
  redirecting to BlackBerry, 29-30
  replying, 83-84
  saving in progress, 79
  sending, 80-81
  text searches (View Email screen), 89
  transmission process
    handheld to server, 213
    server to handheld, 211-212
  web page links, 115
Messages application
  launching, 74
  M icon shortcut, 17
  Message list, 74
  selecting via trackwheel, 16
microphone, location of, 8
Microsoft Excel
  file attachments, 104-105
  worksheets, viewing in file attachments, 107-109
Microsoft PowerPoint
  file attachments, 104-105
  presentation documents, viewing in file attachments, 108
Microsoft Word, file attachments, 104-105
MIDI files, ringtone downloads, 120-121
MIForum.com website, 199
Missed Call message type, 92
Mobile Data Services (MDS), web browser activation, 111
Mobile Information Device Profile (MIDP), J2ME specification, 191
monthly recurring appointments, setting (Calendar), 169
Monthly view (Calendar), 161-162
Multi power-up effect (BrickBreaker application), 189
multiple addresses, grouping (Address Book), 151-152
multiple messages, deleting, 95
MultiTap feature (7100 series handhelds), text typing, 24-25
multitasking, launching applications while on the phone, 136
muting phone calls, 133
MyTip 2.0 application, 196

NAMES

N

names
   email messages, friendly (View Email screen), 90-91
   owner information, setting (Options application), 56
naming ringtones, 121
New Call button (7100 series handhelds), 134
new profiles, creating, 63
new rules, creating (AutoText), 82-83
Next Key (7100 series), 14
No Vibration profile, 63
None rule, alerts (notification types), 61
Not Started status (Tasks application), 174-175
notes
   appointments, adding (Calendar), 167
   call messages, adding, 93
   phone calls, adding (Call screen), 136
notification types (profiles), 61-62

O

old messages, deleting, 95
On/Off behavior for battery, extending life of, 59
One Time Dial (Recent Call list), 128-129
one-handed typing method, 10
one-thumbed typing method, 10
opened status of messages, changing (View Email screen), 91-92
opening
   Address Book, 147-148
   call messages, 92
   file attachments, 106
   SIM Phone Book, 158-159
   SMS messages (View SMS Message screen), 93-94
Options application
   Auto On/Off behavior, 59-60
   date, setting, 55-56
   O icon shortcut, 17
   Owner item information, 56
   Screen/Keyboard options
      font settings, 64
      keyboard settings, 64-65
      screen saver activation, 63-64
      setting, 63-65
   time, setting, 55-56
Options menu (Address Book), 157-158
OTA (over the air) downloads, 200
Out of Holster rule, notification types for profiles, 61-62
OutRoad game, 198
owner information
   entering (Options application), 56
   locked handhelds, screen appearance, 58
   placing under battery, 56
   profiles, generating, 60

P

packages for third-party applications, installing, 195
Password Keeper application
   configuration options, 187-188
   icon (7100 series handhelds), 17
   passwords
      new records creation, 186-187
      storage, 185
      website logins, 187
passwords
   Call Barring screen, 138
   disabling, 58
   lockouts, number of incorrect entries, 58
   protection, enabling, 57, 60
PCs, data synchronization via IntelliSync applet, 42
PDATopSoft.com website, 196-197
   third-party applications, 193
Personal category (Address Book), 152
Phone application
   Call Barring screen, 138
   Call Forwarding Options screen, 139-140
   Call History messages, 138
   Call screen
      conference calls, dropping specific calls, 135
      conference calls, splitting, 135
      creating additional calls, 134
      ending calls, 131-132
      handling call waiting, 133-134
      holding calls, 132-133
      information display, 131
      muting calls, 133
      numeric alphabetic mapping, 131-132
      phone note additions, 136
      receiving calls, 132
      volume controls, 131
   Call Waiting Options screen, 140
   General Options screen, 140-141
   launching via Phone button, 127
   options, configuring, 137
   P icon shortcut, 17
   Phone Status screen, 143-144
   Recent Call list, 127
      integration with Address Book, 128
      One Time Dial dialog, 128-129
      phone calls, deleting, 131
      phone calls, placing, 129

smart dialing rules, configuring, 141-142
TTY options, setting, 143
version 4.0 speed dial feature
    list entries, 129
    mapping changes, 130
    number additions, 130
    number removal, 130
voicemail
    accessing, 130
    options, setting, 142

phone book (SIM), accessing, 158-159

Phone button, 127

phone calls
additional, creating (Call screen), 134
applications, multitasking while using phone, 136
blocking (Call Barring screen), 138
call waiting settings (Call screen), 133-134
conference
    creating (Call screen), 135
    dropping specific calls (Call screen), 135
    splitting (Call screen), 135
deleting (Recent Phone list), 131
ending (Call screen), 131-132
forwarding (Call Forwarding Options screen), 139-140
holding (Call screen), 132-133
logging (Call History screen), 138
message type, 73
muting (Call screen), 133
note additions (Call screen), 136
placing, 81, 129
receiving
    Call screen, 132
    Call Waiting Options screen, 140

phone numbers
alphabetic mapping (Call screen), 131-132
call messages, adding to Address Book, 92-93

Phone Status screen (Phone application), 143-144

pictures
home screens, selecting (version 4.0), 68
saving, 121-122
standby images, selecting (version 4.0), 68

Pictures icon (7100 series handhelds), 18

PIM (Personal Information Manager)
records, category assignments, 152
synchronization settings, configuring (IntelliSync applet), 44-45

PIN messages, 74
composing, 76
forwarding, 84
opening (View Email screen), 88
text searches (View Email screen), 89

Placed Call message type, 92

PocketMac for BlackBerry application, 195

PocketMac.net website, 195

Power button
7100 series handhelds, turning on/off, 6
backlight feature, toggling, 6

presentation documents, viewing in file attachments, 108

prior appointments, deleting (Calendar), 171

priorities of tasks, setting (Tasks application), 175

priority levels (email), setting, 78

privacy options for appointments, setting (Calendar), 167

productivity applications, 195-196

profiles
alert behaviors, 60
    Do Not Disturb rule, 62-63
    None rule, 61
    Tone rule, 61
    Vibrate rule, 62
    Vibrate+Tone rule, 62
changing, 60-61
Default, changing, 60-61
generating, 60
new, creating, 63
No Vibration, 63
notification types, 61-62
selecting, 60

Profiles application
alerts
    customizing, 60
    settings, 60
F icon shortcut, 17

Profiles icon
hiding on Home screen, 65
unhiding on Home screen, 66

Purge Deleted Items folder, 101

Q - R

QWERTY keyboard, 12-14
advantages, 6-7
thumb typing, 9-10
typos, fixing (AutoText), 82
uses, 6-7

rebooting via Reset hole, 8

Received Call message type, 92

receiving phone calls (Call screen), 132

Recent Call list (Phone application), 127
integration with Address Book, 128
One Time Dial dialog, 128-129
phone calls
    deleting, 131
    placing, 129

recharging battery via connection ports, 8
recipients
  email
    adding, 77-78
    Bcc (Blind carbon copy), 77
    Cc (Carbon copy), 77
    To, 77
  SMS messages, changing, 81
records
  categories, viewing, 153-154
  passwords, creating (Password Keeper application), 186-187
recurring appointments (Calendar)
  creating, 167
  daily, setting, 167-168
  monthly, setting, 169
  weekly, setting, 168
  yearly, setting, 169-170
redirecting email messages to BlackBerry, 29-30
Redirector Settings applet (Desktop Manager)
  advanced settings, configuring, 52-53
  filters
    configuring, 48-50
    creating, 49-50
  General tab, configuring, 47-48
  security, configuring, 50-51
  synchronization, configuring, 47-53
refreshing web pages, 115
reminders for appointments, setting (Calendar), 166
replying to email messages, 83-84
  multiple recipients, 84
Reqwireless WebViewer application, 195
Research In Motion (RIM), J2ME extensions, 192
resetting handheld device via Reset hole, 8
Restrict My Identity option (Phone application), 141
RIM (Research In Motion), J2ME extensions, 192
RIMRoad.com website, third-party applications, 194
ringtones
  downloading, 120-121
  installing, 120-121
  MIDI format, 120-121
  naming, 121
  saving, 121
rules (AutoText)
  creating, 82-83
  deleting, 83
  opening, 82

S

Saved Messages application, V icon shortcut, 17
saving
  email addresses while in progress, 79
  messages, 96
  pictures, 121-122
  ringtones, 121
screen
  appearance of, 15-16
  application list, 16
  display options
    changing, 63-65
    font settings, 64
    keyboard settings, 64-65
    screen saver activation, 63-64
  examples, 6
  icons
    application list, 16
    display of, 15-16
    shortcuts, 16
  locked appearance, 57
  trackwheel, navigating, 7
  varieties, 6
screen savers
  7100 series handhelds, lack of, 63
  screen display, activating, 63-64
scrolling
  trackwheel, application icon selection, 16
  web pages, large image views, 113
Search Messages application, S icon shortcut, 17
Search screen
  criteria, entry of, 97
  custom searches, creating, 98-99
  message senders, 99
  message subjects, 99
  messages, searching, 97-98
  previous searches, viewing, 98
searching
  addresses (Address Book), 154
  help topics (version 4.0), 69
  memos in MemoPad application, 180-181
  messages
    customized (Search screen), 98-99
    Search screen, 97-98
  tasks (Tasks application), 176
  text in email/PIN messages, 89
  third-party applications, 192-194
security
  holster placement, 57
  Password Keeper application
    configuring, 187-188
    new password record creation, 186-187

password storage, 185
website logins, 187
password-protection, 57, 60
Call Barring screen (Phone application), 138
disabling, 58
Redirector Settings applet (Desktop Manager), 50-51
screens, locked appearance, 57
web pages, browser settings, 116
senders of messages, searching (Search screen), 99
sending email, 80-81
Sent Items folder (email), 95
serial connection port, 8
Service Packs, downloading, 203
ShapeServices.com website, 196
shutting down (Power button), 6
SIM cards
accessing, 8
device locking features, 9
information transfers to new devices, 9
SIM Phone Book, accessing, 158-159
Slow power-up effect (BrickBreaker application), 189
smart dialing rules, setting (Phone application), 141-142
SMS Message (Short Message Service), 73
composing, 81
forwarding, 84
opening (View SMS Message screen), 93-94
recipients, changing, 81
software
new installations (Desktop Manager), 36-37
upgrading (Desktop Manager), 36-37
sorting tasks (Tasks application), 176
speaker, location of, 8
speed dial feature (version 4.0), 129
entries, viewing, 129
numbers, adding to, 130
splitting conference calls (Call screen), 135
standby images, setting, 68
start times of appointments, setting (Calendar), 165
status of tasks, viewing (Tasks application), 174-175
storage folders, Redirector Settings applet (Desktop Manager), 52-53
storing passwords (Password Keeper application), 185
Street Racer game, 197
subjects of messages, searching (Search screen), 99

SureType feature (7100 series handhelds), text typing, 23-24
Symbol Key, 14
synchronizing
data to PCs via IntelliSync applet (Desktop Manager), 42
conflicts, 44
messages, 101
system lockups, troubleshooting via Reset hole, 8

T

Table of Contents node (outlines), opening file attachments, 106
Tasks application
configuration options, 176
T icon shortcut, 17
Tasks List screen
categories, 175
completion due dates, 174
creation, 174-175
deletion, 175
locator, 176
modifications, 175
priorities, 175
sample screen appearance, 173
sorting, 176
statuses, 174-175
text
documents in file attachments, viewing, 107
edit fields
copying and pasting, 22-23
MultiTap feature (7100 series handhelds), 24-25
SureType feature (7100 series handhelds), 23-24
typos
automatic repair of (AutoText), 82
rules, creating (AutoText), 82-83
rules, deleting (AutoText), 83
themes
7100 series handhelds, 17
version 4.0, selecting, 66-67
third-party applications
games, 197-199
installing, 200-204
locating, 192-194
packages, installing, 195
productivity, 195-196
website sources
Handango.com, 193
PSATopSoft.com, 193
RIMRoad.com, 194
thumb typing
7100 series handheld difficulties, 9
one-handed position, 10

THUMB TYPING

one-thumbed navigating position, 10
two-thumb position, 10

time
backup intervals, Backup/Restore applet, 40-41
GMT (Greenwich Mean Time), calculating, 56
setting, 55-56
zone options, 56, 166

To recipients (email), 77

Tone rule, alerts (notification types), 61

trackwheel
application icons, highlighting, 16
buttons, clicking, 16, 20
list items, selecting, 19-20
menu options, selecting, 19
screen navigation, 7

translators for synchronization settings, configuring (IntelliSync applet), 45

troubleshooting system lockups (Reset hole), 8

TTY (deaf communication) configuration (Phone application), 143

turning on/off (Power button), 6

two-thumb typing method, 10

typing
7100 series handhelds
MultiTap feature, 24-25
SureType feature, 23-24
thumb
7100 series handheld difficulties, 9
one-handed position, 10
one-thumbed navigating position, 10
two-thumb position, 10

typos, automatic repair of (AutoText), 82

U

upgrading software (Desktop Manager), 36-37

URLs (uniform resource locators), 114-115
bookmarks
adding, 117-118
editing, 119-120
folder organization, 118-119
moving order of, 120
removing, 120
copying, 116
sending via email, 115
web browsers, entry of, 114-115

USB connection port, 8

user profile configurations, Redirector Settings applet (Desktop Manager), 52

V

V-Cards, email address attachments, 78-79, 104

version 4.0
help topics, 69
home screens, setting, 68
Phone application, speed dial feature
list entries, 129
mapping changes, 130
number additions, 130
number removal, 130
standby images, setting, 68
themes, selecting, 66-67

Vibrate rule, alerts (notification types), 62

Vibrate+Tone rule, alerts (notification types), 62

View Email screen
email messages
changing opening status of, 91-92
friendly names/addresses, 90-91
header information, 89-90
long text views, 88-89
opening, 88
text searches, 89
PIN messages
opening, 88
text searches, 89

View SMS Message screen, 93-94

viewing
addresses (Address Book), 150
Calendar application
Agenda view, 163-164
Daily view, 162-163
Monthly view, 161-162
Weekly view, 162
file attachments, 105-107
PowerPoint documents, 108
text documents, 107
worksheets (Excel), 107-109
help topics (version 4.0), 69
messages (Message list), 88
records in categories, 153-154

voicemail
accessing (Phone application), 130
options configuration (Phone application), 142

volume of phone calls, adjusting (Call screen), 131

W - Z

Waiting status (Tasks application), 174-175

wallpapers, downloading, 121-122

WAP (Wireless Application Protocol), 112
web browsers
    activation of, 111
    BlackBerry Internet Browser Service (BIBS), 111
    bookmarks
        adding, 117-118
        editing, 119-120
        folder organization, 118-119
        moving order of, 120
        opening, 117
        removing, 120
    caches, clearing, 125
    configuration options
        Bookmarks Page, 124
        changing, 122
        Confirm Close on Escape, 124
        Confirm Execute Scripts, 124
        Current Mode, 123
        Home Page, 123
        Last Page Loaded, 124
        Show Images, 123
        Start Page, 123
    default home pages, 112-113
    launching, 112
    Mobile Data Services (MDS), 111
    padlock icon, 116
    page addresses
        copying, 116
        viewing, 116
    page caches
        clearing, 115
        loading, 114
    page content
        availability of, 112
        HTML limitations with small devices, 112
        HTTP, 112
        Wireless Application Protocol (WAP), 112
    page history, viewing, 114
    page links
        opening, 113-114
        refreshing, 115
    page loading icon, 116
    security information, 116
    selection criteria
        content restriction issues, 112
        security issues, 112
    URLs, entering, 114-115
    Wireless Markup Language (WML), 112
web pages
    caches
        adding to, 114
        clearing, 115
    default home, 112-113
    history, viewing, 114
    large images, scrolling to view, 113
    links
        opening, 113-114
        refreshing, 115
        sending in email messages, 115
    navigation tips, 112-113
    pictures, saving to handheld, 121-122
    ringtones, downloading, 120-121
    security settings, 116
    URL addresses
        copying, 116
        entry of, 114-115
        viewing, 116
websites
    Beiks.com, 196
    BerryGames.net, 197
    BlackBerry.com
        ringtone downloads, 120-121
        third-party applications, 192-193
    bookmarks
        adding, 117-118
        editing, 119-120
        folder organization, 118-119
        moving order of, 120
        removing, 120
    ConcreteSoftware.com, 198-199
    Handango.com, 196-198
        third-party applications, 193
    Idokorro.com, 196
    JavatekMedia.com, 198
    MIForum.com, 199
    passwords, logging in to (Password Keeper application), 187
    PDATopSoft.com, 196-197
        third-party applications, 193
    PocketMac.net, 195
    Reqwireless WebViewer, 195
    RIMRoad.com, 194
    ShapeServices.com, 196
weekly recurring appointments, setting (Calendar), 168
Weekly View option (Calendar), 162, 172
    appointments, creating, 164
White Ninja game, 197-198
Wireless Application Protocol (WAP), 112
Wireless Markup Language (WML), 112
worksheets (Excel), file attachments, viewing, 107-109
Wrap power-up effect (BrickBreaker application), 190

yearly recurring appointments, setting (Calendar), 169-170

ZIP file attachments, 104-105

SUBSCRIBE TO mobile

The Ultimate Mobile Handbook

Order your FREE ISSUE today!
Call 1-800-266-3312

TRY A FREE ISSUE!

Confused about which of the newest digital devices to buy? Want to know about new technologies coming two years or even two decades from now?

Here's the magazine you've been waiting for!

Mobile celebrates the mobile lifestyle! Anything you ever wanted to know about the hottest gear, Mobile's dream team of experts can tell you, giving you more accurate and usable info than any other technology magazine.

In every issue, you'll discover...

- Brutal reviews of the newest gadgets
- Always entertaining, but never jokey features
- In-depth how-to guides
- Mind blowing updates from the Asian think tanks
- Stunning photography

Get more from your gear while you're on the go!

Act Now to receive your Free Issue – with no obligation.
If you like it, you'll pay just $12.00 for 11 additional issues for a total of 12.
You Save 83%!
(Better grab this offer before it disappears!)

Money-Back Guarantee.
If Mobile ever fails to please you, for any reason, let us know and we'll rush you a prompt refund on all unmailed issues.